Daily Reflections for 2022:

Exploring the Message of Our Lady of La Salette

Edited by Fr. Ron Gagné, M.S.

Missionaries of La Salette Corporation
915 Maple Avenue
Hartford, CT 06114-2330, USA

website: www.lasalette.org

First edition (1990s): ISBN 0-9663546-1-3 (pbk), edited by Fr. Roger Plante M.S.

Third Edition (expanded edition): Copyright @ September 19, 2020 by Missionaries of Our Lady of La Salette, Province of Mary, Mother of the Americas, 915 Maple Avenue, Hartford, CT, 06106-2330, USA

Imprimi Potest: Rev. Fr. Rene J. Butler, M.S., Provincial Superior Missionaries of Our Lady of La Salette, Province of Mary, Mother of the Americas, 915 Maple Avenue Hartford, CT 06106-2330, USA

Editor: Fr. Ron Gagné, M.S.

Booklet Design & Digital Formatting: Jack Battersby and Fr. Ron Gagné, M.S.

This and other La Salette titles are available in paper, e-book and audiobook formats at: www.Amazon.com, itunes.Apple.com, and www.lasalette.org

Note: Please refer to the Appendix for the La Salette Novena.

ISBN: 978-1-946956-44-6

Introduction

An Expanded Edition

This book is an expanded edition of *Great News: Reflections on the weekday Gospels and the La Salette message*, edited by Fr. Roger Plante, M.S. in the late 1990s. We have added reflections for all Sundays and Feasts of the year. This edition is intended for use in the year 2021 with its day-by-day reflections and their daily lectionary numbers for your reference.

Our Authors, Past and Present

All our authors are connected to La Salette and come from all parts of the United States, Canada and, in a few cases, from other parts of the English-speaking world. They have participated in a variety of ministries in the La Salette Congregation and in the Church: parish ministry, retreat and parish missions, missions abroad, education and religious formation, as well as community administration.

They are a great mix of brothers, priests and laity, yet they have one thing in common: a love of the La Salette Event. They were asked to "sit with the mystery " of Mary's Apparition at La Salette which happened in 1846. In these daily Gospel Meditations, they share their personal sensitivity to the Lord's call, "Come, follow me," and his Mother's plea at La Salette, "Make this known to all my people."

Our Authors

Sundays of the Year: Wayne Vanasse and Rev. Fr. René Butler, M.S., Provincial; Feast Days of the Year: Fr. Ronald G. Gagné, M.S.

Advent - Christmas

Advent weeks 1-2: Fr. Camille J. Doucet, M.S.

Advent week 3: Fr. Gilles M. Genest, M.S.

December 17-24: Fr. Donald L. Paradis, M.S.

Christmas and January 2-7: Fr. Edward J. Richard, M.S.

Epiphany: Bro. Robert J. Belliveau, M.S.

Lent – Easter

Ash Wednesday and Week 1 of Lent: Fr. Richard W. Lavoie, M.S.

Weeks 2 and 3 of Lent: Fr. Robert J. Campbell, M.S.

Weeks 4 and 5 of Lent: Fr. George B. Brennan

Holy Week and Easter Octave: Fr. Eugene G. Barrette, M.S.

Weeks 2 and 3 of Easter: Fr. Donald L. Paradis, M.S.

Weeks 4 and 5 of Lent: Fr. John R. Nuelle, M.S.

Weeks 6 and 7 of Easter: Daniel P. Bradley

Ordinary Time

Weeks 1 and 2 in Ordinary Time: Fr. William Kaliyadan, M.S.

Week 3 in Ordinary Time: Fr. Terry E. Niziolek, M.S.

Week 4 in Ordinary Time: Fr. Fernand Cassista, M.S.

Weeks 5 and 6 in Ordinary Time: Fr. Manuel C. Pereira, M.S.

Weeks 7 and 8 in Ordinary Time: Fr. Terry E. Niziolek, M.S.

Weeks 9 and 10 in Ordinary Time: Fr. John F. Gabriel, M.S.

Weeks 11 and 12 in Ordinary Time: Fr. Leo C. Holleran, M.S.

Weeks 13 and 14 in Ordinary Time: Fr. Joseph P. Gosselin, M.S.

Weeks 15 and 16 in Ordinary Time: Fr. Joseph M. O'Neil, M.S.

Weeks 17 and 18 in Ordinary Time: Joseph J. Baxer

Weeks 19 and 20 in Ordinary Time: Fr. James Stajkowski, M.S.

Weeks 21 and 22 in Ordinary Time: Fr. Matthew Manjaly, M.S.

Week 23 in Ordinary Time: Fr. Ronald B. Foshage, M.S.

Week 24 in Ordinary Time: Fr. John J. O'Neil, M.S.

Weeks 25 and 26 in Ordinary Time: Fr. Jeffrey M. L'Arche, M.S.

Weeks 27 and 28 in Ordinary Time: Fr. Roland S. Nadeau, M.S.

Weeks 29 in Ordinary Time: Fr. Normand Theroux, M.S.

Week 30 in Ordinary Time: Fr. John F. Gabriel, M.S.

Weeks 31 and 32 in Ordinary Time: Fr. Raymond G. Cadran, M.S.

Weeks 33 and 34 in Ordinary Time: Fr. Joseph G. Bachand, M.S.

Prologue:

The Story of the La Salette Apparition

On Saturday, September 19, 1846, a "Beautiful Lady" appeared to two children, both from Corps, in France Alps: Maximin Giraud, eleven-year-old, and Mélanie Calvat, almost fifteen, who were watching their herds on the slope of Mont Planeau, approximately 6,000 feet in altitude, not far from the village of La Salette. In a little hollow, they suddenly noticed a globe of fire – "as though the sun had fallen on the spot." Within the dazzling light they gradually perceived a woman, seated, her elbows resting on her knees and her face buried in her hands.

The Beautiful Lady rose, and said to the children in French:

Come closer, my children; don't be afraid. I am here to tell you great news.

She took a few steps towards them. Maximin and Mélanie, reassured, ran down to her and stood very close to her.

The Beautiful Lady wept all the time she spoke. She was tall, and everything about her radiated light. She wore the typical garb of the women of the area: a long dress, and apron around her waist, a shawl crossed over her breast and tied behind her back, and a close-fitting bonnet. Along the hem of her shawl she wore a broad, flat chain, and from a smaller chain around her neck there hung a large crucifix.

Under the arms of the cross there were, to the left of the figure of Christ, a hammer, and, to the right, pincers. The radiance of the entire apparition seemed to emanate from this crucifix, and shone like a brilliant crown upon the Beautiful Lady's head. She wore garlands of roses on her head, around the edge of her shawl and around her feet.

The Beautiful Lady spoke to the two shepherds. first in French, in these words:

If my people refuse to submit, I will be forced to let go the arm of my Son. It is so strong and so heavy, I can no longer hold it back.

How long a time I have suffered for you! If I want my Son not to abandon you, I am obliged to plead with him constantly. And as for you, you pay no heed!

However much you pray, however much you do, you will never be able to recompense the pains I have taken for you.

I gave you six days to work; I kept the seventh for myself, and no one will give it to me. This is what makes the arm of my Son so heavy. And then, those who drive the carts cannot swear without throwing in my Son's name. These are the two things that make the arm of my Son so heavy.

If the harvest is ruined, it is only on account of yourselves. I warned you last year with the potatoes. You paid no heed. Instead, when you found the potatoes spoiled, you swore, and threw in my Son's name. They are going to continue to spoil, and by Christmas this year there will be none left.

Discovery of the Weeping Mother

Mélanie was intrigued by the expression, pommes de terre. In the local dialect, potatoes were called las truffas. She looked inquiringly at Maximin, but the Beautiful Lady anticipated her question.

Don't you understand, my children? Let me find another way to say it.

Using the local dialect, she repeated what she had said about the harvest, and then went on:

If you have wheat, you must not sow it. Anything you sow the vermin will eat, and whatever does grow will fall into dust when you thresh it.

A great famine is coming. Before the famine comes, children under seven will be seized with trembling and die in the arms of the persons who hold them. The rest will do penance through the famine. The walnuts will become worm-eat- en; the grapes will rot.

At this point the Beautiful Lady confided a secret to Maximin, and then to Mélanie. then she went on:

If they are converted, rocks and stones will turn into heaps of wheat, and

4

potatoes will be self- sown in the fields.

Do you say your prayers well, my children?

"Hardly ever, Madam," the two shepherds answered candidly.

Ah, my children, you should say them well, at night and in the morning, even if you say only an Our Father and a Hail Mary when you can't do better. When you can do better, say more.

In the summer, only a few elderly women go to Mass. The rest work on Sundays all summer long. In the winter, when they don't know what to do, they go to Mass just to make fun of religion. In Lent they go to the butcher shops like dogs.

Have you never seen wheat gone bad, my children?

They answered, "No, Madam."

The Beautiful Lady then spoke to Maximin.

But you, my child, surely you must have seen some once, at Coin, with your father. The owner of the field told your father to go and see his spoiled wheat. And then you went, and you took two or three ears of wheat in your hands, you rubbed them together, and it all crumbled into dust. While you were on your way back and you were no more than a half hour away from Corps, your father gave you a piece of bread and said to you: "Here, my child, eat some bread while we still have it this year; because I don't know who will eat any next year if the wheat keeps up like that."

"Oh, yes," answered Maximin, "Now I remember. Just then, I didn't remember it."

The Beautiful Lady then concluded, not in dialect but in French:

Well, my children you will make this known to all my people.

Then she moved forward, stepped over the stream, and without turn- ing back she gave the injunction.

Mary speaks to the children

5

Very well, my children make this known to all my people.

The vision climbed the steep path which wound its way towards the Collet (little neck). Then she rose into the air as the children caught up to her. She looked up at the sky, then down to the earth. Facing southeast, "she melted into light." The light itself then disappeared.

On September 19, 1851, after "a precise and rigorous investigation" of the event, the witnesses, the content of the message, and its repercussions, Philibert de Bruillard, Bishop of Grenoble, pronounced his judgment in a pastoral letter of instruction. He declared that "the ap- parition of the Blessed Virgin to two shepherds, September 19, 1846, on a mountain in the Alps, located in the parish of La Salette,... bears within itself all the characteristics of truth and that the faithful have grounds for believing it to be indubitable and certain."

In another pastoral letter, dated May 1, 1852, the Bishop of Greno- ble announced the construction of a Shrine on the mountain of the apparition, and went on to add:

> "However important the erection of a Shrine may be there is something still more important, namely the ministers of religion destined to look after it, to receive the pious pilgrims, to preach the word of God to them, to exercise towards them the ministry of reconciliation, to administer the Holy Sacrament of the altar, and to be, to all, the faithful dispensers of the mysteries of God and the spiritual treasures of the Church.

Mary melted into light

> "These priests shall be called the Missionaries of Our Lady of La Salette; their institution and existence shall be, like the Shrine itself, and eternal monument, a perpetual remembrance, of Mary's merciful apparition."

The first priests imbued with the spirit of the Apparition and who devoted themselves to the service of the pilgrims, felt from the beginning the call to and the need for religious life. Six of them pronounced their first vows on February 2, 1858, in accordance with their provisional Constitutions, adapted in 1862 to include Brothers. From that time, Fathers and Brothers have constituted one religious family.

Mary's apparition at La Salette is a modern-day reminder of an ancient truth: that Mary constantly intercedes for us before God; that she is the Reconciler of Sinners, calling us back to the message and way of her Son, Jesus.

Reflection Questions:

• What quality do you most admire about Mary's appearance at La Salette?

• When and where did you first hear the message of Our Lady of La Salette?

Prayer:

Mary, Humble Maiden, your message and witness on the Mountain of La Salette is that of a true reconciler. You invite us to draw near, you speak to our hearts and then you send us off to spread your message of faith, forgiveness and good news to all your people.

As Mother of the Church, you are concerned about our daily life with its challenges and blessings. In your goodness, assist us in our journey of faith; guide us with your loving presence and assure us of your Son's grace as we make our way together, back to the Father.

We ask this through your intercession, and in the name of your Son, Jesus, who lives with the Father and the Holy Spirit, one God, fore ever and ever. **Amen.**

La Salette Invocation:

Our Lady of La Salette, Reconciler of Sinners, pray without ceasing for us who have recourse to you.

Saturday, January 1 (#018)
Feast of Mary, Mother of God

Luke 2:16-21: *"As for Mary, she treasured all these things and pondered them in her heart."*

Reflection:

A woman tells of her 105 year old grandmother, Edna. From the time Edna turned 90 her quality of life took a significant turn. Her body ached all over. She couldn't see well enough to read, write, crochet, or even watch TV. She couldn't hear well enough to carry a conversation. Edna spent much of the last 15 years of her life in her recliner, sitting in silence staring out the window at birds she couldn't see. What a way to live! And yet, Edna never grew despondent. She always seemed content and happy. She was never one to complain. One day, her daughter asked, "Mama, tell me, what do you think about all day

The Madonna of the Book **by Sandro Botticelli (1445-1510)**

long?" "O honey," Edna responded, "I've got enough memories to last a lifetime."

What is the job description of the Mother of God? I imagine it might say, "First: do what all mothers do – love them always; be a good example to them; respond to their needs; correct them when it's needed. And when they grow up, accept them as they are. Second: treasure your memories. On this feast of Mary, the Mother of God, we hear in the gospel that she began treasuring her memories of Jesus from his very birth. And fortunately she is our mother from the time when Jesus gave her to us, the members of the Church, on the cross at Calvary.

IF THERE IS ANY QUALITY WHICH MARY SHOWED AT LA SALETTE with the two children it was her mothering of them: *"Come near, my children, do not be afraid... See, let me tell it to you another way..."* Mary was a "mother personified" in her solicitous attention, her love and compassion and even her direction to make her message known. She wanted the children to become loving and faithful members of the Church, true evangelizers of her only Son.

Reflection Questions:

- Can you remember an event or quality which you cherish about your own mother?
- What would Mary say to you about your own life as an active Catholic, as a follower of her Son?

Sunday, January 2 (#020-03)
The Epiphany of the Lord

(Isaiah 60:1-6; Ephesians 3:2-3a,5-6; Matthew 2:1-12)

Meditation: *Where is He?*

Adoration of the Magi by Raphael (1483 - 1520)

The Magi arrived in Jerusalem with a question, "Where is the newborn king of the Jews?"

The questions resound through the ages and down to our time. The answer is not always the same from generation to generation, nor even necessarily from person to person.

We can find Bethlehem on a map, we can visit the Church of the Nativity and the Shepherds' Field, seeking the answer to the question, "Where was the newborn king?" As meaningful as such an experience is, it doesn't answer today's question.

Nor is it adequate to answer that Jesus is now in heaven at the right hand of the Father. That is true, to be sure, but we remember that Jesus promised to be with us to the end of time.

A different approach might be more helpful. Instead of asking where Jesus is "out there," the question could be, "where is he, within us, among us?"

That is the question that lies behind Our Lady's Apparition at La Salette. It is as though she has been observing "her people" to see where Jesus is in their lives. To her disappointment, she cannot see him, except, as she says, in the religious practice of "a few elderly women." Her Son, to whom she was and is so intimately united, has been neglected, even insulted, if not rejected, by so many others.

It makes one think of when Mary and Joseph lost Jesus in Jerusalem for three days. Mary's feelings must be very similar as she looks at many parts of the world. Where has Jesus gone? Where is he? Where are the disciples? Why are they so few?

Jesus asked a similar question in Luke 18:8. "When the Son of Man comes, will he find faith on the earth?"

The Gospels often challenge us to examine the depth and constancy of our faith, and to consider what impact it really has, where Jesus really fits in our lives.

Monday, January 3 (#212)
Christmas weekday
(The Most Holy Name of Jesus)

Matthew 4:12-17,23-25: *"The people that lived in darkness have seen a great light."*

Meditation:

Jesus traveled to Capernaum so that what Isaiah had prophesied might be fulfilled. His disciples are called one by one to follow him. As for them, on being called they left what they were doing, in fact leaving everything behind. In following Jesus they experienced first-hand, so to speak, his ministry, his proclamation of the Good News, his healing of the sick, the lame and the blind. Their eyes, too, were opened and they became Christ's first and most dedicated followers.

WE, TOO, ARE CALLED BY MARY at La Salette to follow Jesus, her Son. She came in radiant light and in tears to remind us of Jesus' love for us all. How do we respond to her message? *"Do not be afraid,"* were the words she spoke to nudge us that we might listen to and proclaim the Good News of her Son in and through our own life. Let us respond as well as we can to her message of reconciliation by truly being her "children" and followers of Christ, her Son.

Reflection Questions:

- How can I share the word of Christ with those I meet today?
- Who were the first people to share their faith with me in my youth?

Tuesday, January 4 (#213)
Christmas weekday

Mark 6:34-44: *"Give them something to eat yourselves."*

Meditation:

On seeing the crowd Jesus *"took pity on them."* He saw – perhaps felt is the better word – their hunger. And so he told his disciples to feed them. Not mentioned, but most probably on his mind, was a deeper and more significant hunger, a spiritual hunger. The crowd was there primarily to hear Jesus' words, his message of love, concern and compassion. So, the gospel tells us, *"he set himself to teach them at some length."*

MARY AT LA SALETTE does the same for Maximin and Melanie, the two witnesses. She too pitied "her people." She taught them, gave them a message, and spoke to them of God's hunger. How often do we pass by the hungry without even a glance in their direction – not to mention stopping to feed them spiritually, with a kind word or a moment's attention? The apparition at La Salette did not last very long, but its message and impact have proven timeless.

Reflection Questions:

- What can I do to relieve the hunger of those I meet?
- When has someone fed me by their presence, their witness, their words of comfort or inspiration?

Wednesday, January 5 (#214)
Christmas weekday

Mark 6:45-52: *"Courage! It's me! Don't be afraid."*

Meditation:

Fear! What a big part of life it can be. In the city at night, one senses how fearful the people can be who must walk alone to their cars or the bus stop after work. Apartment dwellers too are often apprehensive in their neighborhood. A change of work, of ministry, an entirely new situation can often make our stomach fluttery and result in sleepless nights. We are afraid of what an unknown situation may demand of us. We are fearful when the future looks rather uncertain or our job security is shaken. Some of our fears are an appropriate and necessary response to perilous prospects; these fears can help prepare us to adapt to new circumstances, provided we do not allow them to paralyze us. One of the goals of the Christian life should be to live in confidence and trust, free of useless fears. The Lord is with us on the stormy sea. He reassures us not to be afraid.

MARY ADDRESSES OUR FEAR AS WELL. She tells us: *"Come near, my children; do not be afraid."* She bids us draw close to her and to her Son. She came in tears, but not in fear. She also came in love and with much compassion for us, her people, to console us in our anxieties and confusion, just as Jesus did in behalf of his disciples.

Reflection Questions:

- What fears do I bring to my daily encounters?
- What events has frightened me in the past?

Thursday, January 6 (#215)
Christmas weekday

Luke 4:14-22a: *"The Spirit of the Lord is on me.'"*

Meditation:

And then Jesus adds, still quoting Isaiah, *"to proclaim a year of favor from the Lord."* We know from subsequent happenings that the Lord did not simply announce a year of favor but centuries and lifetimes of God's favor, the Good News we call the Gospel. We, among many others, have been blessed by it. A single term which sums up what we've been given is faith. Our parents and godparents were asked at our Baptism what they were asking in our behalf; their response was faith. With the help of parents, under the influence of teachers and mentors, that faith has grown. Faith primarily means trust and confidence in God through Christ. It reassures us that our life and the world are in God's hands. Beyond this, faith means a way of seeing the world and life itself.

Faith conquers the world because it gives us assurance about important things relative to life and this world which mere human eyesight or insight could never detect. And so it is that by faith we know that – despite devastating illnesses, tragic accidents, crimes and war – life, joy and peace will have the final say. "Your world," it tells us, "is a world God has loved and will go on loving forever."

MARY ANNOUNCED this same message of life, joy and peace in Christ, her Son. Her words brought tidings of gospel gladness. They reminded us that God continues to break into our world with the joy of salvation, as sin is forgiven, death is destroyed, and broken hearts are healed.

Reflection Questions:

• How faithful am I in sharing this Good News with those I meet?
• How often have I stopped in prayer to thank God for God's many gifts, especially those people I truly treasure?

Friday, January 7 (#216)
Christmas weekday

Luke 5:12-16: *"Sir, if you are willing you can cleanse me."*

Meditation:

In spite of our faith, despite the fact that we have been baptized, in spite of all our good works, daily Masses and thousands of communions, we still might have those days when we wonder if we are going to heaven or not. Will God really forgive me my sins, especially the real terrible ones? For gossiping, for my unkindnesses, my lies, my insults? There are so many skeletons in our soul's closet that we might well worry from time to time whether or not we have really been forgiven? From experience we have all discovered that once a thing is done, there is no going back and undoing it. Yes, we can surely make a mess of our lives.

Though I most certainly do not advocate wrongdoing, I recognize that if it were not for the sins we have already committed, especially the most grievous, would we be going to Mass every Sunday, even daily? Would we have made Christ so central to our lives? Would we have returned to him again and again, confessed our sorrow to him, and relied so desperately on his love and forgiveness? A question we could ask about the leper in Luke's gospel story: Would he have gone to Jesus if he hadn't been suffering from leprosy? Jesus cured the man's body. He cures our souls. All we need do is ask, and choose to believe.

By her invitation that we *"Come near"*, Mary asks that we too draw near to her Son, the Christ. She invites us to come to him that we may find relief from our burdens and refreshment for our spirits. This desire of the Lord is Mary's as well, that her children, meaning ourselves, should feel welcomed, loved and forgiven.

Reflection Questions:

- What makes me hesitate to come to Jesus for help?
- Who has helped me in the past? Who would unhesitatingly respond to my needs?

Saturday, January 8 (#217)
Christmas Weekday

John 3:22-30: *"He must grow greater, I must grow less."*

Meditation:

Probably all of us at one time or another have wished that we could be President of the United States, at least for a day. We think of all the things we would do. Imagine being the chief resident of the White House for four or eight years. One could do so much good for so many people, not to mention the fabulous parties one would be invited to attend. But what happens when it is all over? And someone else takes your place? I would think it would be a big comedown – to be number one no longer.

Corporation presidents must step down, store managers, pastors, religious superiors, assembly-line workers must all move on to make space for others. Even parents must let their grown children be. Others must come to center stage while we step to one side. The same holds true of our decision-making. Christians are to live according to God's will, not their own. We are to do God's thing, not our own thing. Are we willing to do that – only if we are willing to decrease and let Christ increase in our lives.

Our Lady of La Salette chose two simple children to be her messengers. They certainly could not have been lower in social standing – simple, poor, uneducated shepherds. But they were chosen above all others. Isn't that what we see ourselves as – Mary's chosen sons and daughters, being able to let go of our positions, whatever they may be? We are called to follow the Lord in humble service, living up to what Mary and her Son ask of us.

Reflection Questions:

- How willing am I to "let go and let Jesus" take over every aspect of my life?
- How trusting am I of even my closest friends, allowing them to help me when I need them the most?

Sunday, January 9 (#021c)
The Baptism of the Lord

(Isaiah 42:14,6-7; Acts 10:34-38; Luke 3:15-16,21-22, optional gospel for year C)

Meditation: *Beloved*

The first Ecumenical Council, held in 325 AD, stated emphatically that Jesus was the Son of God, "God from God, Light from Light, true God from true God." The Bishops who gathered at that Council summed up in that way the teaching they had received from their predecessors, based in turn on the preaching of the Apostles and the whole New Testament.

They reflected on texts such as we find in today's Gospel. The voice from heaven says, "You are my beloved Son; with you I am well pleased."

The Baptism of Christ in the 1550 Frankfurt edition of the Small Catechism of Martin Luther by Hans Brosamer

This is only one of many passages that indicate the relation of Jesus to God as his Father.

The Mother of Jesus can therefore be called, according to another Council in 430 AD, "Mother of God."

AT LA SALETTE SHE DIRECTS OUR ATTENTION TO HER SON. Even before speaking a word, she shows him to us in the large, dazzlingly bright crucifix she wears on her breast. It bears repeating here that Mélanie and Maximin said that all the light that made up the Apparition seemed to flow from that crucifix. (One could almost say that, in this sense, the Beautiful Lady, too, was "light from Light.")

But she speaks of her Son as well. "I shall be forced to let go the arm of my Son... Those who drive the carts cannot swear without throwing in my Son's name." All together, "my Son" occurs six times in her discourse. She doesn't say "beloved," but who could doubt it

"My people" occurs three times. Again, "beloved" is not used, but who could doubt it?

A striking difference between the Gospel scene and the Apparition, is that the Father is "well pleased" with his beloved Son, whereas Mary came to tell us that her Divine Son was not well pleased with her people. She offered simple, very basic means of remedying that situation.

But our sinfulness does not mean we are not beloved. Why else would Mary have come?

Monday, January 10 (#305)
First Week in Ordinary Time

Mark 1:14-20: *"And at once (the disciples) left their nets and followed (Jesus)."*

Meditation:

The gospel reading tells us about Christ calling some fishermen to share with him the responsibility of gathering God's family and proclaiming the Good News of salvation. Soon after he had begun his public life Jesus wanted to lay a solid foundation for the continuation of his mission. Although he was not as popular at this early stage of his ministry as his miracles and acts of mercy would later make him, Jesus succeeded with his plan to build up his staff. His presence and words must have been tremendously powerful and marvelously inviting. As both God's message and messenger, he is the cornerstone of the Kingdom. He must gather to himself a small band of kindred spirits to whom he can unburden his own heart and upon whose hearts he may write his message. Christ approaches these men in their own life situation, as they were carrying out their daily chores. In response to the call, the fishermen left behind their precious nets and began to walk the dusty roads of Palestine with Jesus.

AT LA SALETTE Mary spoke the words of her Son, *"Come near, my chil-*

dren...." God's invitation is continuously extended through Mary. She comes to us with a plea that we abandon our sinful ways and turn back to Christ. She calls us near him, because as a person she knew the pain of being in this world of alienation and suffering. She is truly our mother whose heart yearns to help us find lasting refuge in Jesus, the Savior. Her entire conversation focused on him. He comes to us, as he did to his first recruits, in our daily struggles and tasks.

Reflection Questions:

- Like Mary should we not center our focus on Christ?
- What holds us back from abandoning our nets and favorite shores?

Tuesday, January 11 (#306)
First Week in Ordinary Time

Mark 1:21-28: *"What do you want with us, Jesus of Nazareth?"*

Meditation:

Jesus began his preaching in the synagogue, primarily an institution of learning. In tone and method, his teaching struck his listeners as a new revelation. He did not teach like the scribes, the experts in the Law. He was a man with a message. He spoke that message with authority and power. He himself was the new Torah, the supreme rule of faith and life. Such authority astonished his audience and the evil powers. "What have you to do with us? Mind your business. Go away. Go anywhere so long as you don't interfere with our ways." The powers wished to go on exploiting men, women, youth, and children, wanted to keep them addicted, bound by hatred and jealousy, burdened by inhuman abuse and cruelty. To this cry of the evil spirit, Jesus answered, *"Be quiet! Come out of him."* He makes the same answer today. He is concerned with every burden that weighs heavily on human shoulders.

At La Salette Our Lady brought a message of freedom to her people. A freedom that requires complete trust in God and obedience to his will. *"If my people will not submit, I shall be forced to let fall the arm of my Son."* Mary's words were spoken from her heart. They were not meant to alarm us with the fear of punishment but to sharpen our concern about our personal relationship with Jesus. She urges us to cultivate that relationship so that he might become more transparent in our lives as we grow more confident in his power. His power can and must own and possess us.

Reflection Questions:

- We all need to be owned and possessed. By whom shall I be possessed?
- Have I allowed Jesus to manifest his authority over my whole life?

Wednesday, January 12 (#307)
First Week in Ordinary Time

Mark 1:29-39: *"(Jesus) went in to her, took her by the hand and helped her up."*

Meditation:

Peter's mother-in-law was ill; the simple household was upset. And for the disciples the most natural thing in the world was to tell Jesus about it. After the exhausting experience of the synagogue service, Jesus could have claimed the right to rest. But once again nothing could keep him from doing good. The need of others took precedence over his desire for rest. He could feel the anxiety and concern of his disciples. He did not wait for an audience in order to exercise his healing power. He was there to heal Peter's mother-in-law. That world is our world, a world full of men and women haunted by fear, burdened with worry. This world seeks a healer. Personal fatigue could not keep Jesus from performing an act of kindness and healing. We must learn to look at people with compassion, to feel their anguish of heart. We are never blessed for ourselves alone, but for *others*.

THE APPARITION AT LA SALETTE is rooted in the vision our Mother has of us, her needy, poor, sinful and wretched children. Her never-tiring and endless love finds expression in the tears she shed at La Salette. There she opened her heart and spoke to Maximin and Melanie in a soft and tender voice. Through them, she was speaking to us as well. Like that of Jesus, Mary's compassion overflowed in tears. We are eternally grateful to God for giving us such a mother. She appears to us in our daily lives with a helping hand. Since we long for healing, she will certainly lead us to Christ, her Son.

Reflection Questions:

- Isn't it true that tiredness is often used as an excuse for not doing good?
- *"And let us never slacken in doing good"* (Galatians 6:9) How can I put this sound advice of the apostle Paul into practice?

Thursday, January 13 (#308)
First Week in Ordinary Time

Mark 1:40-45: *"Feeling sorry for him, Jesus stretched out his hand, touched him."*

Meditation:

The psychologist Erich Fromm wrote: "Alienation as we find it in modern society is almost total; it pervades the relationship of man to his work, to the things he consumes, to the State, to his fellowmen and to himself." Today's gospel speaks about this sort of alienation. In the New Testament no disease terrified people nor moved them to pity more than leprosy. The leper's fate was indeed hard. Ritually unclean, the leper was to remain segregated from the community, avoid all contact with others. Though he had no right to approach or to speak to him, the leper sensed that Jesus' compassion was his only recourse. Upon receiving his healing the man could not contain his inner joy. His heart overflowed with boundless gratitude. The Lord could have cured him from a distance, but chose to do so by touching him. We, too, must help others; but we must be ready to touch one another's lives. We must make sure that our care, our concern and our love touch those who need our help.

"SHE WEPT ALL THE WHILE SHE SPOKE TO US," the children of La Salette reported. Mary's tears spoke more loudly of her inner beauty, one of her most attractive characteristics as a woman. Mary was present, as always, to bring life, to give care, to show love. It is a wonderfully feminine virtue to be there with passion for those one loves, especially in moments of affliction and distress. She was there in tears on the mountain with Maximin and Melanie, representatives both of our broken world.

Reflection Questions:

- Can we see Our Lady's tears as a reflection of the sorrow and pity of the Son as he looks upon an ailing and wounded world?
- What attitude of mine might repel those in my life circle?

Friday, January 14 (#309)
First Week in Ordinary Time

Mark 2:1-12: *"... some people came bringing him a paralytic carried by four men."*

Meditation:

The crowd had jammed the pavement around the door to listen to Jesus. Into this crowd came four men bearing on a stretcher a friend who was paralyzed. We are not told his name nor the names of those who brought him to Jesus. They are referred to simply as "four men." Where would this world be without such people? They were the first of an endless company of those who have made it possible for others to reach the healing hands of Christ, anonymous apostles doing good quietly, unselfishly and without fanfare. People whose names never make the headlines. When he saw the faith of these four men Jesus must have smiled an understanding and affirming smile. In his sight, this was a loud proclamation of living faith. In what was perhaps one of the most joyous moments in his ministry, he looked at the man, and said, *"My child, your sins are forgiven."* Healer of soul and body, Jesus is truly Lord of life.

Mary's words at La Salette reiterate the baptismal call of every believer. She appeared not to add fame or glory to her credit but to bring us her Son's healing touch. Her persistent and enduring love compels her to intercede for us and to carry us to Jesus. Probably that is why her appearance and intercession are known in every corner of the world. Her message is a worldwide call to rediscover Jesus as Savior; it breaks down our self-erected barriers that we might immerse our paralyzed selves in Christ's healing love.

Reflection Questions:

- What hinders me from going out of my way to help others?

•Where should I look for the motivation to deal with pockets of inertia in my own Christian life?

Saturday, January 15 (#310)
First Week in Ordinary Time

Mark 2:13-17: *"(Jesus) said to him, 'Follow me.'"*

Meditation:

Jesus was walking by the lakeside, teaching like any rabbi of his day. He must have stopped when he saw Matthew, a tax collector in his booth. Tax collectors extracted from people as much as they possibly could and filled their own pockets with the surplus once the law's requirements had been met. Matthew was, therefore, thoroughly hated. He was sitting in his office, sitting in his sins, in his own world of alienation and public scorn.

But he had the will to respond to the entirely unexpected call of Jesus, *"Follow me."* He had probably heard about Jesus; he might have listened on the fringes of crowds to his message, and some-thing must have stirred in his heart at Jesus' words. He sprang to his feet, followed Jesus and spent his life in the service of the one who lifted him out of his emptiness and sin. Matthew manifested his gratitude by hosting a banquet, a tangible expression of reconciliation with God. A meal shared is, in fact, a life shared.

WE LEARN ABOUT PERSONAL INVOLVEMENT from the children of La Salette. They were called to proclaim their Beautiful Lady's good news. Her apparition blessed and marked their lives. Every blessing comes with a corresponding duty, a responsibility they did not shirk. Before and after the apparition, we see in them an amazing willing-ness to move freely with the Spirit. Leaving their beloved mountains and their untroubled way of life behind, they lent their words, their hearts and their sufferings to this stirring message. Discipleship in-volves extra sacrifice and a life-long commitment.

Reflection Questions:

•How does the Eucharist, the meal I share with my Lord, affect my personal conversion?

•When counting my blessings, do I give a thought to the responsibility each of them entails?

Sunday, January 16 (#66)
Second Sunday in Ordinary Time

(Isaiah 62:1-5; 1 Corinthians 12:4-11; John 2:1-11)

Meditation: *Do whatever He tells you*

Jesus turns water into wine

There are two places in the Bible where we find the phrase, "Do whatever he tells you." The first in in Genesis 41:55, when during the famine in Egypt the people are told, "Go to Joseph and do whatever he tells you." The second is in today's Gospel, when Mary tells the servants at the wedding feast to do whatever Jesus tells them.

In this scene the Mother of Jesus took the initiative, drawing his attention to the embarrassing situation of the wedding party, about to run out of wine, and overriding his objection that this was none of their business.

I remember a conference on the Apparition of Our Lady of La Salette that I heard when I was a seminarian in the 1960s. The speaker made the point that the Beautiful Lady didn't say, "I have been sent," but rather, "I am here," meaning that this was her idea. At La Salette, in other words, Mary again took the initiative.

THE MESSAGE OF LA SALETTE IS THE SAME AT CANA. It can be summed up in the words, "Do whatever he tells you." Perhaps this is why one of the newest murals painted on the walls of the Basilica of La Salette in France represents the wedding feast at Cana.

While Mary at La Salette highlights a number of basic Christian duties, the sense of her words goes well beyond those. They provide a necessary framework for the whole of Christian life.

In Egypt Joseph helped not only the Egyptians in a time of famine, but also preserved his own people, providing grain to the descendants of Abraham. At Cana, Jesus preserved the dignity of the newlyweds by providing wine. Isn't it interesting that at La Salette, Our Lady speaks of wheat and grapes, dietary staples of so many nations and cultures?

It is easy for us to make the connection to the Eucharist, which is chief among the basic Christian duties mentioned above. Our Lady of La Salette does not want us to go hungry—not physically, not spiritually.

Monday, January 17 (#311)
Second Week in Ordinary Time

Mark 2:18-22: *"As long as they have the bridegroom with them, they cannot fast."*

Meditation:

In the Jewish faith fasting was mandatory only one day in the entire year, and that was the Day of Atonement. Stricter Jews fasted two days each week. Jesus did not oppose fasting as such. It could help people learn to appreciate and value God's gifts, gain spiritual strength against evil and focus entirely on God. He faulted the Pharisees for making their fasting a way of drawing attention to their own righteousness, rather than a genuine expression of devotion to God. Fasting accompanied the rites of mourning in Israel. Jesus was with his disciples still; so there was no need to fast. It was time to celebrate and feast with him at table. We touch here the interplay between Advent and Christmas, between Good Friday and Easter. Our entire life in Christ is interplay between fasting and feasting. The Lord is truly present to us, yet we await his coming in glory. We receive the Lord in our hearts in the Eucharist, but that presence will not be complete until he comes again.

WHEN SHE HELPED HIM RECALL the day he saw the fragile wheat at Coin with his father, Mary at La Salette reminded Maximin that God's care is constant. Eucharist is an everlasting reminder of God's love for us. Our attitude, experience, understanding, and our voice are all-important to our appreciation of God's coming to us in the Eucharist. Each moment of our lives must be a crystal clear reflection of the Lord who comes to us through bread, broken and shared. Our abstinence and our sacrifice will enable us to savor the Eucharistic mystery and center our lives on the Lord's table.

Reflection Questions:

•*"As long as they have the bridegroom with them, they cannot fast."* Have we lost this joy?

•Have we lost the sense of the Lord's presence in our midst whether we are at home, at Mass or elsewhere?

Tuesday, January 18 (#312)
Second Week in Ordinary Time

Mark 2:23-28: *"The Son of man is master even of the Sabbath."*

Meditation:

In their deep reverence for God's command that the Lord's Day be kept holy, the Pharisees elaborated some thirty-nine rules governing its proper observance; they ranged from a prohibition against harvesting grain to a ban on carrying heavy loads. What made their attitude devious was their use of God's command to impose burdens on people, thereby complicating their lives. "What is the purpose of the law?" is a question we should often ask ourselves. Blind obedience to law, whether civil, moral or spiritual, is never enough. This can make narrow-minded or scrupulous Christians of us. We need to educate ourselves to each law's intent, the reason behind God's inspiration of that particular precept. Does our fondness for gossip reveal a hidden desire to appear wiser and holier than others? The Pharisee in us often talks louder than Jesus in us.

WHEN THE BEAUTIFUL LADY APPEARED AT LA SALETTE she said to the children, *"The seventh day I have kept for myself."* In doing so she revealed the deep-seated reason for the Sabbath. The Lord loves us so much, she reminded us, that he wants us to spend this special day in his company. Sunday worship cannot be a mere matter of fulfilling an obligation. It should be the joyful act of a grateful heart. Mary wishes us to grow in gratitude, to journey in faith, not alone but in the big family of believers. She wants us to don the garment of integrity and sincerity as we take our place at table with Jesus.

- Is the Pharisee or Jesus my standard of behavior?
- Am I overly narrow-minded in my Sunday observance?

Wednesday, January 19 (#313)
Second Week in Ordinary Time

Mark 3:1-6: *"Is it permitted on the Sabbath day to do good, or to do evil; to save life, or to kill?"*

Meditation:

Jesus takes time off from his lakeside preaching and healing. Once again he enters the synagogue on the Sabbath. The leading Jews and members of the Sanhedrin were there to scrutinize hi every move. They wanted no unlawful act from him that might mislead the people and entice them from the right way. It was the Sabbath; all work was forbidden. Had he been a fearful prophet, Jesus would have managed not to see the sick man. He well knew that to see him was to heal him, and to heal him could only mean trouble. *"Is it lawful on the Sabbath day,"* Jesus asks, *"to save life, or to kill?"* He thus discloses the priority God assigns to compassion in all his dealings with humanity. The law was meant to enhance the community's sense of human dignity. How can healing the paralytic jeopardize this intent? It can't. Jesus was frustrated with the Pharisees, not because they observed the Law, but because they were narrow-minded and burdened others in its application.

Mary's appearance and intervention at La Salette was rather necessary and most timely in a world become licentious and self-centered. More than an appeal, her message carried transforming power and served as a salutary reminder that evil is to be rejected energetically, that God is to be embraced enthusiastically. Mary stands at La Salette as our spiritual mother and a woman, committed and faithful, dedicated with all her feminine heart to what is good and right. The voice she raised at La Salette needs to be heard even today.

Reflection Questions:

- How do I utilize God-given opportunities to do acts of mercy?

• What might I learn if I write a list of God's commands and their underlying intent?

Thursday, January 20 (#314)
Second Week in Ordinary Time

Mark 3:7-12: *"great numbers... heard of all that (Jesus) was doing."*

Meditation:

The synagogue authorities and the community elders were set for a conflict with Jesus over the good works he did on the Sabbath. Jesus discreetly avoids the situation, however, and keeps the focus on his mission. Leaving the synagogue, he went out to the lakeside and the open sky. It was not that he withdrew through fear, but that his hour had not yet come and that he had much more to do. Undaunted by the controversy, the crowd fearlessly followed Jesus. *"(They) heard of all that (Jesus) was doing."* Reports of his deeds, his assistance to all in need, served as a magnet that drew them. Most were drawn to Christ by an inner desire to taste and see divine acts. The region was electrified. Everyone wants to see a miracle at least once in a lifetime! Miracles in themselves do not sustain faith. For the believer, no miracle is necessary; for the unbeliever, no miracle is possible. What we need most is the courage and strength to decide resolutely for Jesus in the difficult moments of our lives.

THE LA SALETTE MESSAGE focuses on people's refusal to give God the time he re-quests, their disrespect for his name, and the hardness of their hearts. It was addressed to people who refused to welcome the word of God into their lives. Maximin and Melanie were so very blessed to hear Mary's comforting and energizing words. They were set free from fear and anxiety. The miracle of the apparition did not come in answer to any desire of theirs, it simply dawned in their lives. They afterwards gave their whole lives to make the Lady's message known to all. Having freely received, they freely gave.

Reflection Questions:

• How fearless a follower of Christ can I truthfully say I am?
• What is it about Jesus and his teaching that excites me?

Friday, January 21 (#315)
Second Week in Ordinary Time

Mark 3:13-19: *"(Jesus) appointed twelve; they were to be his companions and to be sent out to proclaim the message, with power to drive out devils."*

Meditation:

Jesus takes one more step forward in carrying out his mission. He had articulated his message; he had selected his method; he had shown his divine authority over evil spirits and illness. He had seen large crowds following him, eager to taste divine love. He had felt this flock's inner thirst. Now he had to find an effective way to make his message a lasting one, one that would extend beyond Galilee. To further his mission he chose ordinary men who were willing to give their lives for the sake of God's Kingdom. He called them *"to be his companions and to be sent out to proclaim the message, with power to drive out devils."* These three charges are essential components of the disciple's calling: to be with Jesus, to understand him, to capture his spirit, to share his trust in God, to go out and preach the Word of life, the Word made flesh, to heal the world of all evil spirits. Each of these blessings carries with it a responsibility. To love God is to love his works and his children beyond measure.

At La Salette Mary is indeed sent by God and speaks the words of God. She unabashedly refers to her two most precious possessions: her Son and her people. Her pleading in behalf of her children was ongoing, and sinners were drawn to her Son that they might find in him forgiveness, healing and reconciliation. In a world broken and divided, the La Salette message remains relevant. To take the Word of God, called to our attention by Mary, to the ends of the world is our primary baptismal responsibility. Jesus' death and resurrection have earned us heavenly citizenship. Mary's apparition reminds us that sacred duties and responsibilities accompany blessings such as this.

Reflection Questions:

- As a disciple of Christ do I recognize the responsibilities my discipleship entails?
- Do I act accordingly?

Saturday, January 22 (#316)
Second Week in Ordinary Time

Mark 3:20-21: *"They said, '(Jesus) is out of his mind.'"*

Meditation:

The crowd follows Jesus with great affection and excitement. They have seen him performing miracles and have heard his powerful words. Still we see them thirsting for more of his wisdom and miracles. Certainly a good number of them believed in him and their hearts were yearning to be formed in the ways of God. All these things sounded so bizarre and strange to his own family, who then decided that the time had come to take him home. They perhaps feared the consequences of such acts and preferred not to be condemned by the Jewish leaders. The language of Mark's Gospel here offers a dramatic picture of Jesus' humanness: his reaction and the wide range of emotions he displays are so much like our own. He was pained when people disappointed him. For the good things he was doing, he was anything but appreciated by those closest to him. His own relatives said, "He is out of his mind." We sometimes do good and are suspected of having ulterior motives.

THE LA SALETTE EVENT INVITES US TO LOOK AT THE EVENTS OF OUR LIVES and our world with the eyes of faith. Whatever causes pain in our relationships must be viewed from a faith perspective. It was the absence of a faith perspective that made Mary's presence at La Salette so necessary. Her single-minded focus on her Son should be ours as well. Our modern world and self-congratulatory attitude have created blind spots and denials that challenge us to stand up for Jesus with integrity and proclaim his word with unflagging enthusiasm.

Some Reflection Questions:

- How do you react when your loved ones do not appreciate you?
- Why does affirmation by those closest to you perhaps mean so much to you?

Sunday, January 23 (#069)
Third Sunday in Ordinary Time

(Nehemiah 8:2-4a, 5-6, 8-10; 1 Corinthians 12:1-30; Luke 1:1-4, 4:14-21)

Meditation: *Today*

Twice in today's first reading and once in the Gospel we find the word "Today." It's a word we use often without giving it much thought, but once in a while it has a certain weight or urgency.

That is certainly the case in the Gospel. When Jesus says, "Today this Scripture passage is fulfilled in your hearing," he is saying in effect, "This is the big day! This is the day you have all been waiting for."

That certainly got their attention. We see this also in the reading from Nehemiah. "Men, women and children old enough to understand listened attentively to the book of the Law"—for about six hours! Many, it seems, had never heard it before and they wept on learning how, without knowing, they had violated the Law. That was a big day for them, and they were told not to weep but to celebrate. Now that they had come to know the Law, they would be able to observe it. In this way they could hope to avoid the punishments and exile inflicted on their ancestors who had not observed the Law. They would be in a right relationship with their God.

Jesus Unrolls the Book in the Synagogue
by James Tissot (1836–1902)

In the message of La Salette, Our Lady wants to help us rediscover our right relationship with her Son. She gives examples of how we have endangered it, and indicates how we might begin to repair the harm that has been done or, more accurately, allow the harm to be repaired.

There is an urgency to her words, accentuated by her tears. She says the arm of her Son is so heavy she can no longer hold it. She tells us that she has been suffering a long time for us, so much so that there is no way we could even attempt to repay her.

Is the Beautiful Lady a prophet of doom? No, but like all the prophets she recognizes, as we do not, the consequences of our sin and neglect. She echoes in her own words the sentiments of the prophet Joel, "Even now, says the Lord, return to me with your whole heart," and those of St. Paul, "Now is the acceptable time."

In other words: Today is the day! Why wait?

Monday, January 24 (#317)
Third Week in Ordinary Time

Mark 3:22-30: *"In truth I tell you, all human sins will be forgiven, and all the blasphemies ever uttered; but anyone who blasphemes against the Holy Spirit will never be forgiven, but is guilty of an eternal sin."*

Meditation:

There is something in us that wants to believe that all can be forgiven. After all, Jesus does battle with the powers of darkness and he just doesn't win, he actually crushes the powers of death and raises all life to share victoriously in his glory. The entire ministry of Jesus is a series of conflicts between the powers of God at work in him and the power of evil at work in the world. In every instance the power of good prevails. Resisting that power, denying its strength, dismissing its presence is the great sin.

The world we live in is filled to overflowing with examples of the powers of hell seemingly winning the day. But it may all be summed up in the spirit of the young Columbine student who died for believing that goodness prevails while she stared evil in the face. Not only can a house divided against itself not stand, neither can a faith, nor a heart, nor a marriage, nor a family, nor a community. Indeed, "united we stand and divided we fall." The great sign of the Kingdom actually being built happens when we work together confronting the evils of the day.

Mary weeps at La Salette because her children try to live without the communion of God's love. She comes to call us to communion, to reconciliation. Her apparition at La Salette is a reminder of the will of the Father so intimately known in the life and teachings of her Son. We too are her children for whom she prays for unity and oneness. We are neither Jew nor Greek, neither male nor female, neither slave nor free. We are her children loved with the same heart that loved Jesus, brothers and sisters all.

Reflection Questions:
- What divides our hearts?
- What unites our hearts?

Tuesday, January 25 (#519)
The Conversion of Saint Paul

Mark 16:15-18: "*Jesus… said to them: 'Go out to the whole world; proclaim the gospel to all creation.'*"

Meditation:

There is a contradiction in the life of Saul of Tarsus that seems to be an impediment to his becoming Saint Paul, the apostle to the Gentiles. It is his fierce faith, his devotion to God. After all he is a learned Jew who eats and drinks the Word of God and waits for the all-powerful Messiah who was, in the common view of the Jewish nation, to overcome their enemies and make the Jewish people powerful in the eyes of all the world. Instead Saul realizes, once he meets Jesus "on the road", that his kingdom is not of this world and that his hopes for secular power for his nation are now turned into a life of sacrifice and humble service to Jesus of Nazareth, a carpenter's son. Yet by the grace of God, the conversion makes this staunch Jew into an apostle of Jesus to the gentiles – who could have believed it could come to this!

Mary's appearance at La Salette is also rife with contradictions. She chooses to appear in a most remote place to two seemingly insignificant children instead of in a public place, witnessed by a cast of thousands, addressing a Bishop or other Church notable. Yet her choice miraculously was the right one! The two children received from her a mandate similar to that which Jesus gave to his own disciples: "Go out to the whole world (all my people)" and make the message known. Yet by the grace of God, her words and their effect have truly been miraculous – first, in the life of Maximin's father who came back to the sacraments, and then thereafter to countless pilgrims whose faith was renewed and strengthened by Mary's message of respect for the name of her Son, the importance of daily prayer, Sunday worship and a responsibility to share her message with others.

Reflection Questions:

- How have you acted like Saint Paul, encouraging people to believe, reaching out to others in their need?
- What particular words or actions of Mary at La Salette touched your heart?

Wednesday, January 26 (#319)
Third Week in Ordinary Time

Mark 4:1-20: *"Listen! Imagine a sower going out to sow."*

Meditation:

The people to whom Jesus speaks are being encouraged to be good soil, to be good listeners. Jesus isn't simply asking that his words be given a hearing, but that they be cultivated and allowed to produce an abundance of meaning. The measure that they produced, whether thirty, fifty or a hundred percent according to their abilities, wasn't what concerned Jesus. What he demanded of his hearers was that his words receive a response, that they make a difference. At his word, people are healed, forgiven, saved. He speaks not merely to enlighten our minds but to touch our hearts. To hear with our hearts is to put faith in him, to believe. Without faith the words can be confusing: *"Love your enemies," "The last shall be first." "Happy are those who mourn."* In *The Little Prince*, we are told that what is essential is invisible to the eye and that it is only with the heart that one sees rightly. And so it is that only with the heart can one hear rightly. The heart is the core of hearing and seeing. We can see and hear in those who are in good soil the power of an abundant response to the word of God. We can hear and see gentleness and generosity and undying hope. An abundant harvest is unmistakable.

"Come near, my children, do not be afraid. I am here to tell you great news." Like the words of the Gospel, the words of La Salette are meant to be heard again and again. They weren't addressed only to those who heard them the first time. They were meant for a wider audience, for repeated proclamation. *"Make this known to all my people."* They have a claim upon us because they speak to our deepest yearnings for meaning and healing, for an abundance of life and love.

Reflection Questions:

- Who, in my life, speaks gentleness, generosity and undying hope?
- Whom do I know who has been most generous to me?

Thursday, January 27 (#320)
Third Week in Ordinary Time

Mark 4:21-25: *"Take notice of what you are hearing. The standard you use will be used for you -- and you will receive more besides."*

Meditation:

Listen carefully! To whom do we listen? Do we listen only to the loudest, the most articulate, the most pleasant? Do we listen with the Lord to the cries of the poor, the inarticulate, the lonely? Do we listen to people or just to words? Do we listen for new ideas, for gossip, for the sensational? Do we listen to the Good News? Henri Nouwen spoke of "learning about God as the very opposite of piling up ideas." To truly listen is to embrace the silence that allows us to hear others speak to us about God.

If we listen carefully, "God can be listened out of people." Whose love, whose welcome, whose compassion reflects the love, the welcome and the compassion of our God? From whose life do we receive the Word of God? There is a full measure of revelation awaiting those who have ears to hear. The power of God's word is not confined to our limited hierarchical and holy expectations. The alien, the outcast, the sinner spoke to Jesus of God and so he listened. "Real learning" said Nouwen, "in a spiritual sense, is a growing willingness to listen."

WHEN MOTHER MARY says to Melanie and Maximin, *"I am here to tell you great news,"* she asks for a hearing from her children. She asks for a hearing of her suffering and pain on our behalf. She asks us to listen to the meanings of the signs of the times. She asks to hear our prayers. She asks for our voices to tell the world the Good News of God's reconciling love.

Reflection Questions:

- Where and when and by whom does God surprise you with his revelation?
- When have you felt inspired when you someone doing something good?

Friday, January 28 (#321)
Third Week in Ordinary Time

Mark 4:26-34: *"The reign of God... is like a mustard seed... the smallest of all the seeds on earth...it grows into the biggest shrub of them all."*

Meditation:

Expect the kingdom to happen in small ways. The kingdom is like the innocent heart of a small child eager to love and to learn. It is like the smallest gift of the widow who gives all that she had. It is like the tiniest of seeds that produces the largest of plants. The smallest of beginnings can have great results. God works his wonders among us in very subtle almost unnoticeable ways ac-cording to his own timetable and manner.

The kingdom grows unnoticed while we go about our lives as usual. It happens constantly, mysteriously. The message of the mustard seed encouraged us to face the world with our small resources and trust that God will accomplish great things through them. If God can take the smallest of seeds to produce the largest of shrubs, how much more can he do with our lives. The images of the reign of God are hidden in the obvious, waiting for the recognition of those who have faith to believe, eyes to see and ears to hear.

If the kingdom can be seen in the gospel images of a child's innocence, in the generosity of a widow and in the beauty of creation
then it can also be seen in the love of someone who quietly enlarges
our life and time and world. There are always some people in whom
the seed takes root and flourishes. God is never without kingdom
people. They touch our lives with little acts of kindness and love
which by the world's standards seem insignificant. But the unfolding
mystery is in plain sight for those who have faith to see.

THE KINGDOM OF GOD IS LIKE A MOTHER who gave her all when she gave
the world her son. He grew in grace and love, offering himself for the
salvation of the world. But it is a story that is all too often ignored,
denied, rejected and opposed. So the story needs to be told again and
again. La Salette is an invitation to faith, the planting anew of the
seeds of hope and the cultivating of the kingdom of reconciling love.

Reflection Questions:

• Where do you see the kingdom taking root and flourishing?
• When have you been touched by the reconciling love of God in
another person?

Saturday, January 29 (#322)
Third Week in Ordinary Time

Mark 4:35-41: *"Master, do you not care? We are lost!...Then (Jesus) said to
them, 'Why are you so frightened? Have you still no faith?'"*

Meditation:

Jesus reassures the apostles that when he is with them they have
nothing to fear. He also reassures them his own serenity comes from
trusting in the Father who is always with him. That false sense of
isolation that exists in our imagination, that sense of separateness is
usually at the bottom of all our fears. St. Augustine once said: "The
tragedy of human life is that so many of us walk through life side by
side thinking no one else has a problem like ours and all the way to
the grave the people at our side were experiencing the same things."

The popularity of support groups and Twelve Step programs today, however, suggests that drowning people are calling out for help. When we cry out in our panic, like Peter, we have to believe that it does matter to God and that he does send help to quiet the storms. There is no disgrace in calling out for help as Peter does. Jesus may not solve the problem or change the situation but he will change us and give us peace, which in reality does calm the storm. Being in the boat with Jesus doesn't mean that there won't be any storms. It does mean that we won't have to face them alone. It just takes a little faith and some capacity for surprise.

MOTHER MARY'S FIRST WORDS AT LA SALETTE to Melanie and Maximin were, *"Come near, my children, do not be afraid."* She does this while sharing a worried mother's concern for her children. She came to encourage her children to put aside their fears, to be reconciled to God's loving, merciful presence in their lives. Mary's words at La Salette echo across the years and miles to all her children, *"Come near, do not be afraid."*

Reflection Questions:

• Where in your life do you hear the Lord saying to you, "Why are you so terrified? Why are you lacking faith? Be still!"
• In what situation did you feel the peace of the Lord in your life?

Sunday, January 30 (#072)
Fourth Sunday in Ordinary Time

(Jeremiah 1:4-5 17-19; 1 Corinthians 12:31to 13:13; Luke 4:21-30)

Meditation: *Acceptance*

Jesus, after making a great first impression, was ultimately rejected by the people of his hometown.

Most of us at some time have felt the pain of not being accepted. We might not have been invited to an event we really hoped to attend. Our contribution to a project might not have been appreciated. We might even have been laughed at!

That was certainly the experience, at least initially, of Maximin and Mélanie when they began to tell people what—whom—they had seen on the mountain. In the months following that September 19, 1846, both civic and ecclesiastical officials set out to prove that they were either liars or else victims of a very clever hoax. Fr. Félix Dupanloup, soon to be named bishop of Orléans, actually disliked Maximin intensely when he met him in 1848, but even he came away from the encounter convinced of the truth of what the boy had said.

There were others, of course, who simply dismissed the possibility that the Blessed Virgin could have appeared at all—the secular press was openly hostile to the whole idea—or at least not to two such children as these.

Deep down, it may have had less to do with Mélanie and Maximin than with a certain resistance to the message they were passing on. No one likes to be told to change. We settle into a way of being and doing that suits us, and we don't appreciate having that disturbed.

Nazareth people didn't want to see Jesus as the Savior fulfilling the words of prophets. That attitude is shared by many today. After all, to accept Jesus as Savior implies I need saving, which is not easy to accept. The same was—and is—true of La Salette. It is easier to object to certain words or expressions in the message (as some theologians have done) or to point to the ordinary human failings in the lives of Maximin and Melanie than it is to adopt an attitude of acceptance and really take Mary's words to heart.

Monday, January 31 (#323)
Fourth Week in Ordinary Time

Mark 5:1-20: *"Then (Jesus) asked, 'What is your name?' He answered, 'My name is Legion...'"*

Meditation:

We, like the man in the Gospel, sometimes find ourselves in the grip of things and habits that are not life-giving and keep us restrained or prevent us from growing as persons. Jesus found it important to ask the name of the spirit in this man. Once he was able to name the demon, he had power over it and could cast it out. The same is true for us. We can grow only if we call our demons and fears by their names, and, "they are many," both personal and communal. Only in acknowledging or naming these weaknesses can we begin to allow God to help us change our destructive habits. Only when we have done so, when we've allowed God to help us see rightly, can we progressively change and be renewed. Then, like the man in the Gospel who is healed, we are better able to proclaim the news that God has been powerful in our life, and that God can give us a new heart, if we allow him to do so.

At La Salette Mary urges us to do the same. She calls us to a change of heart. She names some of the demons of the time, which still apply today: indifference to prayer, to the Eucharist, to respect of the Lord's Day and the Lord's Name. Mary tells us that God cares, as she does. God desires to be the true God in our life. She reminds us to what great extent God has gone to reveal the mystery of divine love in Jesus. Mary in tears urges us to return to her Son, with our whole heart.

Reflection Questions:

• Are you able and willing to name your "demons"?
• Which of these is the greatest obstacle to your spiritual growth and relationship with Jesus?

Tuesday, February 1 (#324)
Fourth Week in Ordinary Time

Mark 5: 21-43: *"Who touched my clothes?"*

Meditation:

We have all had the experience of being in a crowded place where people jostle one another, bumping and pushing, oftentimes for no other reason than that there are too many people present. The jostling, though obtrusive and aggravating, truly means nothing except that the place is overcrowded. The pushing and touching mean nothing. On the other hand, if in the same crowd, someone reaches out and touches us gently on the shoulder, to get our attention, we respond immediately. We can tell the difference between a push or a shove and a call for our attention.

The woman with a hemorrhage is desperate. Her need and desire are deep. She timidly, yet confidently and trustingly, reaches out and touches Jesus' garment in the hope of being healed. His sensitivity to her hand and touch as well as to her profound need and prayer causes him to react, to respond and to heal her.

AT LA SALETTE, in no way does Mary push or shove or even demand. She invites, she urges, she "touches" our hearts with her tears and her motherly concern. She gently places before us the glowing and resplendent image and reminder of her crucified Son. She reminds us that he desires to heal and renew. He aches to see us suffer as a result of our human blindness, so he "glows" and "shines" to attract our attention, to touch our hearts, to lead us to repentance and conversion. His hope and Mary's hope for us is that once we have truly seen him as the light of our life, we will cling to him, "touch" him, seeking a change of heart. He desires to grant that gift. Do we choose to receive it?

Reflection Questions:

- In some way do I fear getting too close to Jesus? Do I fear what conversion and healing will demand of me?
- Can I allow myself to trust completely in his love for me?

Wednesday, February 2 (#524)
The Presentation of the Lord

(Malachi 3:1-4; Hebrews 2:14-18; Luke 2:22-40)

Meditation: *The Lord in his Temple*

Malachi has a vision in which *"the Lord whom you seek will come suddenly to his temple,"* and who will purify the Levites, ministers of the temple. Only then will their sacrifices be pleasing to God, *"as in the days of old, as in years gone by."*

Purification is a painful process. The "refiner's fire" conjures up

The presentation of Christ in the Temple
By Hans Holbein the Elder (1465–1524)

40

the image of gold or silver being melted over an intense heat so that the impurities will float to the surface and can be skimmed off. The "fuller's lye" was a caustic substance used to clean and whiten woolen cloth before it was made into garments, especially for worship.

AT LA SALETTE there is a like kind of purification. When Mary says, *"If the harvest is ruined, it is only on account of yourselves"* and catalogues the disasters that have been visited upon her people, she is using images not unlike those used by Malachi. The purpose is not to impose a burden of guilt, much less cause suffering. On the contrary, it is to restore us, to show us where and how we need to be purified. Whatever the pain, sorrow or shame Our Lady's words and tears may cause us, we must not lose sight of the love behind them.

In the Gospel scene of the presentation of Jesus in the temple—a fulfillment of Malachi's prophecy—Simeon says to Mary, *"Look ... a sword will pierce your soul (heart) too."* The image of our Weeping Mother seems to be part of the fulfillment of that prophecy.

In 1 Corinthians 3:16, St. Paul reminds us that we are God's temple. Just as we would expect a physical temple to be as splendid and spotless as possible, so also we ought to be concerned for our inner splendor and integrity, worthy of our indwelling Lord.

Our Lady of La Salette appeared in splendor. Even her radiance is a call, an invitation to be aware of what we might be, if only we would submit simply and humbly to God's will. We are the temple. Let the Lord enter!

Thursday, February 3 (#326)
Fourth Week in Ordinary Time

Mark 6:7-13: *"(Jesus) instructed them to take nothing on the journey."*

Meditation:

It has been said that in Palestine in the time of Jesus, the natives had five articles of clothing: a long inner tunic, an outer cloak, a belt, sandals and the oriental headdress. Travelers carried a bag for food. In sending the disciples forth to preach and teach, Jesus recommends that they take only the bare essentials: clothing and a traveling stick for support and protection. No food, no extras. But they were to take the Word – the good news, the message of freedom and liberation. How challenging for the disciples and for us. No extras! No cumbersome distractions and burdens! An invitation to trust in the power given them by Jesus, the power of the Word. Their mission is accomplished. Their joy and amazement are profound!

ON THE HOLY MOUNTAIN OF LA SALETTE, Mary sends the visionaries forth with nothing but their innocence and simplicity and their experience of the Mountain Vision. It is the Beautiful Lady herself and what she said, and the dazzling crucifix on her breast that would sustain them. She sends them forth as they are, innocent and undeserving visionaries who have been blessed with a transforming experience. *"Well, my children, make this known to all my people."* The tenderness, the warmth and intimacy of this experience are enough to convince her people and lead them to a change of heart. The people will know that the message and meaning here are more than these ignorant and innocent children could fabricate. Her people were converted, then and ever since.

Reflection Questions:

- As a disciple of Jesus and a son/daughter of Our Lady of La Salette, have I been "touched" by my experience of Jesus and Mary at La Salette?
- Are there any "extras" that I probably carry along to fill in the gaps, lack of experience or lack of trust in the power of the Word?

Friday, February 4 (#327)
Fourth Week in Ordinary Time

Mark 6:14-29: *"When (Herod) heard John (the Baptist) speak he was greatly perplexed, and yet he liked to listen to him."*

Meditation:

This gospel scene is a flashback interjected in the middle of the story of the mission of the disciples and their return to Jesus. The flashback serves to give us an insight into what Herod thought of Jesus. The scriptures say, *"King Herod has heard about (Jesus), since by now his name was well known."* Mark takes the occasion to remind his readers that it was this Herod who had John the Baptist beheaded. The flashback also tells us of Herod's weakness, Herodias' grudge against John and Salome's famous dance and her being manipulated into requesting the head of the Baptist as a reward for pleasing Herod. In addition to telling us about these people, the flashback serves to not only dredge up painful and sorrowful events of the past but to bring forth, as well, happy memories of blessings received.

AT LA SALETTE, Mary reminds people of things they have done and are doing. Her message includes flashbacks which most people find to be disturbing reminders of our human weakness and sinfulness. But the apparition also includes two very positive flashbacks. The first is the reminder of Jesus' crucifixion and death which is the sign that "God loved the world so much," as John the Evangelist tells us. The crucifix on Mary's breast is the blinding reminder. The second is the famous reminder of the episode in the field of Coin where Mary reminds Maximin and us that, in her motherly love and concern, she is present to us in the details of our life. How wonderful to be reminded!

Reflection Questions:

• What recent flashbacks in my own life and prayer have helped to make me more grateful for God's love and presence in my life?
• When have I been reminded of a good experience which I had forgotten?

Saturday, February 5 (#328)
Fourth Week in Ordinary Time

Mark 6:30-34: *"Come... and rest for a while."*

Meditation:

In this Gospel scene, Jesus is revealed as the "Divine Psychologist" and the "Man with a Heart." The disciples return from their mission excited and happy with the success of their work but exhausted by its demands. Jesus encourages them to get some rest, to balance their work with leisure and prayer. He invites them to enjoy a mini-Sabbath experience. He knows that one cannot be whole nor even survive long without the necessary physical rest and relaxation. He has seen to this balance in his own life. Here he reveals his loving concern for the disciples, for their wholeness and well-being. Later he is touched with pity for the crowds who were *like sheep without a shepherd.*" He teaches them and leads them to "green pastures," to "still waters" where he refreshes their souls.

Our Lady of La Salette appears in the desert highlands of the Alps. Her very presence there is an invitation for us and for all pilgrims to "come away and rest a while." She invites all her children to enter into that mountain retreat in order to be quiet, to rest, to reflect and to be refreshed by the good news of God's love that she brings. *"Come,"* she says, *"be not afraid. I have come to tell you great news."*

Reflection Questions:

- How often do I allow myself to go into that sacred place of retreat, to hear Mary's motherly message and call to repentance, conversion and reconciliation?
- What is a favorite place which reminds you of the joy of the simple pleasures of life?

Sunday, February 6 (#075)
Fifth Sunday in Ordinary Time
(Isaiah 6:1-2a; 1 Corinthians 15:3-8, 11; Luke 5:1-11)

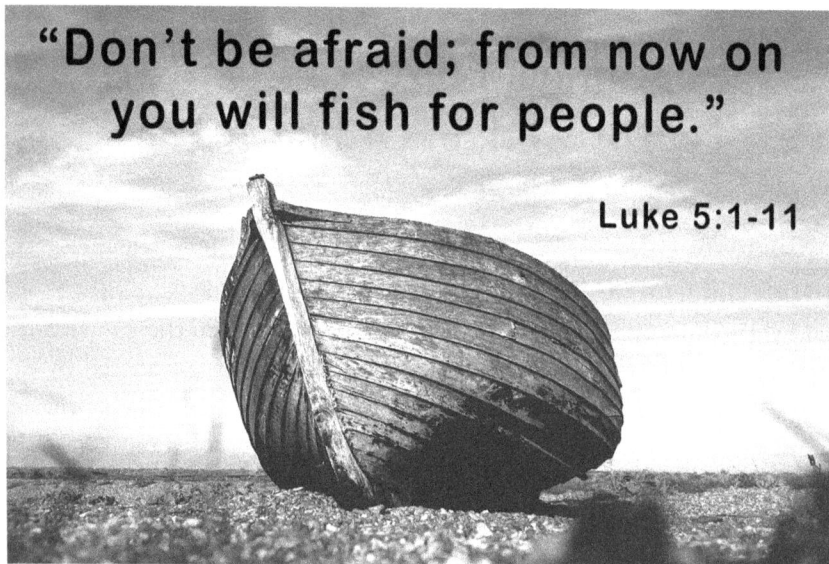

"Don't be afraid; from now on you will fish for people."

Luke 5:1-11

Meditation: *Whom Shall I Send?*

If you were embarking on a career as an itinerant teacher, where would you look for associates or assistants or companions? If you were about to publish the greatest novel the world has ever seen, who would be your proofreader? If you had a really important message to communicate... well, you get the idea.

You certainly wouldn't choose people who had no skills to recommend them for the purpose. And from the opposite perspective, if you lacked the qualifications, you would not expect to be chosen. That's plain common sense.

Simon Peter definitely felt out of his depth when he witnessed the miraculous catch of fish. Jesus shouldn't be associating with the likes of him!

But Jesus, apparently, wasn't looking for saints, or even teachers to help him in his mission. Scribes and Pharisees would later criticize him even just for associating with sinners. What must they have thought of his Apostles!

At La Salette Mary chose two highly unlikely persons to make her message known: a scatterbrained 11-year-old boy who hadn't even the good sense to keep his pet goat from strangling itself, and a slight 14-year-old girl who rarely spoke unless spoken to, who, after returning to the village, went right off to her chores without saying a word about having seen a Beautiful Lady!

Jesus knew what he was doing that day on the Sea of Galilee. Mary knew what she was doing that day in the French Alps. Both needed reliable witnesses, and the most reliable witnesses are those who couldn't possibly have made up the things they are saying, who have no reason to do so. Our legal expectation of witnesses in court is that they tell the truth, the whole truth, and nothing but the truth.

The Apostles did that. Mélanie and Maximin did that. They were faithful witnesses. Who and what they were personally is of no importance compared to the witness they bore.

Monday, February 7 (#329)
Fifth Week in Ordinary Time

Mark 6:53-56: *"And all who touched (Jesus) were saved."*

Meditation:

This final verse of Mark 6 reinforces a theme that is of special significance to the evangelist and to us who make our pilgrim way to the Father's house. The theme of healing. We are all in need of healing, whether physical or spiritual. We seek a confessor, a doctor, or a therapist that we may find the healing we need. Jesus said, *"It is not the healthy who need the doctor, but the sick."* (Mark 2:17). All four gospels attest to the fact that, in the power of the Spirit, Jesus ministered God's healing to all who were in need of it. In response to people's faith, healing poured forth from Jesus, like a never-ending flow of living water. Thus were fulfilled the words of the prophet: *"He who pities them ... will guide them to springs of water"* (Isaiah 49:10b). The wholeness Jesus brings is healing at its deepest level. God's love, incarnate in him, gushes forth as a saving fountain, curing body, mind, spirit. Its power pulsated in the very "tassel of his cloak."

To the bewilderment of her two chosen witnesses, Mary showed herself at La Salette in tears. Her tears bring to mind the healing water flowing from Christ's pierced side (John 19:34). *"The thirsty land,"* Isaiah had prophesied, will become *"springs of water"* (Isaiah 35:7a). The frequency of the word sin in the Bible and its almost total absence from contemporary talk point to a contemporary "thirsty ground." The recognition that human life is infected by sin is, one would think, an essential part of any realistic description of the human condition. How well-inspired those peasant villagers were who, from the beginning, invoked their heavenly Visitor as Our Lady of La Salette, Reconciler of *sinners*!

Reflection Questions:

• Do I find it easy or difficult to admit that I am in need of healing?
• Can I imagine what it might be like to feel the healing touch of Jesus?

Tuesday, February 8 (#330)
Fifth Week in Ordinary Time

Mark 7:1-13: *"In this way you make God's word ineffective."*

Meditation:

One of the controversial things Jesus did in the course of his ministry was to redefine the proper application of Jewish ritual purity laws. By no means was he opposed to the Torah. He had little tolerance, though, for what he considered to be abuses of religious authority inflicted on the little people by the so-called spiritual leaders. We know that many struggle with God's will as stated in divine law and the observance of certain customs and practices that nullify and make a mockery of God's Word.

How often are we ourselves torn between the law of God and man-made laws? The Pharisees in our gospel passage accuse Jesus and his disciples of eating with defiled hands. In reply Jesus unambiguously states that what matters is our inner life with our God and not its outward trappings. What comes from within – a pure heart and a well-formed conscience – interests him a great deal. Cleanse your hearts, put your faith in me, he tells us, and keep from performing empty rituals for others to see.

THE DUTY OF OBEYING GOD'S law goes largely ignored in our secular world. Mary at La Salette underscores her children's disrespectful attitude toward commandments that spell out the duties of humble gratitude and service we owe to our Creator: *"If my people will not submit, I shall be forced to let fall the arm of my Son."* The initiative she showed that September day at La Salette means, essentially, that even in glory the Queen of heaven is ever engaged in the reconciliation of her people on earth.

Reflection Questions:

• Do I set time aside each day to go within and allow Jesus to speak to my heart?
• Is it true that laws make good servants but poor masters?

Wednesday, February 9 (#331)
Fifth Week in Ordinary Time

Mark 7:14-23: *"For it is from within, from the heart, that evil intentions emerge."*

Meditation:

We choose to hear only what we want to hear, or we interpret teachings so that they will fit into our own self-serving scheme of things. Jesus was a fine teacher. He taught with wisdom and clarity. His message provides no loopholes, it leaves no room for excuses or false interpretations. He always speaks the truth clearly and further illustrates it with concrete examples. He tells us today that high ideals are not to replace our heart's need of God. It is not through the perfect observance of dietary laws, Jesus points out, that we are saved. We must rather pay attention to the inner designs and movements of our own heart and respond heartily to God and to our neighbor. He cautions that our ideals can become our idols! Real defilement dwells in the inner person. Jesus calls not so much for a change of outward behavior but for a change of heart.

OUR LADY OF LA SALETTE speaks of inner change, of spiritual transformation in the most dramatic of terms: *"If they are converted, rocks and stones will be changed into mounds of wheat and potatoes will be self-sown in the fields."* Jesus the Savior, she reminds us, came to change the world – from the inside out. Yes, he chose to bring that radical transformation about by changing human hearts, one by one.

Reflection Questions:

• Does my need to be perfect keep me from seeing where my heart is truly centered?
• How conscious an effort have I invested in the cultivation of my inner world?

Thursday, February 10 (#332)
Fifth Week in Ordinary Time

Mark 7:24-30: *"But she spoke up, 'Ah yes, sir,' she replied, 'but little dogs under the table eat the scraps from the children.'"*

Meditation:

We have all heard the saying: Good news travels fast. St. Mark stresses that Jesus "could not escape notice." Jesus' fame had spread far and wide, even into Gentile territory. So it is that we meet a Syro-Phoenician woman, the mother of a sick child, who beseeches him to drive out the demon besieging her daughter. Jesus tells her that God must look after his own first and that his healing power must first benefit the members of his chosen family.

He puts her faith to the test and, surprisingly, really tries her composure and self-control: *"It is not right to take the food of the children,"* he tells her, *"and throw it to the dogs."* Hers was a deep and strong faith; it passed Jesus' test with flying colors. She gave as good as she got: *"Please, Lord,"* she insisted, *"even the dogs under the table eat the family's leavings."* The refreshing resourcefulness of faith!

THE FINAL NEW TESTAMENT REFERENCE to Our Lady presents her as calling the early church community to prayer, *"They devoted themselves with one accord to prayer, together with some women, and Mary the Mother of Jesus"* (Acts 1:14). In her apparition at La Salette, the Mother of the Lord calls our attention to the need to pray well and unceasingly: *"Do you pray well, my children? ... If I want my Son not to abandon you I must plead with him without ceasing."* Personal and communal needs and problems challenge us to claim prayer's unique power: *"Will not God secure the rights of his chosen ones? Will he be slow to answer them? I tell you he will see that justice is done for them speedily"* (Luke 18:7-8).

Reflection Questions:

• How willing am I to accept and love all persons – including "outsiders" – as Jesus did?
• Does the resourcefulness of faith show itself in my prayer?

Friday, February 11 (#333)
Fifth Week in Ordinary Time

Mark 7:31-37: *"Everything he does is good, he makes the deaf hear and the dumb speak."*

Meditation:

The hymn says, "Jesus, you are wonderful!" I love to sing this song over and over again. It soothes my soul and helps me give glory to God the Father for the gift of his Son to me, to us all. In the exercise of my healing ministry I have been given many opportunities to sing the wonders of the Lord. It is perhaps because his love and mercy endure forever, that he is so full of surprises. The cure of the deaf man is a classical gospel miracle story. A person in need of healing is brought to Jesus. By deed and word Jesus restores wholeness. People's utter amazement and exuberant praise attest to, and validate, the wonderful deed. Such works manifest Jesus as the agent of the Father who is *"rich in faithful love"* (Ephesians 2:4) and *"generous to all, his tenderness embraces all his creatures."* (Psalm 145:9). The man's ears were opened, he heard God's saving word; he believed in its transforming power, his tongue was unleashed; joyful praise gushed forth from a heart as thankful as it was astounded.

AT LA SALETTE Mary invites her children to set fear aside and draw near in their brokenness. She bids them approach Christ, the wounded healer, whose crucified image she wore on her breast. Familiar with human need and mindful of the first of Jesus' signs given *"at Cana in Galilee,"* Mary repeats the advice she offered then: *"Do whatever he tells you"* (John 2:5). Appropriate and wise counsel for today's disciples as well.

Reflection Questions:

- Can I hear the voice of Christ through the deafening distractions of life around me?
- How much enthusiasm do I bring to my praise of the Savior?

Saturday, February 12 (#334)
Fifth Week in Ordinary Time

Mark 8:1-10: *"(Jesus) took the seven loaves, and after giving thanks he broke them and began handing them to his disciples to distribute; and they distributed them among the crowd."*

Meditation:

Mark sets a crowd scene before our eyes. A multitude of people. A hungry multitude. Jesus performs a miracle of striking compassion; he feeds them all. When all have had their fill, plenty of loaves and fishes remain. This miraculous feeding obviously looked back to the feeding of the Israelites with manna in the wilderness; it also pointed to our own communal celebrations of the Eucharist. *"(Jesus) took the seven loaves, and after giving thanks he broke them and began handing them to his disciples to distribute; and they distributed them among the crowd."*

God's good creation faithfully and humbly provides for us all each year. But earth's crops are, for better or for worse, in our hands. We hold God's bounty and lavish gifts in trust. We must share them. Our world is not without its own multitudes of homeless, naked and hungry people. Hungry not only for bread, but for love. Naked not only for clothing, but for human dignity and respect. Homeless not only for want of a brick shelter, but because of indifference and rejection.

IT IS WITH THE DEEPEST SORROW, we are entitled to believe, that Mary spoke these words at La Salette: *"A great famine is coming."* She well knew that some of her children would suffer from famine brought on by natural causes; that many others would suffer from famines of human making, she was also painfully aware. The psalmist offers an encouraging promise: *"Yahweh will himself give prosperity, and our soil will yield its harvest."* (Psalm 85:12). The land's increase, however, remains in human hands.

Reflection Questions:

- Am I aware that pity without service to others is mere sentimentality?
- Am I convinced that God's gifts are to be shared, that love must be put into action?

Sunday, February 13 (#078)
Sixth Sunday in Ordinary Time

(Jeremiah 17:5-8; 1 Corinthians 15:122, 16-20; Luke 6:17, 20-26)

Meditation:

Blessed are you who are poor, for yours is the kingdom of God.

Blessed are you who hunger now, for you will be satisfied.

Blessed are you who weep now, for you will laugh.

Blessed are you when people hate you, when they exclude you and insult you and reject your name as evil, because of the Son of Man.

Pope Francis, in his Angelus Message in St. Peter's Square comments on St. Luke's passage on the Beatitudes (Luke 6: 17, 20-26): "Jesus proclaims the poor, the hungry, the suffering and the persecuted blessed, and he admonishes those who are rich, satisfied, who laugh and are praised by the people. The reason behind this paradoxical beatitude lies in the fact that God is close to those who suffer, and intercedes to free them from their bondage.

"Jesus sees this; he already sees the beatitude beyond its negative reality. And likewise, the "woe to you" addressed to those who are doing well today, has the purpose of "waking" them from the dangerous deceit of egotism, and opening them up to the logic of love, while they still have the time to do so... With his paradoxical Word he stirs us and enables us to recognize what truly enriches us, satisfies us, gives us joy and dignity; in other words, what truly gives meaning and fullness to our lives."

At La Salette Mary, after greeting the children warmly, also has assertive and sharp words to begin her message. They are Mary's way of speaking like a prophet with warnings: *"If my people refuse to submit... If I want my Son not to abandon you... I gave you six days to work... And those who drive the carts cannot swear without throwing in my Son's name... I warned you last year..."*

Yet she also speaks with the love and concern of a Sorrowful Mother, announcing with hopeful words of encouragement: *"If they are converted, rocks and stones will turn into heaps of wheat, and potatoes will be self-sown in the fields."* She is indeed the Mother of Prophets, who like the Prophets of old, trusts that "the One who is to come" will bring us abundant blessings if we follow God's will for us.

Pope Francis concludes his homily by saying: "May the Virgin Mary help us listen to this Gospel passage with open hearts and minds so that it may bear fruit in our life and that we may become witnesses of the happiness that does not disappoint, that of God who never disappoints." (La Salette reflection: Fr. Ron Gagne, M.S.)

faithful witnesses. Who and what they were personally is of no importance compared to the witness they bore.

Monday, February 14 (#335)
Sixth Week in Ordinary Time

Mark 8:11-13: *"And with a profound sigh (Jesus) said, 'Why does this generation seek a sign?"*

Meditation: This Markan passage strikes a sharp note of taunting and testing. The Pharisees argue with Jesus, hoping to discredit or entrap him. They insist that he guarantee through "some heavenly sign" the authority he claims. Such profound misunderstanding on their part disturbs Jesus deeply. He himself is the "heavenly sign," a powerful sign. A sign that stands every human notion of power on its head, however. He bans anger and name-calling (Matthew 5:22), he teaches non-resistance to evil (Matthew 5:39), he preaches love of enemies (Matthew 5:44), he will wash the disciples' feet (John 13:3-11), and the humiliation of the cross will be his exaltation (John 19:32). Seeking a sign is natural enough. Have we not at times thought, "If only I were given a sign, my faith would grow stronger"? "Open your eyes, remove your blinders," the Lord says. "Signs of my loving presence surround you." How much smaller, how much more hidden could he have made himself than a bit of bread? Who but God Almighty would come to us in such self-emptying?

"If the harvest is ruined, it is only on account of yourselves," Our Lady admonishes in her apparition at La Salette. *"I warned you last year with the potatoes. You paid no heed."* She rests her reasoning on a cause-and-effect inevitability. To do the same things over and over again, expecting better, different and new results is tantamount to folly. *"I gave you a warning sign last year. You paid it no mind."*

Reflection Questions:

- Does my faith allow me to put my complete trust in the Lord's word?
- Do I go on trusting the Lord even in the absence of clear signs?

Tuesday, February 15 (#336)
Sixth Week in Ordinary Time

Mark 8:14-21: *"Do you still not understand, still not realize? Are your minds closed?"*

Meditation:

His disciples were very close to Jesus. They ate, shared shelter and traveled with the Master. They saw him interact with the blind, the deaf, the lame and had a hand in two amazing multiplications. His patience sorely tried, he plies them with rapid-fire questions: "Do you have eyes and not see? Do you remember when I broke the five loaves for the 5000? The seven loaves for the 4000? How many baskets of leftovers did you collect? Do you still not understand?" What is it they failed to grasp?

They should not have seen Jesus as the *wonder worker* walking across the water but as the *unifier* who calmed the storm in order to secure passage to the Gentile side of the lake. They had missed the point of the lesson. Two feedings had taken place, one on each side of the lake. A first benefited a Jewish population; a second, Gentiles. In showing them how to feed God's flock, Jesus had taught them to be bridge-builders. 12 baskets left over, Israel's 12 tribes, Jewish Christians; seven baskets left over, seven deacons, Greek Christians. So much to learn, so much to let go of?

In contrast to Lourdes and Fatima, for example, Mary at La Salette did not directly indicate who she was. Her opening statement, however, made her identity quite clear: *"If my people will not submit, I shall be forced to let fall the arm of my Son."* Sharing deeply in the mediating ministry of Christ, "the one loaf," she reminds us that she stands between the Bread of Life and those he wishes to feed. Our Lady further challenges us to claim our role as bridge-builders between peoples and races.

Reflection Questions:

•Am I convinced that the same loving hand that created me created all those who are outwardly so different from me?
•Have I drawn the logical conclusion that we are all God's chil-

dren, brothers and sisters one and all?

Wednesday, February 16 (#337)
Sixth Week in Ordinary Time

Mark 8:22-26: *"Some people brought to (Jesus) a blind man to Jesus whom they begged him to touch."*

Meditation:

Jesus healed many people by touching them. I, like most, like to touch things, to feel their texture. The familiar advertising slogan, "Reach out and touch someone" strikes a responsive chord within us. We are surrounded by compassionate people who have touched us and others deeply, people whose caring has impacted the lives of many. The miracles of Jesus recorded in Mark's Gospel do more than cure symptoms; they are signs of God's ultimate victory over the power of evil.

In Christ's humanity God touches our humanity and makes it whole. In this particular encounter at Bethsaida, Jesus gave the blind man very personal attention, made use of spittle and touched it to his eyes. God's grace, he taught us, is mediated through physical signs, through the five senses, and through ritual actions. Given our condition as creatures of both faith and imagination, otherworldly realities are more accessible and touch us more deeply when they take flesh in images and symbols.

THE SYMBOLS ASSOCIATED WITH THE LA SALETTE apparition are a network of signs devised by Our Lady herself to set us on the path to understanding the entire message she delivered there with such loving attention to detail. Natural symbolism and biblical imagery offer us a key to the interpretation of apron, chain, cross, crown, hammer, pincers, roses and tears – among several distinctive visuals linked to Mary's visit. Venturing with fresh openness beyond their more obvious meanings, let us take a new look at them.

Reflection Questions:

• What struck you most when you first encountered the La Salette apparition?

• Over the years, what aspect of the La Salette mystery has become most meaningful to you?

Thursday, February 17 (#338)
Sixth Week in Ordinary Time

Mark 8:27-33: *"Who do people say I am?"*

Meditation:

Jesus was a human being. As such he must have been curious about what was being said about him. We spare no effort in putting our best foot forward so as to impress others favorably. In the defining moment this classic scene at Caesarea Philippi recalls, Jesus puts *the* crucial question to his disciples: *"And you, ... who do you say that I am?"* In the depths of his frustration with their slowness to understand, Jesus thrills to hear the long-awaited word: *"You are the Christ!"* We have here a first confession of Christian faith, of faith in Jesus as our loving God's Only-begotten, come to save us. Amid the many questions our life, its changing circumstances and our relationships constantly raise, we must ask life's ultimate questions: Where do I come from? What is my final destination? A kind of vague understanding and ambivalent commitment simply will not do here.

"**MARY'S MATERNITY** in the order of grace continues uninterruptedly from the consent she gave at the Annunciation and sustained without wavering beneath the cross until the final fulfillment of all the elect. By her maternal charity she cares for the brothers and sisters of her Son, who journey still amid dangers and difficulties until they reach their blessed homeland" (Vatican Council II, *Constitution on the Church*, no. 62). As her appearance at La Salette reminds us, Mary's solicitous love for us has, in God's providence, added to that of intercession the role of prophetic intervention: *"I am here to tell you great news."*

Reflection Questions:

• Who was Jesus Christ to your earlier years?
• Who do you say that Jesus Christ is for you today?

Friday, February 18 (#339)
Sixth Week in Ordinary Time

Mark 8:34 to 9:1: *"Anyone who wants to save his life will lose it."*

Meditation:

Losing and saving. In this passing world, people expend huge amounts of energy on attempts to increase their holdings and to insure that they neither lose nor misplace what they have already acquired. Many go to gambling casinos in the hope they might supplement their earnings and add to their savings. In this very gain-and-loss perspective, Jesus calls us, his disciples, to follow in his own footsteps. He cautions that doing so will be anything but easy, will, in fact, mean taking up one's cross and losing one's life. His word here, as always, *"cuts more incisively than any double-edged sword"* (Hebrews 4:12a). The Apostle Paul expresses the fundamental law of Christian living in these terms: *"... anyone who sows sparsely will reap sparsely as well -- and anyone who sows generously will reap generously as well."* (2 Corinthians 9:6); *"... whatever someone sows, that is what he will reap. If his sowing is in the field of self-indulgence, then his harvest from it will be corruption; if his sowing is in the Spirit, then his harvest from the Spirit will be eternal life"* (Galatians 6:7-8).

THE MOTHER OF JESUS appeared in tears at La Salette on the eve of the feast of her Sorrows: *"A sword will pierce your soul too that the secret thoughts of many may be laid bare"* (Luke 2:35). **"Well, my children,"** she said to Maximin and Melanie and says now to us, **"You will make this known to all my people."** Her words challenge us to forego passivity, forfeit our comfort and forsake our untroubled routine in the cause of Christ and his Gospel of Life.

Reflection Questions:

- If Christ asks me on the Day of Judgment what I was truly passionate about in my lifetime, what shall I answer?
- What point can there honestly be in the following statement: *"What gain, then, is it for anyone to win the whole world and forfeit his life?"* (Mark 8:35)?

Saturday, February 19 (#340)
Sixth Week in Ordinary Time

Mark 9:2-13: *"There in their presence (Jesus) was transfigured: his clothes became brilliantly white..."*

Coming right after his teaching about the cross, Jesus' Transfiguration put into perspective what must have been a devastating blow to the disciples' understanding of the Messiah. Their exhilarating mountaintop experience, not surprisingly, was not destined to last. We ourselves know how disheartening our own descent from the summit, whether of delight or success or from a peak spiritual experience can be. As St. Paul understood it, though, our entire Christian life is an ongoing painful/joyful growth process, a gradual transformation: "It is God who said, 'Let light shine out of darkness,' that has shone into our hearts to enlighten them with the knowledge of God's glory, the glory on the face of Christ" (2 Corinthians 4:6). Jesus went from the Mount of Transfiguration to Mount Calvary, and from the ordeal of the cross to the glory of the Resurrection. Should we not expect to follow in his footsteps?

A stained glass window of the Transfiguration in the facade of the shrine church built on the mountain of La Salette faces the site of the apparition. It appropriately portrays the Transfiguration. The young herders who conversed with her there related that they "could not look at the Beautiful Lady for any length of time without rubbing their eyes, so dazzling was her brightness, and that all the radiance of the vision came from her cross." In tears, yet clothed with the glory of the Risen One, his Mother tells us that though endless struggles await us, Love Crucified will triumph.

Reflection Questions:

• What transforming events have occurred in your life?
• Have you yet managed to carry a cross and remain inwardly joyful?

Sunday, February 20 (#081)
Seventh Sunday in Ordinary Time
(1 Samuel 26:7-9, 12-13, 22-23; 1 Corinthians 15:45-49; Luke 6:27-38)

Meditation: *What is the Law of Love?*

Pope Francis, during Mass at Santa Marta, says: "Jesus gave us the law of *love*: to love God and to love one another as brothers. And the Lord did not fail to explain it a bit further, with the Beatitudes which nicely summarize the Christian approach...

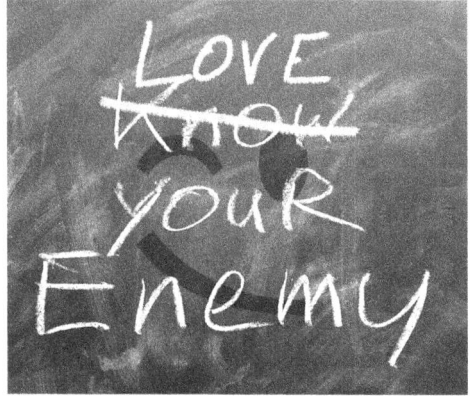

"In [this] Gospel passage, however, Jesus goes a step further, explaining in greater detail to those who surrounded Him to hear Him... the Lord also asks us to do good. And if we do not ask him, to whom? He tells us straight away, 'to those who hate us.' And this time too, we ask the Lord for confirmation: 'But must I do good to those who hate me?' And the Lord's reply is again, 'yes'... "All of Jesus' reasoning leads to a firm conclusion: 'Love your enemies instead. Do good, and lend, expecting nothing in return. Without interest. And your reward will be great.' And thus, you will be [children] of the Most High...

"The passage of St. Luke concludes with the invitation *not to judge* and to be merciful. However, it often seems that we have been appointed judges of others: gossiping, criticizing, we judge everyone. But Jesus tells us: 'Judge not and you will not be judged; condemn not, and you will not be condemned; forgive, and you will be forgiven.' And so, we say it every day in the Our Father: forgive us as we forgive. In fact, if I do not first forgive, how can I ask the Father to forgive me?...

"Of course, being Christian isn't easy and we cannot become Christian with our own strength; we need '*the grace of God.*" Therefore, there is a prayer which should be said every day: 'Lord, grant me the grace to become a good Christian, because I cannot do it alone.'"

Mary at La Salette, as a powerful prophetic voice, ... invites us to do 'improbable things' such as to 'Come closer' when our instinct is to step farther away from the Lady in the globe of light. She delivers warnings yet these are spoken as the prophets of old did when the people were disappointing their God. Mary asks us to '*submit*' in faith to her Son yet many of us hesitate; to rest and worship on Sunday and revere her Son's name and pray daily.

Why should we do all this? Because Mary in essence is reminding us of the core of our baptismal call. And she says: "*If [we] are converted, rocks and stones will turn into heaps of wheat, and potatoes will be self-sown in the fields.*" In other words, if we follow Jesus faithfully, God will bless us abundantly. (La Salette reflection, questions and editor of Papal text: Fr. Ron Gagne, M.S.)

Reflection Questions:

- What good do I do "just for the love of it"?
- How do those who love me show it?

Monday, February 21 (#341)
Seventh Week in Ordinary Time

Mark 9:14-29: "*At once the boy's father cried out, 'I have faith. Help my lack of faith!'*"

Meditation:

The response of the sick boy's father is one we can all identify with, "*I have faith. Help my lack of faith!*" Trusting is about finding light in the darkest moments. It is believing that we are joined to a powerful God who works miracles even with lukewarm faith like ours and who can dissolve the sinfulness that oftentimes envelops us. It is seeing possibilities where we could see none before. It is apparent defeat becoming victory when we could see nothing but discouragement and loss before. Reaching that kind of trust, Jesus says in his final words of instruction to his apostles, can only happen through prayer. Apart from him, we can do nothing (see John 15:5). But in him, as he himself assures us, everything is possible to the one who trusts (see Matthew

19:26).

WHEN MOTHER MARY tells the children of La Salette to *"make her message known to all her people,"* he is not merely asking for a reporter's objectivity. There exists between her and her confidants a mutual trust. Mary trusts that these children will tell the story honestly, just as they heard it, and the children trust in the truth of their encounter with the Beautiful Lady. The father in today's gospel trusted in his love for his son as well as in Jesus' power to heal the boy. Mary, in this same spirit, trusts in the love she bears us and in the abiding love of the God who alone can heal us.

Reflection Questions:

- Can I feel any of the intensity Jesus obviously felt in this gospel scene?
- Do I believe that faith makes all things possible?

Tuesday, February 22 (#535)
The Chair of St. Peter the Apostle

Matthew 16:13-19: *"You are Peter and on this rock I will build my community."*

Meditation:

We all need heroes or examples of good qualities to encourage us on the road of life. Jesus sees in Simon Peter and his faith-filled response – "You are the Christ, the Son of the living God" – a man worthy of the position of leadership. He professed a faith that only the Spirit could give him. He was, in a sense, speaking for all the disciples present. From this moment on, Jesus would no longer call him Simon-bar-Jonah but rather Peter, meaning *rock* (Greek *petros*).

With this change of name, Jesus was also commissioning him to be the solid foundation upon which Jesus would build the Christian community, the Church. Peter became the speaker and the example of faith in Jesus. Yet later even though Peter would deny Jesus during Christ's passion, his life powerfully reminds us that we must always

remember our innate need for Jesus and his strength that will help us persevere in our mission or vocation in life. We cannot live our

Christian life without the center of our faith, Jesus Christ.

MARY AT LA SALETTE emphasizes constantly the centrality of Jesus for our life of faith. She stresses the importance of weekly Eucharist, of reverence for Jesus' name, daily prayer, respect for the Lord's Day, and Lenten habits of faith such as (fasting and) abstinence. All these can strengthen our faith in the Lord from which marvelous blessings will flow. Peter, in his strength as well as his weakness, shows us how faith can triumph over our weakness and failures. God will lift us up through the power of his love and mercy.

Reflection Questions:

• Who first taught you about faith and prayer, about Jesus' love and forgiveness?
• Who for you is an example of strong faith? How does Mary inspire you in your faith?

Wednesday, February 23 (#343)
Seventh Week in Ordinary Time

Mark 9:38-40: *"Anyone who is not against us is with us."*

Meditation:

Who decides who is in and who is not? Who sets the arbitrary standards that determine acceptance or rejection? The teaching of Jesus offers absolutely no basis for this way of thinking, for this exclusivity. When his own followers attempt to use his teachings against others he will have none of it. They object to others invoking his name and casting out demons. That these others might be succeeding better than they themselves are annoys them. One can almost see an exasperated frown cross Jesus' features. Why he should extend himself to the most unlikely people, to people who are different, who are anything they themselves are not, the disciples simply cannot understand. The more of Jesus' story is that we should not be busy building fences that divide and keep people apart. Rather, Jesus insists, we should be building bridges that unite and bring people together. Very simply, isn't that what he meant when he said, "Anyone who is not against us is with us"?

Essential to the definition of reconciliation is the need to come face-to-face with the sources of conflict in our lives. It requires that we face the people and the issues involved; that we open ourselves to whomever or whatever divides us and keeps us apart. Our Mother Mary teaches us at La Salette to put aside whatever makes us look upon others as objects of our diffidence, distrust, ridicule or suspicion. The opening words she spoke at La Salette challenge us in our defensive tendency to distance ourselves from others: "Come near, my children; don't be afraid."

Reflection Questions:

- Do you notice those people you meet whom you initially judge to be somehow below you?
- Do you pray for those "different" people you encounter in church, at school, at work, in another part of town? The wisdom in doing this is that it's often difficult to hate someone for whom you are praying?

Thursday, February 24, (#344)
Seventh Week in Ordinary Time

Mark 9:41-50: *"If your hand should be your downfall, cut it off."*

Meditation:

In rather graphic and startling language Jesus makes clear the need to root out of our lives anything that threatens the advancement of God's reign. The reign of God is worth any sacrifice. "Cut it off" and "tear it out" seem to mean that we must amputate our dependence on those things we grasp at, our possessiveness, our need to have it all. We must excise from our lives, he insists, our struggle for power, our reliance on our own devices. He says we need to tear out of our lives all justification of our anger and arrogance. Franciscan Fr. Richard Rohr emphasizes that authentic spirituality always demands that we let go. We must let go of our need to be right, to be effective, to be successful, to control. Jesus asks that we honestly recognize his own self-emptying, his willingness to be powerless, to depend on his Father's will in all things, and to share in the world's pain.

Throughout human history, a history often concerning lies and sin, God's love must reveal itself as mercy. And so it is that "his mercy is from age to age" (Luke 1:50). In the parables of the lost coin, the lost sheep, the lost son, Jesus invites us to claim this ever-present mercy of God. But as Pope John Paul II wrote in his 1980 Encyclical, Rich in Mercy: "The present day mentality seems opposed to a God of mercy and tends to remove from the human heart the very idea of mercy. It causes uneasiness. Human dominion over the earth seems to leave no room for mercy" (no. 2). Through her tears at La Salette, our Mother Mary appeals to us in Christ's name to let go, to claim God's mercy and allow ourselves "to be reconciled to God" (see 2 Corinthians 5:20).

Reflection Questions:

• What was your honest reaction to this gospel's glimpse of Jesus' strong personality?
• What is it that the Lord asks you to "cut off" or "tear out" from your own life?

Friday, February 25, (#345)
Seventh Week in Ordinary Time

Mark 10:1-12: *"What God has united, human beings must not divide."*

Meditation:

It would be wonderful if all whom God has joined remained together in blissful union. Yet as we all know, such is not universally true of marriage or of other major commitments. Those who experience divorce not only know the pain of seeing a solemn promise, once made in love and hope, unfortunately broken while often accompanied by a distancing from the church. Divorce, of course, is about more than rules. It means a radical transition: to be a husband or a wife one day and then to see that end. It must bring a wrenching loneliness to the hearts of those whose marriages have ended. The anguish of replaying all those arguments, of asking "What if" over and over again, of no longer hearing oneself saying, "I love you," of no longer being assured, "I love you." While plainly making a plea for the ideal, Jesus seems to be asking that reflection on marriage and divorce take into account the real people involved, the real hopes they had cherished, the real lives they must go on living.

Beautiful Lady of La Salette, what is it that you see in your children that moves you to come and plead for their conversion? What hope do you cherish and cling to for your wayward children? What is it that you see in us that we either cannot or refuse to see in ourselves? What lies beyond our indifference and lack of submission that you believe we have lost and beg us to reclaim as a God-given heritage? What is it about us that keeps you from abandoning us, despite our constant breaking of covenant promises? Perhaps it's your own experience of such a generous love in your only Son.

Reflection Questions:

•Are you a person of your word? Do you follow through on your commitments?
•When is the last time you renewed your promises to God or to others?

Saturday, February 26, (#346)
Seventh Week in Ordinary Time

Mark 10:13-16: "*Let the children come to me and do not stop them.'... Then he embraced them, laid his hands on them and gave them his blessing.*"

Meditation:

Jesus calls the children to himself despite the objections of his disciples in yet another manifestation of misunderstanding on their part. Children in Jesus' day enjoyed neither legal nor social standing. They were utterly defenseless. In his mind, though, they exemplified the indispensable inner qualities membership in the kingdom demanded. They were loving, trusting and eager to explore and learn. Jesus asks us to get in touch with the childlike spirit deep within us which alone can free us to grow and change. Because he wishes to instruct us, Jesus embraces and blesses the children who are able to accept and respond to his kingdom invitation. In fact, it is we who are blessed – blessed by these very children. It is we who hunger for attention, who ask a thousand questions in our ongoing life's search for meaning, and who need to be held, comforted and reassured.

Our Mother Mary comes to two children at La Salette, because she wants a guileless hearing of her message. She does not come to argue her case but to tell of her immense love. She doesn't need sophisticated interpretation; she needs transparent simplicity. Through Melanie and Maximin she asks only that we hear and heed her admonition that we grow in the giving and forgiving love of our elder brother, Jesus (see Romans 8:29). That is what any loving mother would do.

Reflection Questions:

- Who are the children who have taught you about the reign of God?
- In what specific way might you become more childlike in your approach to life and to the Gospel?

Sunday, February 27 (#084)
Eighth Sunday in Ordinary Time

(Sirach 27:4-7; 1 Corinthians 15:54-58; Luke 6:39-45)

Meditation: *What is the path to follow in order to live wisely?*

NO GOOD TREE BEARS BAD FRUIT

"During the Angelus in St. Peter's Square, Pope Francis said: 'With the question: can a blind person lead a blind person?' (Luke 6:39), he wishes to emphasize that leaders cannot be blind, but must see clearly, that is, they must have wisdom in order to lead wisely, otherwise [they] risk causing damage to the people who are entrusted to them...

"In today's passage we find another significant phrase, which exhorts us to be neither presumptuous nor hypocritical. It says: 'Why do you see the speck that is in your brother's eye, but do not notice the log that is in your own eye?' (v. 41). So often, as we all know, it is easy or convenient to see and condemn the flaws and sins of others, without being able to see our own with such clarity. We always hide our flaws; we even hide them from ourselves; while it is easy to see the flaws of others...

"How can we understand if our view is clear or if it is obstructed by a log? And again, Jesus tells us so: 'no good tree bears bad fruit, nor again does a bad tree bear good fruit; for each tree is known by its own fruit' (vv. 43-44). The fruits are actions but also words. A tree's quality can also be understood from words. Indeed, those who are good draw good from their hearts and their mouths, and those who are bad draw bad, by practicing the most damaging exercise among us, which is grumbling, *gossiping*, speaking ill of others. This destroys...

At La Salette, Mary outlines well the habits of faith to which the followers of her Son must attend. First of all, "submitting" our will to God's will; in other words, she asks who is in charge of our life?; the answer should be Jesus alone. Secondly, keeping Sunday holy by resting and participating in the Eucharist, doing all this in memory of him.

Thirdly, honoring her Son's name; as Paul said: "...the name that is above every name,.. the name of Jesus" (Philippians 2:9b-10a). Fourthly, daily prayer is of central importance; namely, praying at least the Our Father and the Hail Mary. Fifthly, observing Lent with its emphasis on self-reflection, fasting, abstinence and almsgiving. And lastly, making her message known to all her people; that is, evangelizing others well and often.

At the conclusion of his Angelus message, Pope Francis said: "Let us invoke Mary's support and intercession in order to follow the Lord on this journey." (La Salette reflection, questions and editor of Papal text: Fr. Ron Gagne, M.S.)

Reflection Questions:

- What are the habits of faith to which you are faithful?
- What habits of faith could you do better?

Monday, February 28, (#347)
Eighth Week in Ordinary Time

Mark 10:17-27: *"Good Master, what must I do to inherit eternal life?"*

Meditation:

"God alone is good," Jesus says and dismisses the title, Good Master. He is saying that we should put an end to our obsessive concern for looking good. What Jesus wants is humility and honesty, because those who are humble and honest will hear and accept his teachings. Those who are concerned with their own goodness are too self-absorbed to hear him. They are too busy protecting their own positive self-image to take the drastic step of letting everything go and follow him. In response to the man who asks what he must do "to inherit eternal life everlasting life," Jesus offers a radical change of perspective. He invites the inquirer to turn things around. The Teacher bids him set his acquisitive desire aside: "Rather than view it as one more possession you wish to acquire, why not give yourself over to this unending life? Life eternal is not for sale!"

Our Mother Mary's message to us at La Salette focuses sharply on our grudging refusal to grant God the time Jesus asks us to spend on the Lord's Day in rest and worship. She points out our lack of respect for Christ's holy and saving Name, our ready dismissal of the sacred – in a word, our violations of those commandments that set forth our duties toward our life's Creator and Redeemer. Her words cut deepest when they call for the submission of spirits immersed in a world of their own making, attuned only to the call of their own wants.

Reflection Questions:

• In what ways is Jesus now offering you a deeper share in everlasting life?
• What does this meditation motivate you to do?

Tuesday, March 1 (#348)
Eighth Week in Ordinary Time

Mark 10:28-31: *"We have left everything and followed you."*

Meditation:

In reaction to the man in yesterday's gospel who felt Jesus had asked for too much, Peter takes credit for having "left everything and followed Jesus," for having given up family and possessions. He now wonders aloud what's in it for him. He has stayed on, he points out, and in doing so has lost everything he was formerly familiar with. He implicitly asks, "What's my reward?" Comparing himself to the man "who went away sad," Peter too claims to know how costly following Jesus can be. So now what can he expect to get in return? Everything! Jesus gives his word. Everything that has been put aside for the sake of the kingdom will be returned a hundredfold. He gives Peter this solid assurance and asks him not to worry because God is generous and never to be outdone in generosity. Why think in terms of personal reward? Why not think in terms of the divine reversal where "the first shall come last and the last shall come first"?

At La Salette the Mother of Jesus asks that we measure all that we are – all that we could hope to be – against all that her Son offers for the building of God's reign and the fulfillment of those chosen. Beyond the undeniable alienation and pain our sinfulness brings, there is the healing and wholeness, pardon and peace God gives. The Gospel promise, dramatically echoed in her apparition, is a pledge of unfailing divine generosity: "If they are converted, rocks and stones will turn into heaps of wheat and potatoes will be self-sown in the fields."

Reflection Questions:

- What have you put aside to follow Jesus?
- What more must you put aside in order to serve him more faithfully?

Wednesday, March 2 (#219-03)
Ash Wednesday

Matthew 6:1-6,16-18

Meditation: *Ashes remind us of our call to repentance.*

Pope Francis said: "We are now embarking on our Lenten journey, which opens with the words of the prophet Joel. They point out the path we are to follow... Lent is a journey of return to God. How many times, in our activity or indifference, have we told him: 'Lord, I will come to you later, just wait a little... I can't come today, but tomorrow I will begin to pray and do something for others.' We do this, time and time again. Right now, however, God is speaking to our hearts. In this life, we will always have things to do and excuses to offer, but..., brothers and sisters, right now is the time to return to God...

"Lent is not just about the little sacrifices we make, but about discerning where our hearts are directed. This is the core of Lent: asking where our hearts are directed... Once again, the word of God asks us to return to the Father, to return to Jesus. It also calls us to return to the Holy Spirit.

"The ashes on our head remind us that 'we are dust and unto dust we will return...' We will always be dust, but as a liturgical hymn says, 'dust in love.' Let us pray once more to the Holy Spirit and rediscover the fire of praise, which consumes the ashes of lamentation and resignation.

"This, then, is the Apostle's plea: 'Be reconciled to God' (v. 20). Be reconciled: the journey is not based on our own strength. No one can be reconciled to God on his or her own. Heartfelt conversion, with the deeds and practices that express it, is possible only if it begins with the primacy of God's work. What enables us to return to him is not our own ability or merit, but his offer of grace. The beginning of the return to God is the recognition of our need for him and his mercy, our need for his grace. This is the right path, the path of humility. Do I feel in need, or do I feel self-sufficient?"

At. La Salette, Mary had only to repeat the many invitations given by her Son to those he met on his journey from Bethlehem to Calvary. We, during this 40-day retreat we call Lent, are invited once again to follow her Son. Her breast displayed in radiant glory the special La Salette crucifix with its hammer and pincers. They are no doubt symbols of our two choices in life: through our sins, to hammer the nails into his hands or, through our good actions, to mercifully remove those nails. It's all up to us, but we are supported in our efforts through her intercession and the grace of her Son, Jesus. (La Salette reflection, questions and editor of Papal text: Fr. Ron Gagne, M.S.)

Reflection Questions:

• What if anything is holding you back from wholeheartedly fol-

lowing her Son, Jesus?
•Who is an example to you of active faith?

Thursday, March 3 (#220)
Thursday After Ash Wednesday

Luke 9:22-25: *"What benefit is it to anyone to win the whole world and forfeit or lose his very self?"*

Meditation:

That's the bottom line?" This is a question often asked when people face an undertaking. There is more than a bottom line to look at. What's beyond the bottom line? How does our activity affect our health, our relationships with family members, community or friends? The bottom line may indicate a profit, but at what cost? The gospel tells us that the ultimate bottom line is salvation. That's the reality lens through which we should look at our lives. That lens is not rose-colored. Jesus makes it very clear. *"If anyone wants to be my follower, he must renounce himself and take up his cross every day and follow me."* The bottom line here is salvation attained through the victory of the cross.

MARY LIVED THE GOSPEL FULLY at La Salette. She reminds us, *"However much you pray, however much you do, you will never be able to repay the pains I have taken for you."* Mary carried her cross. She asks us to do the same.

Reflection Questions:

•Can I look beyond the bottom line and carry my cross daily?
•What people do I know that carry their crosses, their burdens with much faith?

Friday, March 4 (#221)
Friday After Ash Wednesday

Matthew 9:14-15: *"… when the bridegroom is taken away from them, and then they will fast."*

Meditation:

Fasting isn't what it used to be. I remember my grandmother weighing out on a postal scale the exact amount of meat allowed back then – a long way from the modest fasting rules for today. Fasting is ordinarily thought of in terms of reducing food consumption. Fasting can, however, be applied to other areas of our lives as well. We can fast from television viewing and instead engage in a real conversation with others in the household.

We can fast from music or news in order to allow ourselves, in the ensuing quiet, to get in touch with what is going on inside ourselves. We can fast from our opinions – this, admittedly, is a tough one – to put aside our view of things, our way of doing things, our way of praying and allow another to touch our mind, our heart, and even our soul.

MARY, AT LA SALETTE, reminds us to fast. *"During Lent they go to the meat markets like dogs."* Fasting is not strictly a Lenten practice. As we abstain, we simply make room for God in our lives. That should be a daily practice.

Reflection Questions:
- How am I called to fast? What should I be fasting from?
- With whom do I need to be more positive in my attitude toward them?

Saturday, March 5 (#222)
Saturday After Ash Wednesday

Luke 5:27-32: *"I have come to call not the upright but sinners to repentance."*

Meditation:

Myopia, Webster's dictionary says, is a "deficiency of foresight or discernment." So myopia is not only a matter of our eyes; our minds can be myopic as well. Lack of discernment makes it difficult to see ourselves as we really are. Somehow we overlook our shortcomings, our character blemishes, our sins. Yet only when we see ourselves as we really are can we respond to Jesus' invitation to a change of heart, to conversion.

If we see ourselves as healthy, we don't go to a doctor even though we may need care. If we see ourselves as spiritually healthy, we don't go to Jesus for a change of heart. No matter where we may be on our spiritual journey, there is always room for change, for conversion. Jesus called Levi to a change of heart. He is calling us also.

AT LA SALETTE Mary came to call us to a change of heart, for the purpose of focusing our entire life on her Son. She assures us of our abundant harvest – *"if they are converted."*

Reflection Questions:

- Can I hear and respond to Jesus' call no matter what my myopic vision sees in me?
- Do I look at myself and accept myself as I truly am? Do I do that for others as well?

Sunday, March 6 (#024)
First Sunday of Lent

(Deuteronomy 26:4-10; Romans 10:8-13; Luke 4:1-13)

Meditation: *Not by Bread Alone*

Lent is upon us, and many of us have decided what to give up, or what kind of penance to practice, or what we might do to reach out to others in need.

Fasting is traditionally associated with this season. Now required only on Ash Wednesday and Good Friday, it is still encouraged. In fact, it is a discipline that is sometimes encouraged for health reasons even outside the religious context. In the religious context, however, fasting is always paired with prayer and a change of heart.

Today's Gospel reminds us that

The Temptation of Christ
by Ary Scheffer (1795–1858)

we do not live by bread alone. Our physical needs, important as they are, do not constitute the whole of life.

That said, in the Scriptures we find that God sometimes imposed a kind of fasting on all the people through drought and famine. In some instances, this was a punishment, in others it was part of God's plan to save his people.

At La Salette, Mary appeared during a time of famine. Unfortunately, her people were blaming God and swearing with the name of Jesus.

She needed to show people that the famine was not just a punishment for sin but that it was a way of leading her people away from sin and back to God. In other words, for God, as for any good parent, punishment isn't for its own sake, much less just a way to vent anger.

Bread (along with potatoes and the other foods that Mary mentions) is vitally important, often called the "staff of life." But more important still is the life of faith and all those means provided through the Church to nourish it: the Scriptures, the Eucharist, the Sabbath rest, and—as the Beautiful Lady explicitly mentions—Lent.

This is a time, then, to remember various things: that we are dust and unto dust we shall return; that we do not live by bread alone. But there is so much more to remember during Lent—such as God's infinite and unfailing love for us, and our call to respond to his love so that truly we may not live by bread alone.

Monday, March 7 (#224)
First Week of Lent

Matthew 25:31-46: *"... so far as you did this to one of the least of these brothers of mine, you did it to me."*

Meditation:

As children our parents would ask us, "How much do you love me?" We would stretch out our arms as far as we could and reply, "This much." Jesus asks us the same question in today's gospel, "How much do you love me?" We cannot simply answer by extending our arms and saying, "This much." The answer that Jesus expects of us is that we should love him this much – namely, that we have fed the hungry,

75

clothed the naked, ministered to the sick, the lonely or the imprisoned. Arms that are simply extended do not necessarily respond in action. We are challenged to put our arms to work in response to those in need. As we respond to Jesus by our actions, he assures us of our place in his Kingdom.

At La Salette Mary expresses her love for us in her tears. She loves us so much that it pains her to see us neglecting her Son. Mary's very presence says that she loves us enough to come and remind us to express our love for her Son by ministering to others in need.

Reflection Questions:

- How much do you love Jesus? How have you shown that lately in your household or your circle of friends?
- How do you respond to needy strangers?

Tuesday, March 8 (#225)
First Week of Lent

Matthew 6:7-15: *"So you should pray like this..."*

Meditation:

What was one of the first prayers your parents taught you? Chances are that What the sign of the cross it was the *Our Father*. That prayer, said more or less accurately, was the launching pad of our communication with God. Prayer has since taken on many shapes and forms – vocal prayer, quiet prayer, sitting and thinking about God, conversation with God, letting our being be awed by the beauty of creation. No matter how we now choose to pray, the fundamental element in all forms of prayer is that God is God and that we are not. Prayer is the creature standing before the Creator with open hands ready to receive, ready to surrender all. In the *Our Father* Jesus put our relationship to God into words.

At La Salette Mary speaks of her own prayer. *"I am compelled to pray to (my on) without ceasing."* She also invites Maximin and Melanie to prayer, *"You must say your prayers well in the evening and in the morning, even if you say only an Our Father and a Hail Mary when you can't do more. When you can do better, say more."*

Reflection Questions:

- How well do I pray? How much time do I give to prayer?
- What forms of prayer do I most enjoy?

Wednesday, March 9 (#226)
First Week of Lent

Luke 11:29-32: *"The only sign (this generation) will be given is the sign of Jonah."*

Meditation:

Jonah spoke God's word; the Ninevites changed. The name of this change is conversion. Conversion is not only for bad people; we are all called to conversion. Conversion is that change of heart which makes us see things differently and adjust our lives accordingly. Every time we experience Jesus at a new and deeper level, we are called to conversion. It's our response to Jesus' invitation to know him and love him more intimately. Conversion is not exclusively our doing. It is our response to Jesus' intrusion in our lives, our response to grace. The invitation to conversion may come in any form – a book, a sermon, a word spoken by a friend, even a child's question. We respond only to the degree that we are aware of Jesus' invitation. Our "yes" opens the door to a new relationship with him.

At La Salette Mary invites the shepherds to *"come nearer,"* an invitation to conversion. Her presence, her words, her whole being pleads with us to respond "yes" to her Son, Jesus.

Reflection Questions:

- Have I become so entrenched in my relationship with Jesus that I no longer hear his invitation to deeper conversion?
- Who is a good example to me of openness to growth in faith?

Thursday, March 10 (#227)
First Week of Lent

Matthew 7:7-12: *""Everyone who asks receives."*

Meditation:

"How come I've been praying for a special grace for a long time and I haven't received it yet?" We've all made a similar statement at one time or another. But are we putting the cart before the horse? Before storming heaven for our special grace, did we ask God if we really needed that grace? Often what we need is evident to us, after all, it's what we need. But do we see with God's vision; do we really know what is best for us? Praying to be enlightened to our need is the first step, then with God's answer in mind we ask and we will receive. Jesus did everything in the will of the Father, for the Father's glory. Jesus gave us the example of perfect prayer; we do well to imitate him.

At La Salette Mary promised *"rocks and stones will be changed into mounds of wheat and potatoes will be self-sown in the fields."* Her promise is preceded by *"If they are converted,"* which means, if they are conformed to the Father's will.

Reflection Questions:

• As we pray, are we one with the Father and his will for us?
• When we ask for forgiveness from the Father, do we also promise to "forgive those who trespass against us"?

Friday, March 11 (#228)
First Week of Lent

Matthew 5:20-26: *"... leave your offering there before the altar, go and be reconciled with your brother first."*

Meditation:

Forgiveness is the decision of one person. We decide to forgive and it is done. Reconciliation requires two people, one to forgive and one to accept the forgiveness. Jesus asks us to go one step beyond forgiveness to reconciliation and reach out to the one who has offended us. Jesus challenges us to seek out not only the one we have offended, but the one who has offended us. We wouldn't think of going to a wedding without getting ready and bringing a gift. Jesus invites us to the altar to share his Body and his Blood with one another. He also tells us to get ready to do this by seeking forgiveness and by bringing a gift, reconciliation with our sister or brother. Together then we may approach the altar.

At La Salette Mary leaves the altar of Jesus' presence to invite us to reconciliation. Her Son forgives; she wants us to accept that wonderful gift.

Reflection Questions:

- Can we respond to Mary's call? Can we be reconciled with her Son, and with each other?
- Whom do you know is a good example to you of active forgives?

Saturday, March 12 (#229)
First Week of Lent

Matthew 5:43-48: *"Be perfect, just as your heavenly Father is perfect."*

Meditation:

Impossible. We cannot be as perfect as the Father! What does that sentence in Matthew really mean? William Barclay tells us, "A thing is perfect if it realizes the purpose for which it was planned, human beings are perfect if they realize the purpose for which they were created and sent into the world." We are created in the image of God. God is love and love knows no bounds. God reaches out to everyone. Our perfection then consists in loving others and reaching out to them no matter who they are. We cannot love to the degree God loves. We can love to the fullest degree possible for us. The U.S. Army recruiting poster says it very well, "Be all you can be." Therein lies our perfection.

At La Salette Mary lives her perfection. Her love for us calls us to full and utter reconciliation with her Son. She is all she can be – a mother concerned for all her children.

Reflection Questions:

- Can I ask God to make me "all that I can be"?
- Where in my life is reconciliation still needed?

Sunday, March 13 (#027)
Second Sunday of Lent

(Genesis 15: 5-12, 17-18; Philippians 3:17 to 4:1; Luke 9:28b-36)

Meditation: *It is Good for Us to Be Here*

La Salette, whether at the original Shrine in France or at Shrines like ours in many countries, attracts both pilgrims and tourists. They come for different reasons, but with very few exceptions they all conclude, "It is good for us to be here." It can be the beauty of the site, the welcome they receive, the impact of the message, or some other deeper, more personal experience.

And, like Peter in the scene of the Transfiguration, they are sorry to leave. I have seen many pilgrims spending their last minutes at the site of the Apparition, making their sometimes tearful goodbyes, praying to be able to return.

Such encounters are indications that, as St. Paul writes, "our citizenship is in heaven." Any true encounter with the divine seeks to be prolonged.

The Transfiguration

In Luke's account of the Transfiguration there is a striking detail that is repeated at La Salette. We read that Peter, James and John had fallen asleep and then, "becoming fully awake, they saw his glory…" Maximin and Mélanie had fallen asleep after eating, and it was after they awoke that they saw the Beautiful Lady.

Instead of trying to prolong the experience, Maximin, in a gesture that looks like he was waving goodbye, tried to grab one of the roses on Mary's feet as she rose in the air. And when Mélanie said she thought the Lady must have been a great saint, the boy answered: "Oh, if I had known that, I would have asked her to take me with her."

Since we are not usually able to prolong our spiritual encounters with the Lord, we have a useful alternative. We can repeat them. This is why we have daily prayer, weekly Eucharist, and the annual discipline of Lent.

Fr. Herbert Alphonso, S.J., a brilliant spiritual writer, used to say, "Go back to where God is waiting for you." In other words, we can continue to draw strength from past encounters in which we have said, "It is good for us to be here."

Monday, March 14 (#230)
Second Week of Lent

Luke 6:36-38: *"The standard you use will be the standard used for you."*

Meditation:

Jesus has given us a model. The measure we measure with will be given back to us. Mercy and compassion must be the yardstick we use in measuring our daily behavior. What obligation do others have to be merciful, forgiving and compassionate with us if we are unwilling to practice these virtues in their regard? Jesus puts his teaching plainly in today's gospel. *"Do not judge and you will not be judged."* Just as we expect our merciful God to look upon us with forgiving kindness, so should we treat others in the same way. We cannot claim to love God and yet refuse to love others. We are encouraged to be people who make it possible for God to reach out to others through us and bring into their lives the compassion and understanding they need. The better we become, the more of God's goodness will others receive. And in this way we become special vessels, carriers of God's love to others.

MARY AT LA SALETTE was the carrier of good news. She was the messenger sent by God to exhort his children to take heed. She came to make us aware that prayer, penance and reconciliation must remain an integral part of our everyday lives. Our Lady highlighted the mission confided to Maximin and Melanie when she repeated these words: *"Well, my children, you will make this known to all my people."* And as a result, many men and women all over the world have found the message of La Salette to be a vessel of conversion, an opportunity for renewed commitment to Christ and to the service of his people.

Reflection Questions:

- How have I become an instrument for the good?
- Have I generously allowed God to use me as his vehicle in giving of my time, my talent, and my presence for the sake of others?

Tuesday, March 15 (#231)
Second Week Of Lent

Matthew 23:1-12: *"Anyone who raises himself up will be humbled, and anyone who humbles himself will be raised up."*

Meditation:

Quite clearly, Jesus teaches us to reject the ways of those who make a show of their status. Listen to sound teachings, but don't follow the path of the hypocrite. Jesus preaches a humble way. And the humble way can be described in one word: truth. The core of humility is a real awareness of who we are as God's creatures. We must not lose sight of this most basic truth about ourselves. God is our Creator and our loving Father. Every gift and talent we have comes to us from God. Humility does not require that we deny our talents but that we acknowledge their source. We do not, therefore, need to put on airs, belittle others, nor should we lord it over them. We do not have to do this. We know the truth, and *"the truth will set you free"* (John 8:32).

During Jesus' public life Mary remained in the background. Very few of the words she spoke have been recorded in the Gospels. Those that have come down to us, however, are filled with meaning and sum up essential aspects of her personality. Faithful obedience: *"Let it happen to me as you have said"* (Luke 1:38). Joy and praise: *"My soul proclaims the greatness of the Lord"* (Luke 1:46). Tenderness and charity: *"They have no wine"* (John 2:3). Faith and humility: *"Do whatever (Jesus) tells you"* (John 2:5).

AT LA SALETTE ministries around the world, today more than ever, the Mother of Jesus, attentive to all her people, draws to her Son all who see God's love reflected in her tears. She comes to a people who refuse to submit. And how long will she be able to withhold the strong and heavy arm of her Son? She can only repeat the words she spoke to the waiters at Cana: *"Do whatever he tells you"* (John 2:5).

Reflection Questions:

- Today will I acknowledge with gratitude and honesty a certain gift (name it here) with which the Lord has blessed me?
- Do I acknowledge very often the source of my abilities and talents?

Wednesday, March 16 (#232)
Second Week of Lent

Matthew 20:17-28: *"... anyone who wants to become great among you must be your servant,n and anyone who wants to be first among you must be your slave."*

Meditation:

The hour of Jesus was drawing near. *"Jesus was going up to Jerusalem, and on the road he took the Twelve aside by themselves and said to them, 'Look, we are going up to Jerusalem, and the Son of man is about to be handed over to the chief priests and scribes. They will condemn him to death...'"*

Yet, even at this late hour, Zebedee's sons and the other apostles as well, failed to understand fully what was about to happen. James and John, their mother speaking in their behalf, wanted ringside seats at the Messiah's triumph. What they did not understand is that the promise of a place in Jesus' Kingdom can be fulfilled only in the life to come, *not* in this one. Once more Jesus had to repeat a fundamental theme of his teaching. Like the master, the disciple is not to *"lord it over others, but serve the needs of all."* Service is what counts with Jesus: a nurse's service to patients, a pastor's service to parishioners, a parent's service to children. *"... anyone who wants to become great among you must be your servant."*

"I am the servant of the Lord," were Mary's words when asked by the angel Gabriel to become the Mother of God. Her calling, her vocation, was summed up in those words. Her dialogue with the angel and her response place her in the line of those whom God calls to a specific mission. This response indicated free and full acceptance of the voca-

tion made known to her.

AT LA SALETTE Mary continues to be the Lord's servant and the servant of her children. Her sensitivity, her concern for us all is a clear manifestation of that. *"Come near, my children; don't be afraid ... If my people refuse to submit ... if they are converted... ."* Her maternal solicitude covers every detail and event of our lives. How can we resist her tears and fail to heed this loving messenger of her Son?

Reflection Questions:

• Whether I hold a position of authority or not, do I ever lord it over others?

• Today how can I exercise whatever authority is mine in a true Christian spirit of service?

Thursday, March 17 (#233)
Second Week of Lent

Luke 16:19-31: *"There was a rich man ... ."*

Meditation:

The rich man in today's gospel enjoyed the pleasures of life and seemed to have no need for God. After his death, he experiences the torture that comes from life without God. Lazarus, on the other hand, spent his life in misery but was at peace in his heart because his life was deeply rooted in faith. It is important for us to note what the rich man's sin was as the parable describes it. It is not that he calls the police to have Lazarus removed from his door. It is not that he objects to giving Lazarus scraps from his table. It is not that he abuses Lazarus each time he passes him.

The rich man's sin is that he ignores Lazarus. He doesn't lift a finger to help him. He even closes his eyes to the fact that Lazarus exists. His sin is not what he *does* to Lazarus. Rather it is what he *doesn't do* for him. We all know many "Lazaruses" in the world. Through no fault of their own, many go without food, medical attention, jobs and, of course, basic opportunities. Television news has often zeroed in on their plight. While we enjoy our privacy and security, they remain outside our gates. How long can we go on ignoring them? Even the dog in the story Jesus told did something. He licked Lazarus's sores.

DURING HER SHORT VISIT AT LA SALETTE, Mary showed us an ailing and suffering world. She spoke of a people *"who cannot swear without bringing in the name of her Son."* She spoke of many who will not observe the Sabbath. *"During Lent they go to the meat markets like dogs,"* she commented. *"A great famine is coming. Before the famine comes, children under seven will be seized with trembling and die in the arms of those holding them. The rest will do penance through the famine."* Those who are rich can be saved if they, like the poor, acknowledge their dependence upon God.

Reflection Questions:

• How sensitive am I to the pain that so many in the world are suffering? Am I listening well to those I meet when they share their painful experiences with me?
• How often do I merely pass by a person asking for help? How often do I pray for them?

Friday March 18 (#234)
Second Week of Lent

Matthew 21:33-43,45-46: *"The stone which the builders rejected has become the cornerstone."*

Meditation:

People in general do not like to rub elbows with excellence. It is much easier to live with mediocrity and the status quo. Alongside an outstanding example of heroic caring and loving, the rest of the community is made to feel that it is far from living up to its potential. So they can begin to feel inadequate. Those who stand head and shoulders above the crowd, in fact, are most often persecuted.

Martin Luther King, Jr., who was assassinated; Nelson Mandela, who was jailed. Both were Nobel Peace Prize winners and yet were mocked and ridiculed for their peacemaking efforts. Ironically, it is these very ones who end up saving the rest of society from its own worst enemy – itself! Today's parable illustrates Jesus' plight. The Father, the owner of the vineyard, has provided his people's livelihood, but they resent his servants and even kill his son. They fail to see that they are killing the one who alone can ensure their salvation. Yet the death of Jesus will still save that society from itself. *"The stone which the builders rejected has become the cornerstone."*

During this season of Lent we must ask ourselves where we stand on that hill of crucifixion. Are we with Mary entering into her Son's agony by our active and compassionate presence? Or could it be that we are part of the mob crucifying the Son of Man again? His mother shared Jesus' suffering not only on Calvary but all through his life. Each mystery of her life is faithfully marked by her loving relationship with God, and with God's Son and hers.

HER MESSAGE AT LA SALETTE bids us share in the sufferings of her children all over the world. The crucifix with hammer and pincers she wears upon her heart makes her call to conversion resonate. It was fitting that the brightness in which she and the children stood should emanate from that crucifix. Jesus is the pivotal point of wisdom, goodness and generosity for all who come to know him. He is in fact the cornerstone of their life.

Reflection Questions:

- Will I pray to the Lord to help me identify a rough edge in my own life today?
- Is Jesus the true cornerstone of my life and future? How does that show in my life and actions?

Saturday, March 19 (#543C)
St. Joseph, Spouse of Blessed Virgin Mary

Matthew 1: 16, 18-21, 24a: *"Joseph her husband… was a righteous man…",* *and able to enter into the mystery.*

Meditation:

Pope Francis, during Mass at Casa Santa Marta, said: "The Gospel… tells us that Joseph was a just man, a man of faith, who lived the faith. A man who can be found on the list of all the people of faith…; those people who have lived the faith as the foundation of what they hoped for, as the guarantee of what they did not see, and the proof of what they did not see.

"Joseph is a man of faith: because of this he was just. Not only because he believed, but also because he lived that faith. He was a just man. He was chosen to educate a man who was a true man but who was also God: only God could have educated such a person but there wasn't anyone like this. The Lord chose a just man, a man of faith. A man capable of being a man and also capable of speaking to God, of entering into the mystery of God.

"And this was Joseph's life: to live his profession, his life as a man and enter into the mystery, a man capable dialoguing with the mystery of God. He wasn't a dreamer. He entered into the mystery. With the same naturalness with which he carried on his work, with this precision of his craft: he was able to adjust an angle precisely on the wood, he knew how to do it; was able to lower, to sand down a millimeter of wood, of the surface of the wood. Right, it was accurate. But he was also able to get into the mystery that he could not control..."

At La Salette, Mary chose to appear to two unassuming children, Maximin and Melanie. They, like St. Joseph, were remarkably able to "enter into the mystery" that is the La Salette Apparition, each in their own way. And we, as devotees of Our Lady of La S alette, as asked to join them. Mary's apparition was certainly an extraordinary event, but it also was a very real event of meeting, communicating, responding and missioning.

As we proceed on our daily journey, let us be mindful of the message of Our Lady of La Salette, one of repentance, reconciliation and evangelization." (La Salette reflection, questions and editor of Papal text: Fr. Ron Gagne, M.S.)

Reflection Questions:

• When in your life have you "entered into the mystery" of some event – perhaps the birth of a child, falling in love with someone, or an event that lifted us up in some wonderous way?
• Who has shared with you a "mysterious event" which was somewhat unexpected?

Sunday, March 20 (#030)
Third Sunday of Lent

(Exodus 3:1-15; 1 Corinthians 10:1 12; Luke 13:1-9)

Meditation: "*The Arm of My Son*"

There are a few elements in the message of Our Lady of La Salette which have undergone a change of interpretation over the years. What seemed obvious in the 1800s and early 1900s is perceived today by many as inconceivable. This is true most especially of "the arm of my Son," which appears twice in the Beautiful Lady's discourse.

The image of Mary's holding back the arm of Jesus raised to strike sinners appears in many of the older paintings and sculptures illustrating these words. But today it is considered scandalous to think that Jesus, who came to save us, would be ready to destroy us and that Mary is now the one saving us—from him!

We can easily see this shift when we compare the older version of the "Memorare" of Our Lady of La Salette to the one we use today.

1880s: "Remember, our Lady of La Salette, true Mother of sorrows, the tears which thou didst shed for me on Calvary; be mindful also of the unceasing care which thou dost exercise to *screen me from the justice of God* ..."

1970s: "Remember, Our Lady of La Salette, true Mother of sorrows, the tears you shed for me on Calvary. Remember also the care you have always taken *to keep me faithful to Christ your Son*."

In today's Gospel, Jesus says, "If you do not repent, you will all perish." And in the parable of the fig tree, he seems to say that there comes a point where there is one last chance. A frightening prospect indeed! And St. Paul writes a similar word of caution to the Corinthians, "Therefore, whoever thinks he is standing secure should take

care not to fall."

The point is not to analyze but to understand the prophetic sense of Mary's words. She uses a biblical image reminiscent of Exodus 32:11 where Moses persuades God not to destroy his people. We read In Psalm 106:23 that Moses "withstood" God. How we visualize the scene is much less important than the call to reconciliation, which may take many different forms.

Monday, March 21 (#237)
Third Week of Lent

Luke 4:24-30: *"No prophet is ever accepted in his own country."*

Meditation:

Jesus is in his hometown. He is among his friends and family – his own people! Yet they hate him enough to try to take him to the top of a hill and hurl him off. Those townsfolk really didn't want to hear anything that might disturb their way of thinking and living. They seemed to have gone to the synagogue only to be comforted, to hear how good they were and how special they were to God. That, however, didn't seem to be what Jesus had in mind. He wanted to make them aware of their faults and invite them to shape up. They were far from believing this, and didn't want to hear anything about it.

It must have pained Jesus very much that the people of Nazareth, where he had been raised, put no faith in him. Likewise, members of our families, parishes and communities often go unheard when they offer observations or recommendations that challenge what we find customary and comfortable. We prefer to bring in outside facilitators, consultants and counselors. We give far more credence to speakers from afar than to the folks with the familiar faces. What we have yet to learn is how powerfully God's truth can be present in our everyday life.

JESUS SENDS HIS WEEPING MOTHER TO LA SALETTE. People have not fully accepted her Son and his message. Will they give his mother a warmer welcome? Following Mary's invitation to *"come near, don't be afraid,"* Maximin and Melanie are reassured that the Lady had come *"to tell us great news."* She comes as an ambassador of peace and reconciliation. Mary helps us to recall those means that have been given to help us return to her Son. Her mission was entrusted to her on Calvary. She now passes it on to us through the two children who saw her at La Salette. We in turn must *"make it known to all (her) people,"* the people of God.

Reflection Questions:

•Can you recall a time when you were slighted or scorned by a family member or a dear friend? Have you forgiven this offense?
•Have you ever had to ask forgiveness of another when you were wrong or acted inappropriately?

Tuesday, March 22 (#238)
Third Week of Lent

Matthew 18:21-35: *"Were you not bound, then, to have pity on your fellow-servant just as I had pity on you?"*

Meditation:

There is something more to the gift of forgiveness we receive from God; it is meant to be accepted but also shared. The merciless official in today's parable pleaded for mercy and received it. *"… the servant's master felt so sorry for him that he let him go and cancelled the debt."* But when that same official was approached by one who owed him, he refused to hear the plea for mercy and demanded what was owed. This official was given a reality check when the master told him: *"Were you not bound, then, to have pity on your fellow-servant just as I had pity on you?"* You must forgive if you want to be forgiven.

The forgiveness we receive must extend to others. To forgive is the greatest gift we can give to others and to ourselves. True, at times, we might be obsessed with feelings of anger or revenge. But forgiveness is given from our will. If we sincerely will to forgive, want to forgive, then we are forgiving. Bad feelings may remain. We may have to struggle to rid ourselves of them but they are not what Jesus is talking about. Let's forgive and get on with our friendship; get on with our good relationship. As the African proverb has it, "The one who forgives ends the quarrel."

THE MESSAGE OF THE BLESSED VIRGIN MARY at La Salette is a renewal of the message we find in Scripture. It speaks to us from the perspective of the cross and exhorts us to conversion and reconciliation. *"If they are converted"*... all will be forgiven... *"for nothing is impossible with God."* The father of the prodigal is forever watching and waiting for his son to return. His only intent is to forgive completely. Mary reassures us that Jesus will do likewise for all his repentant children.

Reflection Questions:

- Do I accept forgiveness from others but fail to forgive them?
- Having received God's forgiveness, do I still find it hard to forgive myself?

Wednesday, March 23 (#239)
Third Week of Lent

Matthew 5:17-19: *"Do not imagine that I have come to abolish the Law or the Prophets. I have come not to abolish but to complete them."*

Meditation:

When Jesus talks about keeping the law he is not talking about a legalistic approach, a literal keeping of the law. He is speaking about the spirit of the law. He came not to abolish laws but to open eyes to the real meaning contained in all that God has ever commanded his people. Jesus found himself in conflict with many of the religious people of his day. A number of them accused him of trying to destroy the old customs and beliefs of their religious heritage. Jesus reassures them that it is not his intent to destroy teachings handed down by the prophets. He has instead come to fulfill them.

We should always remember Jesus' own sense that law is fulfilled in *love* – wholehearted love of God and compassionate love of neighbor. Our problem is that we tend to "abolish the law," indeed to abolish love as soon as we encounter conflict, disappointment or disagreement. If we are honest, we discover that where we most need conversion to the love Jesus requires is in the rather ordinary situations of our everyday life – in our telephone conversations, in our dealings with authority, in our attitude and behavior in traffic, and in our homes.

WE ARE VERY FORTUNATE that Mary appears at La Salette to remind us that God has given us basic laws to follow if we wish to live happily now and with him forever. As a concerned mother, she warns us of the consequences that will follow, if we fail to take heed. In her conversation with the two witnesses, Our Lady does mention specific commandments. She speaks of our lack of submission to God's will, our irreverence toward the name of her Son, our disregard of the seventh-day rest, our need to pray daily, our obligation to participate in weekly Eucharist, and follow the laws of Lenten observance.

Reflection Questions:

- In my view, what of God's laws a blessing or a burden? In what sense?
- How faithfully do I follow Mary's various reminders?

Thursday, March 24 (#240)
Third Week of Lent

Luke 11:14-23: *"Anyone who is not with me is against me."*

For Your Reflection:

People often like to hang quotes on their wall to remind themselves of some important lesson they have learned. Now and then we read one that really makes us think. The one which comes to my mind could make me uncomfortable. It reads, "If you are not part of the solution, you are part of the problem." Suddenly, letting others worry about the homeless makes me part of the cause of homelessness. Not raising my voice against drug abuse, racism, makes me part of those problems. At the close of the gospel passage Jesus offers a similar mind teaser, "Whoever is not with me is against me." As God's people, the members of his audience were invited to join him and enter the Kingdom of God. They refused to do so. Jesus tells them they are part of the problem. They stand against him and are scattering while he tries to gather. Jesus offers us the same choice. By its very nature this choice is not one that should be put off. Lent is a perfect time to become part of the solution.

MARY HAS LEFT MANY TANGIBLE SIGNS IN TESTIMONY TO HER APPEARANCE AT LA SALETTE. She chose shepherd children because her message was a crucial one. She knew the children would share it candidly, truthfully and completely. She wore a crucifix, placing her crucified Son before our eyes. She came not to focus attention on herself, but rather on the Crucified and Risen Lord. The miraculous spring, that has not stopped flowing since the time of the apparition, serves as a perpetual sign of her visit. A large basilica stands at that remote Alpine site. The La Salette religious community of brothers, priests and sisters, now serving in over twenty countries, was founded to proclaim the Beautiful Lady's message and attest to its enduring timeliness.

Reflection Questions:

- Do you seek signs of God's love in the world? Where should you look?
- What signs of God's peace can you find in your own immediate surroundings?

Wednesday March 25 (#545)
The Annunciation of the Lord

Luke 1: 26-38: *"The angel said to her, 'Mary, do not be afraid.'"*

Meditation:

Since the earliest days of the Church, Mary was seen as the first disciple of Jesus. Her vocation, like our own from our Baptism, was to accept God's will and live out our common mission to spread the good news of the Gospel every moment of every day. However in the midst of the various events and preoccupations of our daily lives, we humans can forget that mission. We may lose focus on being children of God and instead concentrate too much on our own will.

At La Salette, Mary continues to carry out that common mission. In fact, she echoes the words of the angel at her Annunciation by greeting the two children at La Salette with: *"Come near my children, do not be afraid."* She had experienced fear when the angel appeared and she identified with the children who were afraid of her sudden appearance within a brilliant globe of light. Her words and attitude during the apparition were a mixture of warnings and promises, reminders and encouragement.

Mary's concern for the daily lives of these two children even extended to the family of Maximin, whose father was seriously concerned whether he could continue to feed his poor family. Her final words to the two children which actually are extended to all those who hear her message were: *"Make this message known to all my people."* She reminds us of the basics of our Baptismal call; namely, daily prayer, the important place of Eucharist in our life, reverence for God's name, a call to constant conversion, the proper place of Lenten customs of faith, and evangelizing others, reminding them of God's love and forgiveness. This is our call as "her children", the children of her loving Son.

Reflection Questions:

• How are you opening your life to God through prayer, the Eucharist, faith practices and spreading the Good News of her Son?
• Where can you do better?

Saturday, March 26 (#242)
Third Week of Lent

Luke 18:9-14: *"For everyone who raises himself up will be humbled, but anyone who humbles himself will be raised up."*

Meditation:

We learn from the tax collector what it means to love. Most tax collectors in his day were accused of being unfair in their dealings with their own people. This tax collector, however, wished to be right with God. His sacrifice was acknowledging that he was a sinner and in need of God's help. He did not raise his eyes nor lift his hands towards heaven. Instead he struck his breast and, confessing the sins in his heart, he implored God's mercy. At the point of realizing that he couldn't pick himself up, pull himself together, set things right, he appealed to God for mercy.

Though he was apparently trying to live according to God's law, the Pharisee boasted of his virtue and looked down on everyone else. It is never tolerable, however, to knock someone else down in order to build oneself up. That is where the Pharisee made his mistake. If we are self-centered and self-seeking, we become too proud and self-righteous. God asks that we be humble enough to admit our sinfulness, our true dependence upon him alone. Facing the truth about oneself is not a pleasant enterprise but face that reality we must!

THE APPEARANCE OF MARY AT LA SALETTE on September 19, 1846, was a major Marian apparition, an exciting intervention by God in Christian history. Saints, pastors and writers – St. John Bosco, the holy Curé of Ars, St. Peter Julian Eymard, Leon Bloy, Paul Claudel, Raïssa and Jacques Maritain, to name but a few – have been profoundly influenced and marked by the gift of La Salette. What influence can it be as we all take up the challenges of our third Christian millennium?

Reflection Questions:

• Can my criticism of others' weaknesses, however true my remarks may be, make me look like a better person?
• What changes do I need to make in my own life as I prepare for Holy Week and Easter?

Sunday, March 27 (#033)
Fourth Sunday of Lent

(Joshua 5:9-12; 2 Corinthians 5:17-21; Luke 15:1-3, 11-32)

Meditation: *Be Reconciled*

The Prodigal Son by **Hans Sebald Beham (1500–1550)**

95

Today's second reading is used also in the Mass of Our Lady of La Salette, and is very dear to the heart of La Salette Missionaries. It describes our mission perfectly. "We are ambassadors for Christ, as if God were appealing through us. We implore you on behalf of Christ, be reconciled to God."

The story of the Prodigal Son in the Gospel illustrates the way in which reconciliation comes about. The destitute son needs what his father can provide. So he decides to humble himself and ask for it. But the father needs something, too. He needs his son to be well, to be happy, to be safe. So, given the opportunity, he makes that happen, he welcomes him home—and with what a welcome!

We cannot be reconciled to God without wanting to, without needing to. Our reasons don't have to be perfect, but we do need to humble ourselves before him. Then we discover that the reconciliation has been there all the time, just waiting for us to accept it. In that moment, too, we discover that the Father desires our return so intensely that we can say that he needs it or, better still, he needs to make it happen.

There are two other parables between Luke 15:3 and the story of the Prodigal Son. They are the Lost Sheep and the Lost Coin. Both end by saying how much joy there is in heaven when a sinner repents.

The older son, who is now the sole heir, has nothing to lose by his brother's return, but he has not desired or needed this reconciliation. It doesn't make sense. For him it isn't fair.

Sometimes reconciliation may require some retribution, or the kind of making amends so essential in 12-step programs. But they are two different things. Reconciliation is less about justice than about relationship. The Prodigal Son's position as legal heir is no more. But his vital relationship with his father is restored.

Monday, March 28 (#244)
Fourth Week of Lent

John 4:43-54: *"The (royal official) believed what Jesus said to him and went on his way home."*

Meditation:

The royal official had much political authority and power, but now he was facing his own powerlessness. He could not save his dying son. Most people in his situation panic when they feel so needy, because it is difficult to know whom to trust at a time like that. Maybe his initial request was not an act of trust; maybe it was panic that became trust when Jesus did not respond in the anticipated way. Instead of traveling to the official's house, Jesus makes a promise and does not explain how it will be fulfilled. *"Your son will live,"* he said. We don't know what enabled the official to trust that promise, but we do know that experiencing God required that he trust.

When the children at La Salette encountered the one they called the Beautiful Lady, they did not know that she was the Mother of God, but they did trust that their story was meant to be retold. How interesting that Grandma Pra was so quick to trust that this was the Mother of God speaking to the two children! The people of that area were perhaps feeling a vulnerability like that of the royal official. There was something about the words they heard that evoked a trusting response in the children. Vulnerable moments do not have to lead to panic; they can be invitations and opportunities to trust.

Reflection Questions:

- Do I find it hard to trust God?
- I believe that he preserved the life of the official's son and continually revives people spiritually. Why should I think God will treat me any differently than he treated them?

Tuesday, March 28 (#245)
Fourth Week of Lent

John 5:1-16: They harassed Jesus because he healed the man on the Sabbath.

Meditation:

How wonderful that someone who had been sick for such a long time was finally well again! How unfortunate that some eyewitnesses were unable to share in the joy of the moment – all because they were rigid in their religious beliefs. So concerned were they about their own actions that they were unable to see what God was doing. They had lost the Sabbath spirit, a willingness to rest, and allow God to speak to our stillness and change our hearts.

At La Salette Mary voiced concern about people's failure to observe the Sabbath spirit properly. Her concern was not limited to what people did on the Sabbath day. She noted that their actions on the Sabbath revealed that something was amiss in their relationship with God on the other days of the week as well. They lacked the Sabbath spirit. They had become so taken with business matters that they were scarcely aware of God. Similarly we can become preoccupied with schedules, future planning, and even church-related activities and still be lacking a genuine Sabbath spirit. Making time for God is a challenge because it means more than simply squeezing a bit more prayer into an already hectic schedule. True Sabbath time is what is needed.

Reflection Questions:

- Do I distort the spirit of the Sabbath by hanging on to certain ideas about God?
- Do I distort the spirit of the Sabbath by maintaining a hectic lifestyle?

Wednesday, March 30 (#246)
Fourth Week of Lent

John 5:17-30: *"(Jesus) spoke of God as his own Father."*

Meditation:

To speak of God as his own Father was one more way in which Jesus challenged people's assumptions about their relationship with God. His concern was not to define God's gender, however, but to invite people to a closer relationship with God. He wanted people to know that God was more concerned about them and more approachable than they had ever thought possible. Nonetheless, some who heard were more concerned about maintaining their assumptions about God than they were about hearing this Good News.

MARY SPOKE OF A GOD WHO DESIRES TO BE INTIMATELY INVOLVED IN OUR

LIVES. She herself was so concerned about us that she wept. She too wanted people to know that God is deeply concerned about them and approachable. Mary's tears and Jesus' use of the familiar term Abba spoke a similar message. God is more concerned about us than we realize. Most people find it difficult to relate to others in an "up-close-and-personal" manner. The experience is all the more challenging when God is involved. We find it difficult to believe that God, or any power greater than ourselves, wishes to bring out the best in us. Individual and corporate lives, as a result, are marked by selfishness, greed and illusions of security. We lower our expectations and eventually stop expecting much of anything from God.

Some Reflection Questions:

- Are you convinced that your God wishes to be close to you?
- Are you ready to take your own first step toward greater intimacy with God?

Thursday, March 31 (#247)
Fourth Week of Lent

John 5:31-47: *"Come to me to receive life!"*

Meditation:

Jesus' words and works did not make sense unless they were understood as part of a divine plan that began with the creation of the world. That plan is an ongoing story of people and events, reminding us that God is faithful, even when we are unfaithful. It also teaches us that the faithful God wants to share life with us. As we respond to the people and events of salvation history, we learn more and more about God, we possess more and more of that life and live our lives much differently.

LA SALETTE IS ALSO AN ONGOING STORY. It is a story about God's people being reminded again and again of the faithful God who calls his own people to possess more of that life that only he can give. For Maximin and Melanie it was a reminder that their failure to pray was preventing them from possessing God's life. Over the years the ongoing understanding of the La Salette story has helped us to see that it is not our personal failures alone that prevent us from possessing God's

99

life. Social systems also can prevent us from experiencing the fullness of God's life. Becoming more aware of God's life begins with personal change but it goes beyond that and must lead to social change.

Reflection Questions:

- Why are you so slow to possess more of God's life?
- Is it because you realize how frightening the prospect of change can be?

Friday, April 1 (#248)
Fourth Week of Lent

John 7:1-2,10,25-30: *"For me the right time has not yet come."*

Meditation:

The invitation to share in God's life is constantly available. Our response to that invitation, sad to say, is not as constant. It seems that we are aware of God's invitation to new life long before we respond. It is hard for us to believe that God wants us to be even happier and more at peace than we have ever been. Every once in a while, however, there is a breakthrough and we know that the time for change is "right" – that the hour has come. People of Jesus' time did not respond to him immediately. Their hour came when they could understand Jesus' hour. Only when they came to a new understanding of his death could they understand that their old ways of thinking would also have to die in order for them to change.

Mary's message to the children at La Salette emphasized that the time had come for people to change and turn back to God. She spoke with urgency: *"How long a time I have suffered for you!"* Hers was a message that required a response, not in the distant future but now: *"I tried to show you with the potatoes last year. You paid no heed."*

Reflection Questions:

- Can you expect the world to know the love of God, if you yourself are not ready to change now?
- What time is it in your life?

Saturday, April 2 (#249)
Fourth Week of Lent

John 7:40-53: *"Would the Christ come from Galilee?"*

Meditation:

Galilee was the geographic place that symbolized acceptance of the Gospel. In keeping with their tradition, the people of Jesus' day had assumptions and expectations about how the saving power of God would become visible in the world. Those assumptions limited their ability to understand what God was promising them. That is why God has often been called a God of Surprises. God reveals to us not only that he is faithful but also that our expectations of him are too low.

No ONE EXPECTED that a place as isolated and unpretentious as the hamlet of La Salette in France would be the site from which God would call his people back to himself; neither did they expect that the call would be spoken by the Mother of God. For that reason, some did not believe the message. Others paid attention to what had happened there by invoking the Visitor as Our Lady of La Salette. Over time, spiritual healings linked to La Salette have by far exceeded people's expectations.

Reflection Questions:

- Are you afraid to expect too much from God?
- Are you reluctant to believe in a God of Surprises?

Sunday, April 4 (#036c)
The Fifth Sunday of Lent

(Isaiah 43:16-21; Philippians 3:8-14; John 8:1-11)

Meditation: The Best is Yet to Come

St. Paul writes that he has accepted the loss of all things for the sake of Christ. What things? In the verses immediately before this passage, he states: "In righteousness based on the law I was blameless." He was a perfect pharisee, in the best sense of the word, one who loved God's Law and strove to observe it perfectly.

In his world that was a lot to lose, but compared to "the supreme good of knowing Christ," he now considered it "rubbish." And he concludes: "Forgetting what lies behind but straining forward to what lies ahead, I continue my pursuit toward the goal, the prize of God's upward calling, in Christ Jesus."

Isaiah even goes so far as to tell us to forget God's former triumphs, because what lies ahead is greater still: "I am doing something new!"

Today's Gospel story is usually titled *The Woman Caught in Adultery*. In the spirit of today's readings, however, we ought to change that to *The Woman Saved by Jesus*. Saved from two things: from stoning and from sin. We must believe that at the same time as Jesus told her, "Go, and from now on do not sin any more," he made it possible for her to live a new life. Her future would be more important than her past.

Trial of the Adulteress by **Julius Schnorr von Carolsfeld** (**1794–1872**)

That hope is the goal of conversion, which is the point of Lent. That was the Beautiful Lady's hope in coming to La Salette. Her people had been "caught" in their sins and were facing due punishment. Her Son was once again in the position of letting the penalty stand or offering salvation. His preference is clear, and the message for us is the same as to the woman: "From now on do not sin any more."

But is that really possible? Actually, it is. Sin means turning our back on God. Conversion means turning to him once again, seeking his grace and strength, rediscovering the joy of his love and putting that love into practice. Our Christian life will have its imperfections, but living in Christ will remind us that it is he who saves. We sow in tears, but by his power we will reap rejoicing.

La Salette calls us to that same conviction that the best is yet to come.

Monday, April 4 (#251)
Fifth Week of Lent

John 8:12-20: *"Neither do I condemn you."*

Meditation:

The Mosaic Law condemned the woman. The crowd condemned her too. But Jesus had a different response. He did not condemn her; he reacted to those who did the condemning. Those who wanted to throw stones were preoccupied with other people's sins and were paying no attention to their own. Perhaps they were unable to show compassion toward others because they had forgotten about God's compassion towards them. Jesus did not interrogate the woman about the accusations; he did not even lecture her about the why and how of God's compassion. He showed compassion by his initial silence and this simple statement: *"Neither do I condemn you."*

AT LA SALETTE MARY SPOKE TO THE CHILDREN about the sins of the world, but she did not condemn. She did not give a lengthy explanation of why her Son was compassionate. Like that of Jesus, her gesture of compassion was a simple one; she wept. Since that time many people have been freed from the burden of past guilt because they were touched by her tears.

Reflection Questions:

• What are the gestures in your life that speak to others of a compassionate God?
• Are you willing to acknowledge your sin that you may be more compassionate towards others?

Tuesday, April 5 (#252)
Fifth Week of Lent

John 8:21-30: *"They did not recognize that (Jesus) was talking to them about the Father."*

Meditation:

Jesus spoke to people about a God who loved them in a way that went beyond their usual understanding of love. In order to understand the meaning of this newly revealed love they would have to look beyond their usual experience. *"You are from below; I am from above."* When people are confused and do not understand a new experience they are inclined to get frustrated and give up. However, people who were persistent in their attempt to understand the newness of Jesus' message came to believe in him. They wrestled with God (and with themselves) in order to discover the life that he was offering.

AT LA SALETTE the children initially did not understand initially what the Beautiful Lady was saying. It is not just that she spoke a different language than they did; she spoke about problems that were beyond their grasp. Nonetheless, they knew that something important was being said and they shared their story with others at home. Their willingness to share their confusion was their way of wrestling with God. Because they did not give up when they were confused, they (and others) came to a new understanding of God's love.

Reflection Questions:

- Is it difficult to believe that God will guide you through life's confusing experiences?
- Are you willing to wrestle with God in order to discover God in new ways?

Wednesday, April 6 (#253)
Fifth Week of Lent

John 8:31-42: *"... the truth will set you free."*

Meditation:

The words of Jesus promising freedom are directed at people who had not realized how enslaved they were. They were the ones who paid so much attention to the details of the Law that they could not appreciate its spirit. They were well intentioned, but they had a shallow understanding of what it means to believe. That kind of belief is itself enslaving.

AT LA SALETTE Mary encouraged people to avoid shallowness in their faith. She asked: *"Do you pray well?"* Praying well was not simply a matter of saying more prayers. It meant that their fidelity to prayer would help them to be honest with themselves and open them to that truth which would set them free.

Reflection Questions:

- If Jesus could accept society's outcasts, do you find it hard to accept them?
- Do you find it difficult to accept the truth about yourself? Are you afraid to be truly free?

Thursday, April 7, (#254)
Fifth Week of Lent

John 8:51-59: *"They picked up stones to throw them at (Jesus)."*

Meditation:

The people who picked up stones to throw at him feared the implications of Jesus' assertion that he was greater than Abraham. It threatened their identity as followers of Abraham. Their stones did not harm Jesus but their fears harmed them. As great as Abraham was, he was a limited human being and as such he experienced death. Jesus offered something timeless that could not be destroyed by death. Unfortunately some people were so fearful that they could not respond to his offer. In their fear they became violent and took stones into their hands.

WHEN THE CHILDREN OF LA SALETTE first saw the Beautiful Lady surrounded by a great light, they were afraid. Maximin considered striking her with his herder's staff: "If it does anything to us, I'll give it a good whack." Mary understood that fright, however, and addressed it immediately: *"Don't be afraid"* she said. The two children did us all a great favor when they decided to come near and let their fear dissolve. Their decision not to be controlled by their initial fear made it possible for us all to hear an invitation to relate to God without fear.

Reflection Questions:

- Is it difficult to see the consequences of your fear?
- Are you afraid to learn from children?

Friday, April 8 (#255)
Fifth Week of Lent

John 10:31-42: *"... even if you refuse to believe in me, at least believe in the work I do."*

Meditation:

It troubled some people to think that this man, Jesus, could also be God. Jesus had taught them a new kind of love that included forgiveness and unconditional acceptance. Some thought that kind of love could only be accomplished by God. To believe that Jesus' kind of loving was the same as God's meant that we were being challenged to love as God himself loves. Those outcasts who had been recipients of Jesus' new kind of love, on the other hand, were more than willing to take up that challenge.

WHEN MARY TOLD MELANIE AND MAXIMIN, *"My children, make this known to all my people,"* she challenged them (and us) to be as compassionate as Jesus is. We should not expect God to love, forgive and accept us unconditionally if we ourselves are unwilling to do the same.

Reflection Questions:
- Are you willing to forgive as God forgives?
- What might help you accept others unconditionally?

Saturday, April 9 (#256)
Fifth Week of Lent

John 11:45-56: *"If we let him go on in this way everybody will believe in him."*

Meditation:

Those who did not understand, feared that unless they took steps to control Jesus' popularity, they might lose the very things that insured their security – their sanctuary and their nation. They feared that the whole world would change entirely and affect the personal security they enjoyed. It never occurred to them that a world transformed by God's love might be a desirable place, not only for themselves but for everyone. It seemed to them too good to be true.

JUST AS THE GOSPEL IS MEANT FOR ALL PEOPLE, the story of La Salette is a story that is meant for the whole world to hear. People who understand that God's compassion is more powerful (and important) than our sinning, realize that they have shared in something that must be passed on – a spirit of reconciliation.

Reflection Questions:

- Do you have a desire to control people and situations, thus preventing others from experiencing God's love?
- Do you feel a need to cling to a false sense of security?

Sunday, April 10 (#038)
Palm Sunday

(Luke 19:28-40; Isaiah 50:4-7; Philippians 2:6-11; Luke 22:14—23:56 or Luke 23:1-49)

Meditation: *Weep for Yourselves*

The outline of the Passion of Jesus is the same in all of the Gospels but there are details that are unique to each one. The "Seven Last Words," for example, are distributed as follows: Matthew and Mark have only "My God, my God, why have you forsaken me?" while Luke has "Father, forgive them, they do not know what they are doing," "Amen I say to you, this day you will be with me in paradise," and "Father, into your hands I commend my spirit. John has, "Woman, behold your son — Behold your mother," "I thirst," and "It is finished."

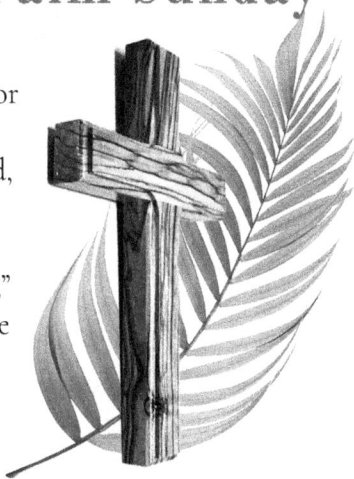

Today we are reading the Passion according to Luke. His is the only Gospel to record Jesus' encounter with the weeping women. He tells them, "Daughters of Jerusalem, do not weep for me; weep instead for yourselves and for your children." A similar painful image is used by our Lady of La Salette: "Children under the age of seven will be seized with trembling and die in the arms of those who hold them."

Anyone who has lost a child—as I write, the funeral of little Annalee Rose Harrington is about to begin—can understand the weight of grief evoked by these words. Mary bore that burden herself, and the prospect of such pain for her people is more than she can bear. At La Salette she weeps, in a sense, for herself and for her children.

This a source of consolation for us. It is also a renewed invitation to return to God with all our heart. Which in turn evokes other biblical texts: "No longer shall the sound of weeping be heard there, or the sound of crying. No longer shall there be in [Jerusalem] an infant who lives but a few days, nor anyone who does not live a full lifetime" (Isaiah 65:19-20); "He will wipe every tear from their eyes, and there shall be no more death or mourning, wailing or pain, for the old order has passed away" (Revelation 21:4).

The "old order" of sin and death has been replaced by the "new order" of grace—of hope, of life, of love—by Jesus' death and life.

Monday, April 11 (#257)
Holy Week

John 12:1-11: *"You have the poor with you always, you will not always have me."*

Meditation:

There is something disturbing about the scene. Mary's profound gratitude to Jesus for what he had done in her life led her to be extravagant. Deep and true love does not count the cost. As the odor of the precious ointment filled the house, so did a sense of awe at this bold act of love. But a voice pierced this atmosphere and declared this a shocking waste that the money could have been used for the poor. (The value of the ointment, made in India, amounted to an ordinary worker's yearly wage, commentators say.) Perhaps we ourselves silently agree? But Jesus did not agree. He reveals what is really happening. This anointing prepares his body for the death and burial he will soon be facing. The poor will always be with us, and when he is gone, they will be a privileged place for ministering to Jesus himself.

There is also a place for devotion, love, reverence, and worship. Our challenge is to discern what, here and now, is the most appropriate response to those myriad ways in which Jesus remains present to us.

AT LA SALETTE Mary wore peasant garb. She spoke to two children from very poor families. The words she spoke were jolting and disturbing yet she was vested with dazzling radiance and glory. The light surrounding her served to identify the Beautiful Lady. Its rare brilliance awakened in Maximin an impulse to reach out and grasp some of this beauty.

Reflection Questions:

- Has your faith ever found inspiration in a magnificent church building or religious work of art?
- Are you able to see and help others see the faith reality and appropriateness behind this kind of "extravagance"?

Tuesday, April 12 (#258)
Holy Week

John 13:21-33,36-38: *"At that instant, after Judas had taken the bread, Satan entered him... It was night."*

The scene is the Last Supper. Judas leaves to tell the officials where they can find and arrest Jesus. Step by step, Judas has been walking the cold, calculated path of betrayal. He deliberately leaves the glow of the light and plunges into the night. Jesus tells the disciples that he must leave them now but that they cannot follow him. Blustering, impetuous Peter immediately leaps into the conversation: *"Lord, why can I not follow you now? I will lay down my life for you."* One can almost see Jesus sadly shaking his head and telling Peter – or is he chiding him? – that before the cock crows he will have betrayed him three times. And so it happened. But Peter's heart, overflowing with love for the Lord, was not a place where Satan might find a welcome. Jesus could see the depths of Peter's heart and the love within it. It is this love that enabled Peter to emerge from that night and confidently claim Jesus' loving forgiveness.

MARY'S RECITATION OF HER PEOPLE'S SINS and neglect of God can at times seem to be a path into darkness. As she breaks open the political reality France was then experiencing and its consequences, we may be tempted to block our ears and run away. That is why the light radiating from her and the crucifix on her breast is what dispels the darkness. From the heart of darkness, the suffering and death of Jesus shines as the light that will transform the night forever.

Reflection Questions:

- Do you make an about-face when your choices make you dim the guiding lights on your path of life?
- What can help you turn what is often a "long day's journey into the night" into a "long day's journey into the light"?

Wednesday, April 13 (#259)
Holy Week

Matthew 26:14-25: *"Better for that man (Judas) if he had never been born!"*

Meditation:

It is not uncommon to be bewildered by Judas. (The film, *Jesus Christ Super Star*, includes a scene of Judas running in the desert, huge tanks pursuing him – powerful images of his fate, his destiny, about to destroy him.) In the divine plan, someone was to betray Jesus. It could have been someone who did not know Jesus personally, a Roman soldier, a member of the Sanhedrin. However it ended up being a trusted friend. And yet Jesus had chosen Judas.

He had given him a position of confidence in the group. Jesus did not shut Judas out. Even on the night of the betrayal, he let Judas know that he was aware of what was going on. Jesus exerted no power to stop Judas. The only power he used was the heartfelt appeal that Judas remain a faithful disciple, a faithful friend but to no avail.

Did Judas die in despair, believing he could never be forgiven? Was his vision so desperately closed in on himself that he neither saw nor entirely understood the extent of Christ's mercy and compassion? Ours is a God of second and seemingly infinite chances! Simply by asking, Judas could have been reborn in Christ's unconditional love. We have no idea what happened during those seconds between the hanging and actual death (Matthew 27:5). Judas may have whispered,

"I'm sorry. Please forgive me."

AT LA SALETTE Mary's message gives us the promise that can break the chain of sin and the consequent sufferings and dyings. "*If* my people are converted..." *If* is the hinge word. *If* smashes "fated" or "destined" punishment. *If* is a precious reminder of our continued second chances. *If* takes us beyond.

Reflection Questions:

- How have you experienced the Lord's powerful forgiveness?
- How do you convey to others this core truth of your faith in Jesus?

Thursday, April 14 (#039)
Holy Thursday

John 13:1-15: "*If I therefore ... have washed your feet, you must wash each other 's feet ... so that you may copy what I have done to you.*"

Meditation:

On this day celebrating the institution of the Eucharist, it is surprising that the familiar words transforming bread and wine into the body and blood of Jesus, as recorded in the Gospels of Mark, Matthew and Luke, are not found in the gospel for the Mass of the Lord's Supper. In John's account, Jesus provides instead a different way of remembering him and making him present to one another. It is the remembrance and presence of loving service.

In washing the feet, Jesus turns our understanding of authority and power upside down. The Lord who holds all power and authority manifests himself as servant. His act is an example that we are challenged to imitate and repeat in our own culture and society, so taken with control, force, might and power. Jesus invites us to believe in the counter-cultural power of humble, loving service.

AT LA SALETTE Mary shows the power of a weeping mother. Her apparition manifests a *kenosis* (Philippians 2:7) or *self-emptying*, all its own. She has bent over her children just as Jesus bent over the feet of his disciples. She does not stand aloof, but comes near. She wants our hearts to be washed with her tears of love. And as she came to call us to conversion; she confers that same task on us. As she has done, so should we do.

Reflection Questions:

- How do I make Jesus present to others?
- How frequently do I engage in "bending down" in service to others?

Friday, April 15 (#040)
Good Friday

John 18:1 –to 19:42: *"I was born for this, I came into the world for this, to bear witness to the truth; and all who are on the side of truth listen to my voice."*

Meditation:

The truth of Good Friday shone in the glory of Jesus' suffering and death. No, we have not yet reached the Easter moment. We are at the foot of the cross. In the words, *"It is finished,"* Jesus declares the astounding truth that all that has happened is part of the Father's plan. "It," the plan, has been brought to its fulfillment, although not in the manner messianic hopes had imagined. In God's plan, Jesus had to undergo such pain, such vulnerability, such darkness, such near despair. This is the truth this day challenges us to walk in and remain in for a while. Jesus has made all of our sufferings, and even our death, his own. All suffering and dying itself have, therefore, been infused with meaning beyond what we can comprehend. This is the truth that Easter has guaranteed us forever.

But let us not move too quickly to Easter. Let us stay with this day's pain and overwhelming truth. All this suffering, and dying, "for love of me … for love of us." There is always the strong temptation to avoid "Good Friday moments" at all cost. It is all part and parcel of *"If anyone wants to be a follower of mine, let him renounce himself and take up his cross and follow me"* (Mark 8:34). It is an intricate part of what we sometimes glibly call the Paschal Mystery. Good Friday's "truth" is that the "no" of death is not the last word; its "truth" is that life ultimately conquers death; its "truth," by now almost a cliché, that there can be no Easter unless there is a Good Friday.

At La Salette Mary helped us to see the "truth" underlying the events of those crucial days. Like the prophets, she sliced open the reality and allowed us to see an even deeper reality beneath it. Prophets help us see the layers of truth in the world. Mary's tears and the brilliant light surrounding this Queen of Prophets invited us to look and see with the eyes of our hearts. The truth of love comes to hearts alert and open.

Reflection Questions:

- How well do I recognize my Good Friday experiences and my Easter experiences? Can I name some of them?
- What impresses me most about Jesus on this Good Friday?

Saturday, April 16 (#041C)
Holy Saturday

Luke 24:1-12: *"Why look among the dead for someone who is alive? He is not here; he has risen. Remember what he told you..."*

Meditation:

It is surprising that those who knew Jesus and followed him closely, still didn't have a clue. The events of Good Friday traumatized them into a numbing forgetfulness. Some of the women go to the tomb to do what they could not do on the Sabbath – the ritual anointing and preparation of the body. These gospel pas-sages all begin with a sense of the finality of it all. Everything has ended in tragedy. No great expectations. But this is quickly changed into a whirlwind of strong emotions – fear, joy, confusion, belief, disbelief. The women have found the tomb empty and have been told by an angel that Jesus has been raised. Some actually see Jesus, very much alive. And thus began the overwhelming realization that Jesus is not to be just a memory, but a living presence with us, as he promised, to the end of time. Do we continue to search for Jesus among the dead? We can fill our heads with all the stories, doctrines, dogmas, and teachings of and about Jesus and yet not have a personal encounter with him, who is very much alive.

At La Salette Mary comes to us, her children. From the cross Jesus gave his mother to us, and us to his mother. Her loving motherhood is accentuated at La Salette by her tears flowing for us, her children. La Salette is a very powerful reminder of Mary's continuing, real, maternal presence to us.

Reflection Questions:

- Have you deeply experienced in your life the move from "knowing about" Jesus to actually "knowing" Jesus?
- In what ways might you now be looking for the Living One among the dead?

Sunday, April 17 (#042)
Easter Sunday

He is Risen

(Acts 10:34-43; Colossians 3:1-4; John 20:1-9. Other options possible.)

Meditation: *Witnesses*

In the first reading, Peter states that he and his companions were witnesses to three distinct realities: 1) Jesus' public ministry; 2) the risen Christ; and 3) that Jesus has been appointed judge of the living and the dead.

Paul, in the second reading, bears witness to the resurrection of Jesus and, in a particular way, to its meaning for our Christian life.

Mary Magdalen, Peter and the disciple whom Jesus loved also were witnesses, in the account we read today from John's gospel. Witness to what, exactly? To nothing, to absence, to emptiness—or, more accurately, to mystery.

The mystery of Jesus' resurrection is so fundamental that it is not easy to express in words what it means to us. In 1972, Easter fell on April 2. That day, the truth of Easter struck me in a way I cannot adequately describe. I can say, however, that it was the most life-changing spiritual experience of my life.

The beloved disciple, John, entered the tomb, saw, and believed. In that emptiness he experienced the deepest possible faith. His goal from then on was to help others to experience the same. Near the end of his Gospel, he writes: "These [signs] are written that you may believe that Jesus is the Messiah, the Son of God, and that through this belief you may have life in his name."

"Life in his name"—Mary at La Salette does not use those words, but that is the meaning of her message. Like Moses in Deuteronomy, she places before us life and death, and begs us to choose life. Those who do so become witnesses to the transforming mystery of what St. Paul calls a life "hidden with Christ in God."

Not knowing, not understanding, is not necessarily a bad thing. Mélanie and Maximin did not know who was speaking to them, nor did they understand everything they heard; but at the Beautiful Lady's invitation, they entered into that mystery, into what a 14th century spiritual classic calls the Cloud of Unknowing.

In telling others, like Peter, what they had seen and heard, the children were actually witnessing to what they did not know. They drew others into the mystery of Mary's love, revealing the fathomless depths of God's mercy, of which we too can be witnesses.

Monday, April 18 (#261)
Easter Monday

Matthew 28:8-15: *"Do not be afraid; go and tell my brothers that they must leave for Galilee."*

Meditation:

What an extraordinary gift it is to have the Lord's peace that can take away our fears. The Lord often prefaces his appearances to the disciples with the greeting that grants this peace. Ultimately, this peace is a fruit of the Holy Spirit and it is very much needed because fear prevents us in many ways from being fully present and attentive. Fear can have us cringe, squint and look away, thus severely limiting our capacity to see and take in the whole picture. Fear can set our heart and mind racing, searching for a defense, looking for an escape. Fear can cause the fight or flight mechanism to kick in. Fear can cause us to run and not stop to look and listen to what is truly happening. This is especially true when we are dealing with a powerful spiritual experience. And fear can be so totally absorbing that it can make us forget.

Good Friday had been so overwhelming that the women and the disciples forgot what Jesus had said about his dying and rising. The encounter at the empty tomb left them "half-overjoyed and half-fearful." Did they dare hope and believe that Jesus was risen? And into this excitement the risen Lord appears. Jesus takes their dramatically renewed energy and sends them off to bring the good news to the others.

AT LA SALETTE Our Lady follows the same pattern. She invites the children to come near and not to be afraid. Her message, however, certainly could raise fear in their hearts and leave them filled with anxiety. Along with her command to *"make this known"* it would seem that Our Lady gave her confidants a special strength allowing them to hold steadfast to their story, even when threatened by authorities.

Reflection Questions:

• What fears at times prevent me from living and sharing the Lord's gift of peace?
• Are there fears that hold me back from witnessing to the Risen Lord?

Tuesday, April 19 (#262)
Easter Tuesday

John 20:11-18: *"(The angels) said to (Mary Magdalene): 'Woman, why are you weeping?'"*

Meditation:

A heavy cloak of sadness is Mary Magdalene's attire this morning. Her grieving heart has tunneled her vision into a single thought, "He is gone. He is dead. All my hopes, all that had helped me make sense out of life, all were dashed on that horrid day. There is nothing I can do now but give final anointing to his dead body. There is nothing else."

It is into this brokenhearted experience that Jesus appears. Just as it is in the confusion and disappointment of the disciples going to Emmaus that Jesus appears. Just as it is into the fear of the disciples barricaded behind locked doors that Jesus appears. Yes, we find and experience Jesus in moments of joy, of love, of celebration. But often Jesus breaks into the weeping moments of our lives – times of painful failure, unfulfilled hopes, broken plans, unattained goals and disappointed hopes. At times Jesus breaks into the hurting fragments of our broken commitments that can appear irreparable, irretrievable. Times and places such as these seem to be favorite entries for Jesus.

At La Salette no one asked Mary why she was weeping. The children thought at first that she was a mother from the area and that her children had beaten her. But her message soon put the reason for her tears beyond speculation – her children were suffering. Hers were tears of love – love so strong that it breaks into her "beatific state of being" and causes anguish and pain. What makes no sense to the theologian's mind makes eminent sense to the loving heart.

Reflection Questions:

•Have I allowed myself to touch the roots of some of the sadness in my life?
•If the Lord were to ask me "why are you weeping," how would I answer?

Wednesday, April 20 (#263)
Easter Wednesday

Luke 24:13-35: *"... how our chief priests and our leaders handed him over to be sentenced to death and had him crucified."*

Meditation:

Our text is found in the account given by the Emmaus disciples of what had recently happened in Jerusalem. Is it farfetched to imagine that part of their pain came from a deep sense that they had been betrayed by their religious leaders? These disciples do not refer to *"the* chief priests and leaders" but to *"our* chief priests and leaders." How could it all have gone so wrong? How could the One who seemed to fulfill their messianic hopes and dreams be destroyed by the very guardians and teachers of their faith, including faith in the expected Christ?

The two disciples welcomed a stranger into their fear, doubts and disillusionment. Jesus the Stranger reviews the Scripture passages relating to the Messiah and helps them to see how the events of recent days fulfilled the predictions of the prophets. What is more, he set their hearts on fire. They understood the deeper meaning of those events. Their hope reborn, they rushed back to Jerusalem to share their experience with the other disciples. Easter's living light had now pierced the darkness of their despondent feelings of betrayal.

THE LA SALETTE EVENT, like other officially recognized apparitions, knew stormy beginnings. But even before canonical approval had been given, thousands flocked to the favored mountain and felt their hearts catch fire as the words Mary had spoken there helped them understand the "meaning" of contemporary events and their link to the providence of God. Many hurried down from the mountain and shared their experience with others.

Reflection Questions:

• What or who has contributed most to my own search for meaning?
• Has my heart ever been "set on fire"?

Thursday, April 21 (#264)
Easter Thursday

Luke 24:35-48: *"Why are you so agitated... See by my hands and my feet that it is really I myself.. Touch me and see for yourselves; a ghost has no flesh and bones as you can see I have."*

Meditation:

The Incarnation has a unique continuance after the Lord has been raised from the dead. In speaking of the post-Resurrection Christ, we stress that we are dealing with his glorified body. That is true. But we must avoid the danger of spiritualizing too much. At the heart of our faith is Jesus' bodily resurrection. In his Easter and post-Easter appearances to the disciples, Jesus went out of his way to have them recognize that he was no phantom or hallucination. He invites them to look at his hands and feet. They are signed with the wounds he suffered for love of us and in obedience to the Father. In these appearances Jesus shows that his glory and the cross must always remain together. We are *incarnational* people. Our faith, our religion, is *incarnational*. Our sacraments offer visible, tangible signs of God's grace and presence. It's not wrong to expect or seek moments of encounter with the Lord that will touch and move us.

AT LA SALETTE the brilliant light surrounding Our Lady, and then embracing the children, was truly a sign of glory. As the two herders observed, this light seemed to emanate from the crucified Christ on the cross that Mary wore on her breast. That dark, dark moment of Good Friday is here revealed in its ultimate reality: Glory.

Reflection Questions:

- How do I respond to Christ's invitation to relate to him in the humanity he shares in with me?
- How do I find and relate to him in the wounds his people bear?

Friday, April 22 (#265)
Easter Friday

John 21:1-14: *"Simon Peter said (to the disciples), 'I'm going fishing'. They replied, 'We'll come with you.'"*

Meditation:

This gospel passage recounts Jesus' third appearance to the disciples. As they had been instructed, they were waiting for the Lord in Galilee. Peter decides to go fishing. The others join him. Fishermen by trade, they returned to what they knew best, giving us a life-goes-on feeling. After an unsuccessful night of fishing, a man walking along the shore tells them they should cast their nets once again. They do so and a tremendous catch of fish results, bringing vividly to mind their very first encounter with Jesus: *"Come after me and I will make you fishers of people"* (Matthew 4:19). John is the first to recognize him. *"It is the Lord!"* he says.

There is something evocative about the scene. The disciples labor in vain. When the as yet unrecognized Lord offered direction they might have been tempted to tell him they were seasoned at their trade, had been fishing all night, and that if there were fish to be caught they would have caught them. As members of our "instant everything" culture, we are quick to toss off one single failed attempt and move on to a new try. "Been there, done that" is a mantra of our age. Yet we often row to shore, nets empty and spirits drooping. Perhaps our attempts need only one more try. The grace moment may be the very next one. And when success does come, do we exclaim: *"It is the Lord!"*?

AT THE TIME OF THE APPARITION AT LA SALETTE, it took a grandmother to realize that the Beautiful Lady was in fact the Blessed Mother. There is much "waiting" in the hearts of our elderly. And it is in that patient waiting that an understanding and recognition of spiritual realities become clearer. The timeless "light on the mountain" reveals the divine presence in the events of our time.

Reflection Questions:

• Can I identify times when the Lord has transformed my seemingly fruitless efforts into blessings?

• Is this patient attitude of "waiting for something" a part of my faith life and Christian ministry?

Saturday, April 23 (#266)
Easter Saturday

Mark 16:9-15: *"(Jesus) showed himself (to the two disciples) under another form."*

Meditation:

The Easter Week gospels have dealt with the post-Resurrection appearances of Jesus. Jesus shows his wounds, invites the disciples to touch him, breaks bread, cooks fish and eats with them. He is not a ghost; he is really present. But he is also able to walk through closed doors, appear and disappear at will, and presents a changed appearance. Sightings and encounters with him were first reported to the apostles by some of the women and two of the disciples. Most of the apostles did not believe them. When Jesus did appear to them by the lake, he reprimanded them for their disbelief and the stubbornness they showed in not putting faith in these witnesses.

We are people called to believe in Jesus as a living presence, but he is very much the Jesus of a changed appearance. Mark, Matthew and Luke identify his presence in the bread and wine consecrated in his memory. For John, it is a presence hidden in humble, loving service to others and the indwelling of the Holy Spirit. The invitation to believe and experience Jesus' presence turns the popular saying upside down. "I'll believe it when I see it" becomes "I'll see it when I believe it."

MARY'S MESSAGE AT LA SALETTE invites us to recognize the presence of God in our everyday lives. The passage about the wheat field at Coin reveals God's ear close to earth, hearing Mr. Giraud's expression of care and concern for his son, Maximin, if the wheat crop continues to fail. The connectedness between the here and the hereafter can be seen, if we believe.

Reflection Questions:

- How often have I recognized Jesus in the unexpected events of my life or that of others?
- How much faith and confidence do I put in the faith experience of others?

Sunday, April 24 (#045)
Second Sunday of Easter

(Sunday of Divine Mercy)

(Acts 5:12-16; Revelation 1:9-11a; John 20:19-31)

Meditation: *Poor Thomas/Blessed Thomas*

It was unfortunate for Thomas that he was not with the other Apostles the first time the Risen Jesus came to them. It was also unfortunate that he refused to believe what the others told him. Worse still, he issued an ultimatum—unless he saw, unless he touched, he would not believe. And so. even though he ultimately believed, he

121

became what the bible often calls a byword, his name forever linked with his unbelief, the original "doubting Thomas."

In early 1847 a French priest named François Lagier came to his hometown of Corps to care for his ailing father. He had heard about the so-called apparition near the village of La Salette in the hills above Corps, which had allegedly occurred about five months earlier. The two children who were spreading this fantastic tale were also from Corps, and Fr. Lagier, who spoke their dialect perfectly, was determined to trick them into admitting that it was all a hoax. He took careful notes.

What he did not expect was that he would become a firm believer in the Apparition, and that the "Lagier notes" would be among the most important documents showing its authenticity. He was by no means the only one who came a doubting Thomas and went away a believer.

It is commonly said that people believe what they want to believe. And in the case of private revelations like Apparitions, the Church leaves us free to believe or not. That said, no one ever succeeded in the effort to prove that Maximin and Mélanie were either deceivers or deceived.

The Gospel of John indicates clearly why this story of Thomas is recorded: "Blessed are those who have not seen and have believed." But let us not forget that Thomas was blessed, too, blessed by a merciful Lord who was not put off by Thomas's ultimatum. He saw, he believed, and never doubted again.

La Salette is not essential to our salvation. We may believe or doubt as we see fit. Still, those of us who do believe feel truly blessed.

Monday, April 25 (#555)
St. Mark, Evangelist

Mark 16:15-20: *"Go out to the whole world; proclaim the gospel to all creation."*

Meditation:

This biblical account of the Ascension of Jesus and the beginning of the Apostolic Mission gives us a glimpse into a post-resurrection event which was only added later to Mark's gospel. Here we hear the words 'the Lord working with them' used to describe the fact that this Jesus who ascended is said, according to Fr. Edward Mally, S.J.: "to cooperate with the endeavors of his own disciples and agents in the spread of the kingdom which (the gospel) was proclaiming (*Jerome Biblical Commentary*, pg. 61)." Jesus, after his ascension, was still involved in proclaiming the gospel through the efforts of his disciples.

SIMILARLY OUR LADY OF LA SALETTE, at the conclusion of the apparition, just before ascending to God, left a call to evangelization as well. She invited all who hear her parting words to "Make this message known to all (her) people." As mother of the Savior, she could do nothing less than echo the words of her Son. She also stated that she constantly prays for all her children, supporting them in their daily journey to follow her Son and, no doubt, in their efforts to evangelize in His Name.

Reflection Questions:

• Do you readily respond to the opportunities to encourage people you know or meet whose faith is not active to become more involved and aware of their faith and their call to follow Jesus?
• Do you pray for those whose faith is not very active?

Tuesday, April 26 (#268)
Second Week of Easter

John 3:7b-15: *"'How is that possible?' asked Nicodemus."*

Meditation:

Trustee of the past, heir to a rich legacy, Nicodemus comes forward, willing and wanting at least to learn about the new. That he is sincere, we discover from the progression in his questions about the reality, the how, and the when of this birth from above. The questions he puts to Jesus, his surprise at the answers he gets, suggest that, although he is thoroughly schooled in the sacred writings and culture of his people, he has not yet discovered what it really means to be lost or saved, to be dead or alive. The questions we puzzle over can take us to the innermost boundaries of our yearning, to the outermost reaches of our desire.

In living her graced life and in fulfilling her exalted calling, Mary asked few questions. She pondered in her heart the words and deeds of the Lord. How to love to the point of laying down one's life, she learned, is the answer to the most basic of life's questions. Knowing only Christ and Christ crucified, she appears on the mountain of La Salette wearing his crucifix upon her heart. "Loveliest of all," as Melanie and Maximin later delighted to repeat, "was the Lady's cross, the source of the light that enveloped her entirely."

Reflection Questions:

- What questions do I raise in my intimate encounters with Jesus?
- What do these questions say about the boundaries of my own yearning?

Wednesday, April 27 (#269)
Second Week of Easter

John 3:16-21: *"... whoever does the truth comes into the light."*

Meditation:

A familiar, if not universally welcome, sight is that of the fellow brandishing the John 3:16 placard before the television cameras in sports arenas and stadiums. If a few people pause a moment and think to themselves: "This is really what it all comes down to"; if several more say to themselves: "This is truly good news"; if yet others flirt with the idea of acting on this reassuring word, our man will have proved to be a clever publicist and an effective evangelist.

Just as God had refused to surrender the first human couple to their fear and shame, but came looking for them, so too did the risen Jesus seek the very ones who had deserted him and fled into the dark night. Our Lady's appearance at La Salette in a globe of resplendent brightness, inviting the children to step into her very light, tells us that our salvation is nothing less than God's relentless effort to find us and lure us out of hiding – from God and from ourselves – in order to strip us of the evasions, pretenses and rationalizations with which we have clothed our shame.

Reflection Questions:

- Am I conscious of any locked, dark rooms in my spiritual house?
- "Fortunately, it is in the nature of cover-ups to be uncovered," William Safire once wrote. How wholeheartedly do I agree with him?

Thursday, April 28 (#270)
Second Week of Easter

John 3:31-36: *"The Father loves the Son and has entrusted everything to his hands."*

Meditation:

Today's gospel reading calls for probing and penetrating reflection as it puts before us such profound realities as discipleship, the community of life and the communion of love. Jesus discloses to us here the decisive underlying pattern of our whole life in him. The love of the Father for the Son, a love that the Son returns in obedience, establishes a community of life between the Father and the Son and this shared life manifests itself when the Son speaks the Father's words and does the Father's works. The love of Jesus for the disciples, a love the disciples return in obedience, establishes a community of love between Jesus and them, and this shared life manifests itself whenever the disciples proclaim his words and carry out his works. The key word here – some would call it the problem word – is obedience.

THE OPENING WORDS SPOKEN AT LA SALETTE by the Mother of the Lord, who herself accepted with loving submission her place and part in God's plan, keynote the entire discourse she delivered there: *"If my people refuse to submit, I will be forced to let go the arm of my Son."* This stark statement of fact contrasts sharply with her own wholehearted commitment as the first among the disciples. The large chain embracing her shoulders tells us we are all interlocking links in a chain of divine life. "All things are yours," she seems to say, "and you are Christ's, and Christ, of course, is God's" (see 1 Corinthians 3:21,23).

Reflection Questions:

- Do I balk inside at the mere mention of obedience?
- In what specific ways will submission to my Lord set me free? What concerns or situations can I let go of when God is in charge?

Friday, April 29 (#271)
Second Week of Easter

John 6:1-15: *"Where can we buy some bread for these people to eat?"*

Meditation:

There can be no doubt that the early church was rather partial to the multiplication story. We find it in all four gospels: twice in Mark, twice in Matthew, once each in Luke and John. It focuses on a most basic and shared human reality – the need to eat. In his gift of bread, Jesus gives himself entirely, feeding our bodies and satisfying the many hungers of the human heart. A bit of bread and a bit of fish wondrously became a lot of bread and a lot of fish. Every year through the good earth, the Creator makes a little barley and a little wheat into much barley and much wheat – enough to feed a world. In the feeding of the multitude, God incarnate does up close, on a smaller scale and at an accelerated pace, in hands just like ours, what he has always done.

WITH TOUCHING SADNESS Mary cautions at La Salette that the wheat will become scarce and that hunger will surely follow: *"If you have wheat you must not sow it. Anything you sow the insects will eat, and whatever does come up will fall into dust when you thresh it."* To bring her poignant message home to us more vividly, she echoes the distress and powerlessness of a father before his child's hunger: *"Child, eat some bread… I don't know who will eat any next year if the wheat continues this way."* How are we to deal with humanity's growing needs? One lad's provision for a day out is where one should begin. The need will never be too great for our resources, if we share them as the Lord bids us do.

Reflection Questions:

- What are some of the deepest hungers of the human spirit?
- How concerned am I about world hunger? What have I done to "feed the hungry"?

Saturday, April 30 (#272)
Second Week of Easter

John 6:16-21: *"The disciples saw Jesus walking on the sea."*

Meditation:

From our vantage point in time we realize that as Jesus came walking toward them on the sea, the disciples were witnessing a miracle of the new creation. That brief glimpse was, so to speak, a crocus miracle. Crocuses, to our delight, break through the earth's winter crust and snow. They signal that a crucial corner has been turned.

In the walking on the waves we see the relations between spirit and nature changed to the point where nature can be made to do whatever the spirit pleases. This new obedience of nature cannot, of course, be separated from the obedience of the human spirit to the Creator.

"IF MY PEOPLE ARE CONVERTED," the Mother of the risen Christ promised at La Salette, "rocks and stones will be changed into mounds of wheat and potatoes will be self-sown in the fields." She well knew that hope must always describe a future that few think possible or even imaginable. Queen of Prophets, she reminds us that language about "what will be later" must necessarily contradict language about "what is now."

Some Reflection Questions:

- Can you honestly say that hope is a favorite virtue of yours?
- How do optimism and hope differ?

Sunday, May 1 (#048)
Third Sunday of Easter

(Acts 5:27-32, 40b-41; Revelation 5:11-14; John 21:1-19)

Meditation: *Who is it?*

Today's gospel presents a curious scenario. An unusual event (a miraculous catch of fish) has taken place. Most of those present don't seem to know who the mysterious stranger on the shore is. And then, with the logic of faith, the unnamed "disciple whom Jesus loved"

The Miraculous Draught of Fishes: **Author unknown circa 1540**

makes the connection between the person and the event and says to Peter, "It is the Lord!"

On a superficial level, this is like the ending of the Lone Ranger episodes where someone always asked, "Who was that masked man, anyway?" But that was always where the story ended. In the life of faith, recognition is where the story begins and where it is deepened.

John's gospel states that the apostles had seen the risen Jesus already on two occasions before this. You would think that this time they would have known who he was. It is important for us to realize that faith, in a sense, "comes and goes." It is often only later that we see that the Lord has again been present and active in our lives.

Even persons of deep faith can be surprised by the Lord. For example, when friends are kind to us in a time of loss, we do not spontaneously hear the Lord's voice or feel his touch in their words and gestures. Upon reflection, however, we see those persons as agents of God's love. We believe we all have a guardian angel, but it can take a "close call" to wake us up to that reality.

For those who have studied the event of September 19, 1846, there is no doubt that the Beautiful Lady seen by Mélanie Calvat and Maximin Giraud was Mary, the Mother of Our Lord.

But the first to realize this was not the bishop or the commission called by him to investigate the matter. It was an elderly lady in the tiny hamlet where Mélanie's and Maximin's employers lived. On the very day of the Apparition, after hearing what the children said, she exclaimed with the logic of faith: "Oh, these children have seen the Blessed Virgin! She is the only one in heaven whose Son reigns."

What a wonderful surprise La Salette was—and is!

Monday, May 2 (#273)
Third Week of Easter

John 6:22-29: *"Do not work for food that goes bad, but work for food that endures for eternal life."*

Meditation:

Food drive sponsors are careful to indicate whether perishable as well as nonperishable items are acceptable. If nature abhors a vacuum, human nature deplores waste. The ongoing project of this world's creation claims from each of us major contributions of effort, energy and work. But our life's work must leave room for us to become more and more the person God is calling us to be. Six days a week we seek to master the world. On the seventh day we try to master ourselves. The world has our hands but our hearts belong to the Creator of the world.

FROM HER MOUNTAINTOP and with the deepest concern, Our Lady of La Salette observes her children trudging their way over life's pathways, toiling for their livelihood. *"I gave you six days to work,"* she says, speaking as prophets do in God's very name, *"I have kept the seventh for myself."* Six days we are to work at the creation of the world, on the seventh we are to enjoy the world of creation. The Lord's day calls us to marvel, to praise, to wonder. "Gather together," it invites us, "eat and drink. Sit comfortably and relax. Rest and be restored. The feast is prepared and ready. It awaits you: body, spirit and soul."

Reflection Questions:

• One year from now which of my currently pressing concerns will I even remember?
• How can what I do benefit me, if I neglect who I am? How am I

taking care of myself?

Tuesday, May 3 (#561)
Saints Philip and James, Apostles

John 14:6-14: *"(You) will perform even greater works (than I)"*

Meditation:

In looking back over Jesus' choice of his first disciples, we would perhaps have chosen differently. If a "report" had been given beforehand to Jesus concerning his proposed choices by a Jerusalem Management Agency, it might have read: "It is the opinion of our staff that most of your nominees are lacking in background, education and vocational aptitude for your proposed enterprise. They have no team concept. Simon Peter is emotionally unstable and given to fits of temper. Andrew has no qualities for leadership. The two brothers James and John place personal interest above company loyalty. Thomas shows a skeptical attitude that would tend to undermine morale. Matthew has been blacklisted by the Jerusalem Better Business Bureau. James the son of Alphaeus, and Thaddeus, definitely have radical leanings, and registered a high score on the manic-depressive scale. One of the candidates however, shows real potential. He is a man of ability and resourcefulness, meets people well, and has contacts in high places. He is highly motivated, ambitious, and responsible. We recommend Judas Iscariot as your controller and right-hand man." How "God's ways are not our ways"!=

WHEN MARY APPEARED TO THE TWO CHILDREN, Maximin and Melanie, an outsider Management Team would certainly have told Mary that these children were the weakest of applicants for the mission she intended to give them. Yet despite all their faults and lack of personal qualities, their attestation to what they saw and heard was remarkable and unwavering. They simply told people what they witnessed and they were faithful to that mission until their death.

As Jesus reminds us in the gospel for today, "whoever believes in me will perform the same works as I do myself, and will perform *even greater works.*" Who would expect that of Jesus' first disciples or of Maximin and Melanie? Yet as we learn repeatedly in the scriptures, "for God, all things are possible" (Matthew 19:26).

Some Reflection Questions:

- Have you heard about or seen people who are examples of Jesus' words, "whoever believes in me will perform the same works as I do myself, and will perform even greater works"?
- Have some of the saints of the past or present (or even people whom you have known personally) shown what great things God can do with the seemingly weakest of followers?

Wednesday, May 4 (#275)
Third Week of Easter

John 6:35-40: *"I will certainly not reject anyone who comes to me."*

Meditation:

Listing the striking qualities of the love Jesus gave to his own requires no effort at all. His love for those first disciples was affirming, compassionate, constant, forgiving, gentle, loyal, patient, trusting, and unfailing. That same love for his own in the world now goes on giving courage and strength; it continues to show endless patience and understanding. Despite our slowness to believe, our lack of spiritual understanding, our less than prompt response, this loving Savior assures us that we are not a burden, but rather a gift to him from the Father, whose will it is that "Jesus should lose none of those given to him."

SEEING HIS MOTHER IN TEARS on the mountain of La Salette, how could we not recall the stirring scene of Jesus weeping over Jerusalem? In each instance a hearty and timely response to the invitation of grace is at issue. *"How long a time I have suffered for you!"* Do we not too often keep the Lord waiting? Our impulsive pride, capricious love and inordinate self-absorption put all but ourselves and our preoccupations on hold. And the Lord does wait. *"I will certainly not reject anyone who comes to me."* He bides his time and will patiently tell us tomorrow what we refuse to hear today.

Reflection Questions:

- Is Christ really my closest friend, sharing in all I do and experience?

- Have I thanked the Lord lately for the privilege of being "one of his own"?

Thursday, May 5 (#276)
Third Week of Easter

John 6:44-51: "*... the bread that I shall give is my flesh, for the life of the world.*"

Meditation:

This promise was fulfilled at the Last Supper, itself the anticipation of Calvary. Now and then the words, "This is my body" take you by surprise, seeping quietly into that void you had forgotten was there. You live a timeless moment as you receive that flesh given for you and feel inwardly linked with the divine, certain that you are looked upon with mercy and love. The person behind you steps up to your place to receive this bread. And it's not just that one person, there are two long lines of them. And over and over again "The Body of Christ. This is my body given for you," until the words mean more than you. Before you and behind you others reach out, having brought there their flushes of fervor, their pulses of doubt, their dearest dreams and their unspoken hopes. We are many and we are one. We are happy and we hurt. We are much in need of grace and we hunger to hear "This is my flesh for you, for the life of the world."

TO PRESERVE FOR THE LORD A PEOPLE he may continue to call his own is the purpose of Mary's ministry at La Salette: "*In the summer only a few somewhat aged women go to Mass. The rest work on Sunday all summer long.*" Once and for all God's love has been given and received. The covenant has been sealed once and for all. The church is the community sealed by this definitive gift of God to us in Jesus Christ. When Christians gather in remembrance of their Lord and celebrate his death until he comes again, they actualize and express their God-given identity and fulfill their God-given mission. If their Scriptures and consecrated signs bear fruit in humanizing love, then the world for whose sake they witness and worship will find them eloquent indeed.

Reflection Questions:

- Is the Eucharist the center of my life?

•At Eucharist do I look to the Word and Body of Christ to transform me?

Friday, May 6 (#277)
Third Week of Easter

John 6:52-59: *"The Jews started arguing among themselves, 'How can this man give us his flesh to eat?'"*

Meditation:

The devil offered Jesus all the kingdoms of the world. He rejected the offer. The tempter suggested that he change stones into bread and satisfy his hunger. Jesus refused to do so. Earlier in this chapter of John's Gospel the enthusiastic crowd wanted to make Jesus king. He fled. Some Pharisees warned him at some point: "Herod wants to kill you. Leave here." That time he did not go away. *"How can this man give us his flesh to eat?"* many ask here in angry disgust. Rather than dilute his statement, as we might advise him to do, Jesus enlarged upon it: *"If you do not eat the flesh of the Son of man and drink his blood, you have no life in you."* How little inclined the Lord was to conform to our standards of accommodation, moderation and reasonableness! The quarreling goes on.

Saint Joseph the Carpenter
by Campin Robert circa (1375–1444)

"IN THE WINTER WHEN THEY DON'T KNOW WHAT TO DO," the Mother of Christ noted, her cheeks wet with tears, *"they go to Mass just to make fun of religion."* How easily we can forget that worship is the joyous acknowledgment that we did not make ourselves but are dependent on the One who must not be made into a guarantor of reality as we would like it to be. A truth tailored to our own measure would be a pitifully partial truth. A God entirely of our own making would be a God far too small.

Reflection Questions:

- How sincerely do I invite the Lord to open my understanding to his Word?
- Do I usually look to Scripture for confirmation of what I am already thinking or doing?

Saturday, May 7 (#278)
Third Week of Easter

John 6:60-69: *"Then Jesus said to the Twelve, 'What about you, do you want to go away too?'"*

Meditation:

Pollsters report the results of their surveys under three headings: agree, disagree, no opinion. In times of crisis, when trying to reach a decision, we usually consider three possibilities: for, against, undecided. God never put three choices before the people of Israel. The alternatives were always these: *"I put before you a blessing and a curse. I set before you life and prosperity, death and doom"* (Deuteronomy 11:16; 30:15). The choice is yours. *"Fully aware that his disciples were murmuring at what he said,"* Jesus at this critical point leaves them no middle ground either. He challenges them to decide: *"Do you want to go away too?"* This approach is rooted in our very freedom. Every moment of our life we move either toward or away from our true fulfillment; we must say "yes" or "no" to the reality that we are. There is no way to say "maybe" or "undecided" to existence.

Recognizing in Gabriel's words the will of the Most High, the Virgin of Nazareth entrusted herself fully and freely to the person and work of her Child. The choice she made in freedom on that blessed day, she would freely ratify each day of her faith pilgrimage to the foot of the cross. It is no surprise then that her entire message at La Salette hinges on the classical "ifs" of free choice: **"IF** *my people will not submit,* … **IF** *my people are converted…"*

Reflection Questions:

- How deeply do I share in my Lord's risen life, a life which death can no longer reach?
- Do I choose to yield or to cling? to hurt or to heal?

Sunday, May 8 (#051)
Fourth Sunday of Easter

(Acts 13:14, 43-52; Revelation 7:9, 14b-17; John 10:27-30)

Meditation: *Why Don't They Get It?*

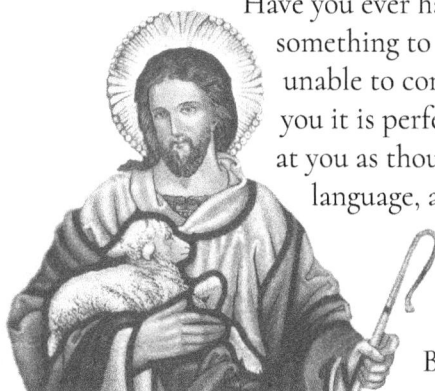

Have you ever had the experience of knowing something to be absolutely certain but being unable to convince others of that truth? To you it is perfectly clear, but everyone looks at you as though you were speaking a foreign language, and you wonder, "Why don't they get it?"

We see this especially in today's first reading. Paul and Barnabas went to the synagogue, eager to share with their Jewish brethren the fantastic news that the Scriptures had been fulfilled and the Messiah had come in the person of Jesus of Nazareth. There was initial interest (see omitted verse 42) and then opposition and finally persecution. And yet, Paul's preaching was all so clear, logical, verifiable. Why didn't they get it?

Mary at La Salette expressed the same feeling when she said: "You take no heed!" Her people were oblivious to her concern for them, and to the ways she had tried to make them aware of the consequences of neglecting their faith.

So she did, you might say, what she had to do to get our attention. She came, she wept, she spoke, sometimes even harshly—whatever it might take to make us see what she saw so clearly.

The Church has often been in the same situation. We Christians have such good news—the Good News—to share, but sometimes we feel like the prophet who asked, "Lord, who has believed our report?"

Anticipating that no one will listen can easily discourage us from speaking. Fortunately that has not been the case with the Church. Missionaries have lost their lives rather than remain silent.

Our Lady of La Salette also chose not to stand by and watch her people bring destruction on themselves.

The whole point of her coming, her tears, her words and even her choice of witnesses, is to try to make sure that we "get it," so that we will be able to give a resounding Yes to Jesus' question in Luke's gospel: "When the Son of Man comes, will he find faith on earth?"

Monday, May 9 (#279)
Fourth Week of Easter

John 10:1-10: *"... one by one he calls his own sheep and leads them out."*

Meditation:

In the Middle East it was the custom of shepherds to bring their flocks together into a secure fold for the night. Here, while their fellow shepherds slept, a chosen few could easily guard many flocks from predators. In the morning each shepherd would enter the fold and call his sheep. They would respond to the familiar voice and confidently follow it – to green pastures; to running water, even through the valley of darkness, on to the fullness of life. In Jesus' time sheep were raised primarily for their wool and milk, not as a source of meat. To the shepherds they were much like domestic animals, even pets. They had names. Shepherds didn't use sheep dogs to nip and snap at the heels of their sheep. Called by name, each of the sheep responded.

ONE OF THE INTRIGUING THINGS about the apparition at La Salette was that the Beautiful Lady never referred to Maximin and Melanie by name. When speaking of prayer she asked: *"Do you say your prayers well, my children?"* When inquiring about spoiled wheat: *"Have you never seen wheat gone bad, my children?"* And when they gave a negative answer, she addressed Maximin: *"But you, my child, surely you have seen some..."* I have often wondered why she didn't use their names, yet she went on to recount a very intimate moment in the life of the lad and his father. Again at the end of the discourse Mary says: *"Well, my children, you will make this known to all my people."*

Reflection Questions:

- Is my God near and supportive, or distant and silent?
- When I think of and pray to God, do I call him by an intimate or more impersonal name?

Tuesday, May 10 (#280)
Fourth Week of Easter

John 10:22-30: *"The sheep that belong to me listen to my voice; I know them and they follow me."*

Meditation:

Words, sounds, voices are such a great part of our lives. From our first conscious moments, they are our major means of expression, of communication. They take on meaning for ourselves and for others, not because they are heard but because they are listened to. Listening requires attention to words and to persons. It involves discernment and leads to choices. How often Jesus felt flustered because people heard without listening, without understanding, without opening their hearts. His teaching was not about dogma but about relationship with a loving God to whom we could cry, *"Abba"* (Galatians 4:6). Rather than listen to his voice, so often we continue to close our ears and cry out, *"Crucify him"* (Mark 15:13).

AT LA SALETTE the children said that once they heard the voice of the Beautiful Lady their fears melted away. They found themselves drawn into her company, standing so close that no one could have passed between them and her. They listened attentively. Enthralled with the person before them, they didn't always understand her words but did grasp the urgency of her message. Their dialogue with her was etched into their memories, into their lives. But it took time to flower, to ripen, to mature into practice. Remember that on the day after the apparition, Maximin didn't even attend Mass after he and Melanie had recounted their story to Father Perrin, the parish priest.

Reflection Questions:

- Where have I matured lately after listening to the gospel message?
- Is my heart afire when a word in Scripture truly challenges me?

Wednesday, May 11 (#281)
Fourth Week of Easter

John 12:44-50: *"... anyone who rejects me and refuses my words has his judge already."*

Meditation:

Coming right before the narration of the Passion, these words reflect how Jesus might have looked at the result of his years of teaching, preaching, working miracles, trying to shed new light on the reality of our world. Was he a success or a failure? Except for a few trusted friends, people didn't perceive him as a shining light. People didn't hear his loving message of forgiveness and conversion. People didn't believe in him but wanted to use him for what they could get out of him. Even Judas thought he could get his thirty pieces of silver and that Jesus would somehow get away. Jesus, however, knew that the end was near –r rather that a new beginning, so far removed from any miracle he had worked till then, was at hand. Yet he had not come to judge or condemn but to save.

At La Salette Mary tries to help us realize the effects of our actions. *"If the harvest is ruined, it is only on account of yourselves... If they are converted, rocks and stones will turn into mounds of wheat and potatoes will be self-sown in the fields."* Our pernicious choices help create a social structure that brings ruin upon ourselves and upon others, extending over and beyond what we imagine. We might feel distant from those who died in the great famine of 1846, but can we think of ourselves as uninvolved in what is happening in the Balkans today? If we believe we can escape the effects of what is going on, we are deaf to Mary's words: *"It is only on account of yourselves."*

Reflection Questions:

- Do I recognize that what I am, what I believe, and what I do all have repercussions on my life and on that of others?
- What actions should this call me to perform? Where should I get involved?

Thursday, May 12 (#282)
Fourth Week of Easter

John 13:16-20: *"Whoever welcomes the one I send, welcomes me."*

Meditation:

We have all heard stories of a Jesus in disguise coming to visit a household as a beggar, a child, a homeless person. Those who welcomed him were astonished to discover him under the disguise. The stories are touching and the reality is even more so. Jesus comes indirectly to us through those who touch our lives. We shouldn't be surprised when we don't recognize him. Mary Magdalene didn't recognize him until he spoke her name. The apostles recognized him only when they saw his wounds. Though they walked with him for hours, looked into his eyes and heard his voice, the disciples going to Emmaus needed to share the bread of fellowship before they recognized him. Welcoming people means receiving them with pleasure, satisfaction and hospitality. It means sharing what we have. It means caring about those we receive as well as for them.

WHEN MAXIMIN AND MELANIE first saw the globe of dazzling light they were afraid. They would have fled had not the globe parted to reveal the Beautiful Lady. Like her Son, Mary came disguised. Maximin naively thought she had come up there to cry her heart out because her children had struck her. When she stood and invited them to come near, their fears melted. As Mary came toward them, they approached her. Each welcomed the other. She brought Christ into their lives, first through the shining crucifix on her breast and then by the conversion which would gradually take place in their lives. Hospitality is considered one of the chief Christian trademarks. It calls us to welcome disguised saints and sinners into our lives, where Jesus can have the pleasure and satisfaction of encountering them.

Reflection Questions:

- What fears hold me back from welcoming Christ into my life today?
- What fears hold me back from sharing the bread of fellowship with my brothers and sisters?

Friday, May 13 (#283)
Fourth Week of Easter

John 14:1-6: *"I am going now to prepare a place for you."*

Meditation:

Jesus must have experienced a whole range of feelings as he bid farewell to his disciples. Things would never be the same. Their solidarity would be broken. Judas would betray him. Peter would deny him. All would flee. As Son of God, he had come down from heaven. As son of Mary, he would be going home for the first time. What expectation, what joy! But to get home, he would have to suffer and die. What horror, what revulsion! Though he would rise from the dead, he would no longer be with his disciples as before. Is it any wonder that he tried to forestall their fears. *"I am going now to prepare a place for you."*

MANY OF US HAVE EXPERIENCED that place which is special to her Missionaries and to all her devotees - Our Lady's shrine in the French Alps. This conjures up a blend of physical, psychological and spiritual attitudes, feelings, judgments and memories. For some La Salette is a picturesque place of prayer, for others it means a barren wilderness of sorts. Some felt at home, while others have been there and known desolation. For those who minister there week after week, routine can set in; whereas for first-time visitors, feelings of anxiety before the unfamiliar could arise. However we view this mountain sanctuary of La Salette, it is a steppingstone in the spiritual lives of countless pilgrims. After her visit to earth on this mountain, Mary returned to heaven. We can echo Maximin's words: "We should have asked her to take us with her." Hopefully, one day she will.

Reflection Questions:

• What range of feelings surges in me when I think of going home to Jesus?
• Is mine a peaceful confidence that I shall indeed follow where Jesus has gone?

Saturday, May 14 (#564)
St. Matthias, Apostle

John 15:9-17: *"You did not choose me, no, I chose you."*

Meditation:

The sad truth is that, despite these many years after Vatican II, many people still feel that only clergy or religious have "vocations." This, of course, comes from the mindset that all vocations comes from and are based on "the main vocation-sacrament – Holy Orders." However the Fathers of Vatican II first reminded us of the "universal call to holiness," saying: "... all the faithful of Christ of whatever rank or status, are called to the fullness of the Christian life and to the perfection of charity ... The classes and duties of life are many, but holiness is one- that sanctity which is cultivated by all who are moved by the Spirit of God... Every person must walk unhesitatingly according to his own personal gifts and duties in the path of living faith, which arouses hope and works through charity. (*Lumen Gentium*, #40-41)" It is therefore our common Baptism that is the basis from this common call to holiness. As today's scripture reminds us, we all need to remember the words of Jesus: *"You did not choose me, no, I chose you."*

AT LA SALETTE Mary spoke similar words to those of the Fathers at Vatican II. She did not choose the local Bishop or a priest but rather two unschooled children to *"make (her) message known."* This was certainly a surprising choice of messengers but just shows us how important each baptized member of the Church is! On this feast of St. Matthias, we hear that "we are all chosen" as the scripture reminds us, no matter what our state. We are all chosen to follow Christ and use the gifts he gave us to build the Kingdom of God where we live and work and serve. What a simple, basic and profound view of the importance of every person!

Reflection Questions:

- In your own state in life, where is your Baptismal call the easiest to live?
- Where is your Baptismal the most challenging to live?

Sunday, May 15 (#54)
Fifth Sunday of Easter

(Acts 14:21-27; Revelation 21:1-5a; `-33a, John 13: 31-33a, 34-35)

Meditation: *Wiping Away Every Tear*

A recurring theme during the Easter Season is that Jesus, by his death, destroyed death, and by his rising restored our life. It occurs to me that we could apply a similar pattern to La Salette. By her tears, the Blessed Virgin reflects the image found in the book of Revelation, where we read that God "will wipe away every tear from their eyes."

When we see someone crying, our first instinct is often to wonder if we can or should do something to "make it stop," to ease the pain or grief that lies behind the tears.

Those who are perhaps puzzled or even offended by Mary's words need to remember the tears that accompanied them. One and the same sorrow is at the source of both

In today's gospel Jesus offers the ultimate key to consoling the disconsolate. "As I have loved you, so you also should love one another." If only we could all live this "new commandment" perfectly! Not only would we do everything in our power to respond to all the suffering around us and in the world at large, but we would likewise devote our best efforts to eliminating the root causes of so much unhappiness.

Like Paul and Barnabas in the second reading, we would recognize that "It is necessary for us to undergo many hardships to enter the Kingdom of God." But these hardships are different from the suffering that leads to despair. They are endured out of love, and the disciples of Jesus can support each other in the midst of them. More than once Jesus made it clear that his disciples could not expect an easy life.

Mary at La Salette looked on the hardships and the sins of her people and wept over them. Moved by the same love that moved her Son, she responded in her maternal way. She cannot make all our troubles disappear, but she offers a way through them, a way of trust, of hope, of faith.

No one person can do everything, but each can do something, however simple, to create "a new heaven and a new earth." We all can do our part to "wipe away every tear from their eyes."

Monday, May 16 (#285)
Fifth Week of Easter

John 14:21-26: *"Anyone who loves me will keep my word, and my Father will love him, and we shall come to him and make a j home in him."*

Meditation:

Dwelling with us is what Jesus is all about. *"The Word became flesh, he lived among us"* (John 1:14a). The Incarnation is more than cohabitation. Jesus came to share every aspect, every fiber of our humanity. He tells us that through the loving observance of his commandments we can share in his divine life. What an exchange! We know how difficult it is to dwell together, to form community. All community is based on perceived needs. Not to perceive needs keeps the community from developing. There are many things that thwart human community: individualism, unwillingness to forgive, aggression, indifference. One thing that fosters community is love, which is why Jesus says he will be found dwelling in those who love.

OF MAHATMA GANDHI, Pandit Nehru said: "Where he sits is a temple and where he walks is holy ground." We can say that of each other, because Christ promised to make us his home, his temple, his dwelling place. Dwelling together in community has always been an integral part of the La Salette Missionary life. This was demonstrated in the document shared with us by our young religious brothers who gathered at La Salette in December 1998-January 1999 to prepare for their perpetual profession of vows.

Based on solid foundations (Scripture, the convictions of our founders, our present Constitutions, Pope John Paul II's apostolic letter, *Vita Consecrata*), community calls us to more than cohabitation, namely: "private and community prayer, especially the Eucharist, interdependence, discernment, dialogue, openness and sharing, respect for others, hospitality, attentiveness to the needs of others, co-responsibility, forgiveness, an active obedience, and sharing in those moments together that manifest human relationship and joy in community."

Reflection Questions:

•How do I perceive these elements as helps to the deepening of my loving commitment to my religious community? to my family? my parish family? my God?
•What moments do I treasure within my family, my friends, my sacraments and other faith-centered events?

Tuesday, May 17 (#286)
Fifth Week of Easter

John 14:27-31a: *"Peace I bequeath to you; my own peace I give you."*

Meditation:

The gift of peace is echoed in every Mass yet it so often eludes us. When it is experienced, it exudes wholeness, a reconciliation, a sense of union with all of creation and beyond. Could that be why Jesus left it to us as his farewell gift? He was about to reconcile the world to himself, to join again the created and the Uncreated in a special relationship. The result would be that peace which he alone could give, a joy for which all of creation had been groaning (Romans 8:22). St. Augustine was possibly describing it when he said that a Christian should be alleluia from head to toe. We are an Easter people and, with that farewell gift in our hearts, *alleluia* is our song.

WHEN WE FIRST HEAR OF LA SALETTE, there seems to be no echo of peace and joy. Rather we find a continual flow of tears, we hear of suffering, of God's arm grown heavy, people swearing, human beings behaving like dogs, famine, worm-eaten crops, children dying. Hardly a reason to sing *alleluia*! But as we look deeper into the meaning of the tears and the message we can distinguish the call to conversion, to reconciliation, to joy and peace. We come to understand the meaning of the word *if* that Mary spoke. Christ left us his farewell peace as a gift that must be received, not as something foisted upon us. He said that we have his life in us, that salvation, peace and joy are ours, "*If you love me.*" Anyone who has experienced the grace of reconciliation knows the profound peace that comes when the *if* changes to *yes*.

Reflection Questions:

- What would it take for me to experience a deeper sense of Jesus' farewell gift of peace?
- How expectant and trusting is my relationship with him?

Wednesday, May 18 (#287)
Fifth Week of Easter

John 15:1-8: "*Anyone who does not remain in me is thrown away like a branch -- and withers; these branches are collected and thrown on the fire and are burnt.*"

Meditation:

Chapter 15 of John's Gospel is a richly constructed monologue in which Jesus goes far beyond a farewell to his disciples. The imagery of the first part is clear – no life in branches separated from the vine, abundant fruit when branches are trimmed. One way or another some part of the vine is going to be trimmed, cut, pruned with branches separated from the stem. These branches will be placed on the vineyard wall to dry, then used for firewood. I remember being in a vineyard once where such precious branches were removed from their drying place and used to make a very hot fire over which to roast our dinner of shellfish. I have also seen them used to kindle a fire in an outdoor oven for baking bread. Even these seemingly no-good twigs are precious and useful.

THE LA SALETTE EVENT often reminds me of these separated branches. When Mary spoke to the children, she was directing her words primarily to people who were like severed twigs – abandoning church, not observing the Lord's Day, swearing, neglecting private and communal prayer. They were surely cut off. Yet there still must have been some life in them. They were precious enough for her to come and plead for their return. A desperate situation surely, but not a hopeless one. It seems that an incision had to be made into the vine so that it might receive as a graft those not completely withered branches.

La Salette, then, is a miracle of hope. Mary was willing to let us see her sorrow, her tears, her maternal solicitude for us when we stray. Perhaps it is because of her tears falling on us that we retain some spark of life and are kept from withering and dying.

Reflection Questions:

• What have I done lately to thank the Lord for not allowing me to wither and die spiritually?
• To what extent have I made the moral and spiritual values of Christian life inwardly my own?

Thursday, May 19 (#288)
Fifth Week of Easter

John 15:9-11: *"I have kept my Father's commandments and remain in his love."*

Meditation:

Fidelity is not a quality particularly required, sought after or cherished in today's society. This is true in business dealings, in interpersonal relationships, in marriage and in religious life. To Jesus, however, it was essential. He was faithful to his Father, to his mission, to his word, to his disciples and friends. His joy came from being loyal and faithful, in loving and being loved. His obedience was shown in his loyalty to his Father. This same loyalty brought Jesus to his death, yes, even death on the cross. It also paved the way for his resurrection – new life for him and for us. Sharing that joy, sharing that life, sharing that fidelity, will bring us completeness.

WE CAN MARVEL AT THE FAITHFULNESS OF MELANIE AND MAXIMIN to what they witnessed at La Salette. These two uneducated children, Maximin – a scatterbrain, and Melanie – an introvert, had to undergo personal scrutiny, long hours of questioning, buffeting by family and friends, and even scorn from churchmen. Yet they remained faithful. We find Maximin's last testament a marvelous declaration of fidelity. "I firmly believe, even were it to cost the shedding of my blood, in the renowned apparition of the Blessed Virgin on the holy mountain of La Salette, September 19, 1846, the apparition to which I have testified in words, in writings, and in suffering. After my death let no one assert that he has heard me make any retraction concerning the great event of La Salette, for in lying to the world he would be lying to himself. With these sentiments I give my heart to Our Lady of La Salette."

Some Reflection Questions:

- How have you shown the quality of fidelity in your life?
- To what and to whom do you feel most firmly attached?

Friday, May 20 (#289)
Fifth Week of Easter

John 15:12-17: *"I commissioned you to go out and to bear fruit, fruit that will last."*

Meditation:

Perhaps the word that best describes the thirst of society today is freedom – freedom of assembly, freedom of choice, freedom of speech, freedom from restraints of all kinds, especially authority. Freedom of choice is foremost. It generally implies the liberty to choose whom and what I want, when and how I want it. It is often said that you can't choose family but you do choose friends. In choosing us to be his friends, though, Jesus puts a damper on freedom. *"You are my friends if you do what I command you."* Does the price of friendship mean taking orders? Now that's counter-cultural! The friendship he offers, however, is not based on one-to-one equality. *"It was not you who chose me; I commissioned you to go out and to bear fruit, fruit that will last.*"

Maximin and Melanie were chosen and given a mission. As wonderful as it may have been to be chosen to witness the apparition, they paid a price. Their lives were disrupted. From obscure, uneventful lifestyles they were thrown first into the path of belligerent critics only to become objects of excessive adulation later on. Free-spirited Maximin was hemmed in too quickly by the walls of the seminary classroom when all he desired was the freedom of the mountain slopes. Taciturn, melancholy Melanie was soon caressed by fame and a following; her chances of living a simple, hidden religious life thus permanently damaged.

Reflection Questions:

• How often do I stop and think about the call and mission the Lord has chosen to give me?
• What counter-cultural efforts can I expect to make, if I choose to be Jesus' friend in this day and age?

Saturday, May 21 (#290)
Fifth Week of Easter

John 15:18-21: "*... in my name.*"

Meditation:

Every name is sacred, yours and mine included. Shakespeare asked, "What's in a name?" Some names still instill fear, some inspire awe, some foster tenderness, others ooze with hate, some leave us indifferent and unmoved. For most people, God's name, be it Yahweh, Allah, Jesus or Zeus, carries a special reverence. In God's name, people have sacrificed their lives for others just as Jesus did for all humankind. In the name of God, wars were waged; infidels, heretics, and innocent people were tortured and put to death; the gospel was preached far and wide; grace was dispensed; innumerable prayers and sacrifices were offered; saints were canonized. Jesus knew his name would be reverenced, cursed, defiled and invoked as a panacea for every ill, and often by the same person – me.

At La Salette, Mary underlines the irreverence people have for God's name. It comes in the form of swearing and is also seen in indifference to what God asks through the commandments, the laws of the church, the requirements of sacramental life. That attitude was not limited to 1846. I have only to consider the extent to which I accept and live the reality of the post-Vatican Council II world and church to realize the necessity of voicing my present-day *mea culpa*. But do I? *"And as for you, you pay no heed."* I know my indifference touches Jesus deeply, because Mary accented it as *"one of the two things that make the arm of her Son so heavy."*

Reflection Questions:

• When I pray in the name of the Father, and of the Son, and of the Holy Spirit, how do I come into the presence of my God?
• Does my prayer continue to have an influence in my life even long after the words have passed my lips?

Sunday, May 22 (#057)
Sixth Sunday of Easter

(Acts 15:1-2, 22-29; Revelation 21:10-14, 22-23; John 14:23-29)

Meditation: *Keeping It Simple*

Compared to Lourdes and Fatima, the message of Our Lady of La Salette is long and appears complex. Still, it is basically quite simple.

In the early Church, as described in today's first reading, the situation had seemingly become very complex, due to the influx of gentile converts to the Christian way of life and faith. Some were convinced that these new believers had to convert first to Judaism. At the

"Council of Jerusalem," as it is sometimes called, an elegant solution was found, a minimum set of conditions, decided not by the power of reason alone, or by majority vote. We read, "It is the decision of the Holy Spirit and of us, not to place on you any burden beyond these necessities."

At La Salette, Mary selected a few such necessities: personal prayer, Sunday worship, respect for the Lord's name, the discipline of Lent.

In the early Church, anyone taking the basic requirements seriously would, of course, not stop there. So too at La Salette. It is a fact of human nature that, when we settle for the minimum, even that in due time gets neglected. The minimum is a foundation of sorts, but a foundation on which nothing is built will sooner or later crack and disintegrate.

In the gospel Jesus says, "Whoever loves me will keep my word." This is another way of saying the same as above. Love of Christ is the foundation of the Christian way of life, but "keeping his word" is a sign of the genuineness of that love and the strength of our personal commitment to him. And yet it all ultimately very simple—follow him in love, learn to know his will, and seek to carry it out.

Experience teaches that this is easier said than done. This is why St. Paul in many of his Letters takes the Christians to task for their failure to understand the implications of their faith. 1 Cor. 13, ("Love is patient, love is kind," etc.) for example, is so beautiful in itself that we can forget that Paul wrote this because the Christians of Corinth were not making the connection between faith and life.

La Salette also helps us make that same kind of connection. Pretty simple, really.

Monday, May 23 (#291)
Sixth Week of Easter

John 15:26 to 16:4: *"... you have been with me from the beginning."*

Meditation:

"Cradle Catholics" often speak of having been "born Catholic." Tertullian, one of the early North African Church Fathers, offered this corrective: "Christians are made, not born." If it is true that we Christians are not born but made, then how is it that we are made? In the same way that Peter, Mary of Bethany, James, Mary Magdalene, John, Martha, Andrew, and the rest were made like Christ: by dwelling with him, by following him. We *become* his disciples, we are not *born* so. It is something we must choose daily. Those of us who have been with him from a time shortly after our birth do sometimes take our Catholic Christian faith for granted. But the Risen Lord comes to stir us out of complacency and into a more mature responsibility for our faith as adults.

BECAUSE OF CHRISTIANITY'S EARLY HISTORY IN FRANCE, the country is sometimes referred to as "the eldest daughter of the Church." Unfortunately today, there is much indifference and some hostility to the Christian faith in this ancient cradle of Catholicism. Mary, Mother of the Church and Mother of La Salette, went to the people of this eldest daughter in order to rouse them from their sleep, to bring their faith to life again in the name of Jesus her Son. Her words apply still to the Church throughout the world. For the renewal Mary sought to bring to "all her people" to be effective, we must continually grow in our faith, coming to a more mature level of trust in her Son.

Reflection Questions:

• In what ways do I take my faith for granted and fail to truly appreciate this gift of God to me?
• Have I thought to pray for the children and adults who were baptized in my parish this Easter Season?

Tuesday, May 24 (#292)
Sixth Week of Easter

John 16:5-11: *"And when (the Paraclete) comes, he will show the world how wrong it was, about sin..."*

Meditation:

We don't usually think of advocates as those who tell us what we have done wrong. We think of them as those who stand up for us and fight for us to the last. The Holy Spirit, our promised Paraclete before the Father, shows us the ways in which we have betrayed ourselves, the ways in which we have contradicted our true selves, the ways in which we have done wrong. We, who are flesh and spirit, must learn from the divine Spirit how to be human. It is the Spirit who leads us to recognize how wrong we are about our sins. The Spirit calls us away from both these extremes: our sins either don't matter at all or they are too great to be forgiven. As this Paraclete helps us to see how wrong we have been, he also shows us how right with God, self and others we can be.

MARY'S MESSAGE OFTEN SEEMS STERN TO ME. That sternness is tempered, however, when I recall that it was spoken by a mother. The image I have of a stern mother always includes that of a child who has just done something to hurt a friend, or him- or herself. "Why did you hit Bobby? ... Get away from that stove now! You'll get burned! ... Go to bed. You need your rest." *"If my people will not repent, I will be forced to let go the arm of my Son,"* said Mary at La Salette. Reading between the lines, I am tempted to insert, "I'm warning you. It's for your own good."

Reflection Questions:

• What warnings have I heard that I do not heed?
• Do I take the counsel of others seriously, or am I a spiritual individualist, insisting on learning *only* from my own experience of God, rather than trusting in the experience of others, like the saints, and my brothers and sisters in the Lord?

Wednesday, May 25 (#293)
Sixth Week of Easter

John 16:12-15: *"... the Spirit of truth ... will lead you to the complete truth ... and he will reveal to you the things to come."*

Meditation:

"Apocalyptic things" (revealing the end-of-the-world) are all around us. There is much talk and fascination about the end of the world. In light of this, we might be tempted to think about the end of the world when Jesus tells his disciples that the Spirit will reveal what is to come. When we look for the magic formula that gives us the day on which the world will end and Jesus will come in glory, we risk forgetting to welcome him into our life this very day, this very moment. Perhaps those *"things that are to come"* refer not to the end of the world, but to this world's evolution toward God's Kingdom and the revelation of God's will for us, our calling and direction in life. Some go through life aimlessly wandering, never sure of their steps, yet hoping to stumble into the right direction. With the Spirit as our guide, however, our steps are sure, and we walk the straight and narrow path of Christ (Matthew 7:14), not out of fear, but out of faith.

MARY'S MESSAGE AT LA SALETTE is apocalyptic in the truest sense of the word. Apocalypse means revelation. Mary's message manifested the divine disappointment over the way things had gone (rotting crops) and also the divine hope that things would be much improved (self-sown seeds). Just as the earth sometimes seems to withhold a harvest from us, so too our hearts sometimes withhold justice from each other, obedience and worship from God. At other times, though, our response seems generous, pure, spontaneous, full of good will. At La Salette, Mary calls us to such Spirit-led spontaneity.

Reflection Questions:

• When is it easy for me to bear good fruit in following the Lord? When does it seems more difficult?

• How can I persevere in the hard times, and show my gratitude in the good times?

Thursday, May 26 (#058C)
Feast of Ascension of the Lord

Luke 24:46-53: *"in (Jesus') name, repentance for the forgiveness of sins would be preached to all nations..."*

Meditation:

When Benjamin Franklin wished to interest the people of Philadelphia in street lighting, he didn't try to persuade them by talking about it. Instead he hung a beautiful lantern on a long bracket near his own front door. Then he kept the glass brightly polished and he religiously lit the wick every evening at the approach of dusk. People went about on the dark street saw Franklin's light a long way off and came under the influence of its friendly glow with grateful hearts. It wasn't long before Franklin's many neighbors began placing the lights in brackets before their own homes and soon the entire city awoke to the value of street lighting and took up the matter with interest and enthusiasm. Such is the power of example.

Jesus was born of the virgin, Mary. He lived with his family until it was time to begin his public ministry. His words were certainly powerful but perhaps his example of healing, forgiving, and bringing people back to life – literally and figuratively – were equally powerful.

At the end of his life and after the resurrection, his wish for his disciples was that "in his name, repentance for the forgiveness of sins would be preached to all nations…" It was an immense task but he also promised the lasting gifts of the Holy Spirit so that his followers, like himself, would do wonderful things for others and that this tradition of love, forgiveness and reconciliation would endure for ages to come.

Our Lady of La Salette came with her message, which indeed was the very same message of her Son: the importance of prayer, Eucharist, and other Lenten habits of faith. She also was a powerful example to us of a person of faith who truly loved even the two young children, Maximin and Melanie, her unsuspecting witnesses. They in turn were also called, like the disciples of old, in her Son's name, to speak about repentance for the forgiveness of sins to all her people. They faithfully did so throughout their lives and people were brought back to God. Such is the power of example.

Reflection Questions:

- Do you have an incident you could share about "the power of example"?
- What was a moment of joy in your life or that of another which touched your heart?

Alternate for May 26 (#294)
Sixth Week of Easter

John 16:16-20: *"What does he mean?"*

Meditation:

Earlier in the Gospel of John it was the Pharisees who failed to understand. Maybe they didn't even want to understand. Now, however, it is Jesus' own disciples, those who welcomed the Kingdom, who fail to understand. Indeed, a few hours after these words are spoken, John tells us these same disciples, who shared in that last supper conversation, will scatter to the four winds for fear of their lives. They will abandon their master. But they will see him again, and the very sight of him will be enough to overcome their fear of the same fate, and the shame of their abandonment. For now, however, they fail to understand this "short time" remaining until he goes away. The Resurrection surprised even those like Peter and John, who had been closest to him. However close to or distant from the Lord we may be, there are parts of our walk as disciples that we do not understand.

PEOPLE WERE NOT QUITE AS PUZZLED BY MARY'S WORDS AT LA SALETTE. To speak of spoiled wheat and rotting potatoes in a time of famine brings immediate recognition of the truth of the message. The famine before their eyes was quite obvious to everyone in 1846. The famine in their hearts was not quite so obvious to them. Often we do not see our own sins. Something needs to happen for the scales to fall from our eyes. The supernatural character of the apparition at La Salette is not attested to so much by crutches left behind as at Lourdes, but by hearts renewed and turned back to God. "Our Lady of La Salette, Reconciler of sinners, pray without ceasing for us who have recourse to you."

Reflection Questions:

• What in Jesus' message do you find difficult to understand and live?
• Would it be appropriate for you to pray that God would remove the scales that blind you to your own sinful ways, and then make a good examination of your conscience?

Friday, May 27 (#295)
Sixth Week of Easter

John 16:20-23a: *"A woman in childbirth suffers, because her time has come; but when she has given birth to the child she forgets the suffering in her joy that a human being has been born into the world."*

Meditation:

In light of his own reference to himself as a mother hen who longs to gather her chicks under her wings, sheltering them from danger, the 14th-century English mystic Julian of Norwich speaks of Christ as our Mother. Christ and the sufferings of his Passion which gave us life readily come to mind. But John seems to have the labor pains of the disciples in mind here. This seems odd since, in their confusion over what was happening to the master and what might happen to them as well, they fled from the pain and suffering. It remains true that the child, too, must endure the trauma of birth. And as the mother rejoices "*that a human being has been born into the world,*" the child finds contentment and reassurance in its mother's arms. What joy the first disciples found, what joy will we also find in the arms of our Risen Lord!

MARY'S PRESENT SHARING IN CHRIST'S GLORY does not insulate her from the trials her children bear on earth. Her tears at La Salette remind us of her constant care and concern for us, and reflect our God's even greater care and concern for our well-being. Her tears and her recollection of the incident on the road to Corps when, out of loving concern for him, Maximin's father gave him a piece of bread, remind us of Mary's unblinking watchfulness over our lives – itself a reflection of the divine concern her Son has for us every moment of our lives.

Reflection Question:

• Look at a crucifix, or call to mind the image of our crucified Lord. Fix in your heart the immeasurable love with which Christ died for you. Carry this appreciation with you throughout the day and reach out to others from that same immeasurable love with which Christ has loved you.

Saturday, May 28 (#296)
Sixth Week of Easter

John 16:23b-28: "*Anything you ask from the Father he will grant you in my name.*"

Meditation:

To ask or pray in the name of Jesus requires more than simply tacking on "We ask this through Christ our Lord," or "In Jesus' name we pray" at the end of our prayers. The *Constitution on the Sacred Liturgy* of Vatican Council II teaches us that in the liturgy all who are gathered are called to fulfill the priestly office of Jesus Christ (#7). This high calling to pray in Jesus' name and fulfill his priestly office by our own prayer means more than just "name-dropping" at the close of our intercessions.

To be a Christian at prayer is to make Jesus' longing for the Father and the coming of the Reign of God one's very own longing ("Thy kingdom come; thy will be done."). It requires that at Mass, in union with the Risen Lord, we put on the altar alongside the gifts of bread and wine, our own lives, our self-offering to be sustained throughout the rest of the day and week. Yes, praying in Jesus' name is no magic formula; rather it is a way of life, a responsibility all Christians are invited, even commanded, to carry out.

MARY'S COMMAND to pray the *Our Father* and *Hail Mary* (and to pray more when we can) at evening and morning is more than just a good way to start the day off right and end it appropriately. We begin and end by praying as Jesus prayed so that all through the day we will live as he lived (with the aid of his Mother's intercession, of course).

Reflection Questions:

• What are the best times for me to pray? What does it mean to me to pray *well*?
• What keeps me from praying regularly, attentively? Does my prayer help me to walk more faithfully in the ways of the Lord?

Sunday, May 29 (#061)
Seventh Sunday of Easter

(Acts 7:55-60; Revelation 22: 12-14, 16-17, 20; John 17: 20-26)

Meditation: *That The World May Believe*

You may recall the controversy that arose when *Jesus Christ Superstar* first appeared on stage in New York. Among other things, some took exception to the very notion of "superstar" as applied to Jesus, as if he were seeking the adulation of his fans.

And yet, in today's gospel Jesus doesn't hesitate to pray to the Father "that the world may believe that you sent me." Two more times in the same passage Jesus expresses the same desire in different words. He also refers twice to his "glory."

It isn't for himself, that's clear. Always his goal has been to bring people to the Father. Still, if you want to bring someone else to a particular place or person, first you have to draw them to yourself, to attract their attention in some way. If you don't, how can you lead or guide them?

Our Lady of La Salette certainly attracted the attention of others— Mélanie and Maximin first of all, then the local people, Church authorities, civil authorities, the press. Even traveling salesmen wasted no time getting highly inaccurate images printed! Some people were, predictably, fiercely opposed; others were prepared to believe even before any kind of investigation took place.

In all this, the two children also attracted a good deal of attention. This was a new experience for Mélanie in particular; but according to Fr. Jean Stern, M.S., who probably knows La Salette history better than any person living, it was not a healthy experience for her. Be that as it may, attention to the children meant attention to the Beautiful Lady, and her purpose was precisely to turn the attention of her people to her Son.

In the first reading, Stephen is an ideal witness to and for Christ. But his adversaries directed their attention and hostility to him instead.

Whoever attracts the attention of others in order to bring them to Christ runs the risk of getting too much attention. It's a delicate balance. Unlike Stephen, we are not ideal witnesses. If our personal integrity is called into question, we become a distraction, turning attention away from Jesus.

How then will the world come to believe?

Alternate for May 29 (#058C)
Feast of Ascension of the Lord

Luke 24:46-53: *"in (Jesus') name, repentance for the forgiveness of sins would be preached to all nations..."*

Meditation:

When Benjamin Franklin wished to interest the people of Philadelphia in street lighting, he didn't try to persuade them by talking about it. Instead he hung a beautiful lantern on a long bracket near his own front door. Then he kept the glass brightly polished and he religiously lit the wick every evening at the approach of dusk. People went about on the dark street saw Franklin's light a long way off and came under the influence of its friendly glow with grateful hearts. It wasn't long before Franklin's many neighbors began placing the lights in brackets before their own homes and soon the entire city awoke to the value of street lighting and took up the matter with interest and enthusiasm. Such is the power of example.

Jesus was born of the virgin, Mary. He lived with his family until it was time to begin his public ministry. His words were certainly powerful but perhaps his example of healing, forgiving, and bringing people back to life – literally and figuratively – were equally powerful.

At the end of his life and after the resurrection, his wish for his disciples was that "in his name, repentance for the forgiveness of sins would be preached to all nations..." It was an immense task but he also promised the lasting gifts of the Holy Spirit so that his followers, like himself, would do wonderful things for others and that this tradition of love, forgiveness and reconciliation would endure for ages to come.

Our Lady of La Salette came with her message, which indeed was the very same message of her Son: the importance of prayer, Eucharist, and other Lenten habits of faith. She also was a powerful example to us of a person of faith who truly loved even the two young children, Maximin and Melanie, her unsuspecting witnesses. They in turn were also called, like the disciples of old, in her Son's name, to speak about repentance for the forgiveness of sins to all her people. They faithfully did so throughout their lives and people were brought back to God. Such is the power of example.

Reflection Questions:

- Do you have an incident you could share about "the power of example"?
- What was a moment of joy in your life or that of another which touched your heart?

Monday, May 30 (#297)
Seventh Week of Easter

John 16:29-33: *"Do you believe at last?"*

Meditation:

Just when we think we have figured it out, something always seems to come along and cloud our crystal clear understanding. We find ourselves back at square one, trying to make sense of life, faith, loss. We who follow Christ in the third millennium can take comfort in the fact that the gospels all tell us of the confusion the disciples often experienced on hearing him speak or seeing him act. No one has ever been so misunderstood in all of history as Jesus of Nazareth. No one is more misunderstood today as he. I sometimes pretend to know more about Jesus and his ways than I actually do know. It is an occupational hazard. As one who is called upon to preach several times a week, I am "supposed" to know who Christ is, what Christ means. The best response I can offer is the one I some-times gave my father when I was younger: shoulders that shrug, a head and heart that hope to understand more and know better the next time.

"YOU DO NOT UNDERSTAND, MY CHILDREN?" Mary asked and then went from flawless French to a more approachable *patois*, Maximin's and Melanie's local dialect. Communication can be difficult when we aren't speaking the same language, or when we are not interpreting words the same way. Perhaps Our Lady was exercising the gift of tongues she received at Pentecost, showing us how language, so divisive at times, can also unite. Whatever her reason for speaking both French and *patois*, she wanted the children to understand her Good News about Jesus as much as he wanted the disciples to understand his about the Kingdom. Neither did the first disciples nor these humble La Salette visionaries comprehend the fullness of what was entrusted to them. As we hear the Gospel today, we are sure to miss the total picture too – but not entirely.

Reflection Questions:

- What puzzles me about Jesus and the call to be his disciple?
- Am I waiting until I understand more before I make a deeper commitment to Christ, or am I willing to trust and to learn as I follow him day by day?

Tuesday, May 31 (#572)
The Visitation of the Blessed Virgin Mary

Luke 1:39-56: *"Why should I be honored with a visit from the mother of my Lord?"*

Meditation:

Many people can look at the experience of their childhood upbringing and honestly say that they basically remember being loved and nourished in their home. What a gift to be able to say that! Others can remember being loved but they also experienced considerable disruption due to sibling or parents who had difficulty getting along. Whatever the situation, we have all been blessed by some people who loved us. This is the purpose of family: to nurture and love those around us. When Mary went to visit Elizabeth it was an arduous journey but Mary went simply because she loved Elizabeth and wanted to help he in her advanced age.

AT LA SALETTE THE REASON FOR MARY'S VISIT to the two children was love, plain and simple. Out of loving concern for "her children" she came to remind all her children of the basics of our faith and express God's concern for our struggles and hardships. She did that so well that, as the children readily mentioned, when they first saw her they were afraid. But upon hearing her invitation to "Come near, my children", their fear dissolved and they gladly approached their heavenly visitor.

Some Reflection Questions:

- Who has surprised me with a visit to say hello?
- Whom might I visit or contact to find out how they are doing?
- Do I appreciate that Mary came to La Salette to bring her concerns for us, her children?
- What do her tears mean to me?

Wednesday, June 1 (#299)
Seventh Week of Easter

John 17:11b-19: *"They do not belong to this world any more than I belong to the world."*

Meditation:

I once caught myself saying in a homily, "... the Mother Teresas of this world." I don't recall exactly what I was speaking about, but I'm sure it had something to do with her exceptional holiness as an example for us to imitate. Months later this phrase came to mind out of the blue, and I realized the irony of it: Mother Teresa was not "of this world." She was simply in it. It was not the benevolence of the human heart that made her what she was for the creatures of this planet, but the greatness of God's grace that made her so. Like the Christ she so humbly followed, Mother Teresa had set her heart on the will of her heavenly Father. She sought no compensation in this world, but to know she was a beloved daughter of God. She excelled in giving Christian witness, because she belonged first to Christ and only in him did she belong to the world to which he gave her. We may not be so great as she in giving our witness to Christ, but we too are called "out of this world" to live in Christ. But he will likely give us back to the world as witnesses to his love.

"BEHOLD THE HANDMAID OF THE LORD, be it done to me according to your word" (Luke 1:38). Mary's *fiat* continued in the apparition and message of La Salette. As she encountered the *no* of the children of God, her *yes* resounded all the louder. Once again, she came to earth to draw us closer to her Son, she brought us the opportunity to be filled with the blessing of the "fruit of her womb." No doubt Mary's yes to Christ echoed in Mother Teresa's life. May it echo in yours and mine as well!

Reflection Questions:

- Do I see myself as one who is "of this world" or "of Christ"?
- Can I see myself as given back to the world by Christ to make it holy by my life of faith, like Mary, Mother Teresa and all the saints?

Thursday, June 2 (#300)
Seventh Week of Easter

John 17:20-26: *"The world will recognize that it was you who sent me and that you loved them as you loved me."*

Meditation:

Jesus clearly turns his attention to the future. He anticipates the success in time of the disciples' mission, praying *"for those who will believe in him through their words"* and foresees their presence in eternity *"with him where he is."* He expresses his Last Will: *"that they may all be one"* and goes on to sketch the essential traits of this ardently desired unity. Its model is the unity of Father and Son. It is a unity in diversity (despite their perfect oneness Father and Son remain distinct persons). This unity must be visible enough to challenge the world, just as he did, to recognize God present and at work in him. The fact that Jesus prays to the Father for this gift tells us that it lies within the sole power of God. It is fitting that this majestic and stirring prayer which concludes the Farewell Dis-course itself closes on the note of the unity of all believers, "the fruit that will remain."

At La Salette the Mother of Jesus expresses concern about various harvests: grapes, potatoes, walnuts, wheat. She is solicitous of earth's produce in field, garden, orchard and vineyard. In biblical language, such productivity mirrors the fruitfulness of the human spirit as it obediently carries out the Creator's purpose. Mindful of the solemn words her Son spoke at the Last Supper, *"You did not choose me, no, I chose you; and I commissioned you to go out and to bear fruit, fruit that will last"* (John 15:16), she cares deeply about the spiritual fruit human hands and hearts are to bring forth for the life and unity of the world.

Reflection Questions:

- Science and technology in future years will be much improved. Their human manipulators, however, won't be. Am I nonetheless hopeful?
- In light of Jesus' prayer can I imagine a day when human life will have been completely transformed?

Friday, June 3 (#301)
Seventh Week of Easter

John 21:15-19: *"Simon, son of John, do you love me?"*

Meditation:

Sometimes one spouse has trouble saying, "I love you." When the question is raised (usually because "I love you" never gets spoken!) the response is defensive: "Yes, you know I love you. … Of course I love you. … I'm hurt. How could you even ask; you know I love you." People cite the many things they do, the hardships they endure, the many things they have sacrificed, the lengths to which they have gone. There is something about hearing it, however, that seems to make a difference. Showing it is walking the talk, but saying it is still important because mere routine, or who knows what, could be what keeps the relationship going. Sometimes the question is asked even when the answer is known for certain. Jesus, who knows what's on our mind before we say it, still seems to want to hear us say it. Maybe he realizes that it will make a difference to us if we say it, and realize we mean it.

NOT HEARING THAT YOU'RE LOVED can lead to tears and much sadness. Maybe that's what Mary's tears were about? "How could someone who had experienced the glory of God in heaven be sad and cry?" Some wondered when the children reported that the Beautiful Lady wept for the entire duration of the apparition. Maybe she realized how much her children – the children of the Church, the children of God – were missing out on when they failed to practice what they professed, and failed to appreciate what they practiced.

Reflection Questions:

- Whom do you love that you have taken for granted lately?
- How can you show those you love that you love them today –

perhaps to strengthen your own awareness as well as theirs?

Saturday, June 4 (#302)
Seventh Week of Easter

John 21:20-25: *"So the word among the brothers that (the disciple that Jesus loved) would not die."*

Meditation:

At a recent gathering of La Salette Missionaries that focused on our Marian roots, we were reminded that apparitions, including that of Our Lady at La Salette, always address "the last things." This doesn't mean that La Salette Missionaries go around predicting a precise day, time or even the extreme nearness of these "last things." Nor does it mean that they are to be dismissed altogether. Talk about the end times in Catholic circles has always intended to bring about repentance here and now and not to cause hysteria or panic. In the midst of our hectic and sometimes reactionary age in which many will vaguely hint or specifically point to Christ's Second Coming, we are to look closely at the signs of the times and recognize that, whether or not his return is imminent, now is always the moment for repentance. Whether they live until Jesus comes or whether generation upon generation will yet follow, Christians know it's never too early to return to their Lord with all their hearts.

THE AUTHORITIES WERE WORRIED that if Mary's dire predictions about the crops were to get out, no one would risk planting anything. Reasons for opposing the La Salette message were not just anti-religious, but very practical. Mary's words expressed concern about the kind of daily bread that would feed spirits, not just stomachs, however important the latter may be. The authorities may have been aware that "people don't live on bread alone," but they also knew that at least a little bread was needed. In the story of Maximin's father offering him a piece of bread on the way home to Corps, we have evidence that Mary is aware of both the bread of this world as well as the bread of the Kingdom to come. She knows the role each of these must play, and is willing to intercede in order that body and soul be kept together and ordered rightly to our ultimate good.

Reflection Questions:

- What am I feeding my body? What am I feeding myself mentally, emotionally, morally, and spiritually? Is it all healthy? Is it what I should be feeding myself? Is it what I need?
- How am I taking care of the physical, emotional and spiritual parts of my life?

Sunday, June 5 (#063c)
Pentecost Sunday

(Acts 2:1-11; 1 Corinthians 12:3b-7,12-13 or Romans 8:8-17; John 20:19-23 or John 14:15-16,23b-26)

Meditation: *In Our Own Language*

After the coming down of the Holy Spirit upon them, the Apostles addressed an international audience, presumably speaking Aramaic while people of different nationalities heard them speaking in their own languages. This, of course, was the work of the Spirit, a unique sign.

Wouldn't it be wonderful if this sign had continued to our own day? But this particular manifestation of the gift of tongues seems to have been reserved to that one event. Today missionaries spend a long time learning languages that only a few will truly master.

At international gatherings of La Salette Missionaries, I have often provided simultaneous translation, and I am keenly aware of how inadequate that can be at times. Finding the right turn of phrase on the fly is always a challenge.

Mary spoke two languages at La Salette. She started in French, and then at a certain point saw that the children were confused. She said, "Oh, you don't understand? I'll say it another way." The rest of her discourse was in the local dialect, except for the final command to "Make it known."

One would think that Mary might have anticipated this problem.

But, as the sign of many tongues at Pentecost showed that the Gospel message was universal, the Beautiful Lady, through the sign of just two languages, showed that her message was likewise not restricted to one place.

As Fr. Marcel Schlewer, M.S. points out, Our Lady spoke her people's language in more than one sense. In the local dialect, in fact, she spoke of the things that mattered in their life—blighted crops, famine and children dying—showing that these things mattered to her, too. This was her "mother tongue," that is, her speaking as a mother. She also spoke to their hearts through the language of tears.

It is not surprising that different aspects of the Apparition of Our Lady of La Salette speak to each of us in different ways. We are each unique, after all, and we might say that the Holy Spirit, as at Pentecost, was at work to ensure that each of us would hear Mary "in our own language."

Monday, June 6 (#572)
Mary, Mother of the Church

Luke 1:39-56: *"Why should I be honored with a visit from the mother of my Lord?"*

Meditation:

Many people can look at the experience of their childhood upbringing and honestly say that they basically remember being loved and nourished in their home. What a gift to be able to say that! Others can remember being loved but they also experienced considerable disruption due to sibling or parents who had difficulty getting along. Whatever the situation, we have all been blessed by some people who loved us. This is the purpose of family: to nurture and love those around us. When Mary went to visit Elizabeth it was an arduous journey but Mary went simply because she loved Elizabeth and wanted to help he in her advanced age.

AT LA SALETTE THE REASON FOR MARY'S VISIT to the two children was love, plain and simple. Out of loving concern for "her children" she came to remind all her children of the basics of our faith and express

God's concern for our struggles and hardships. She did that so well that, as the children readily mentioned, when they first saw her they were afraid. But upon hearing her invitation to "Come near, my children", their fear dissolved and they gladly approached their heavenly visitor.

Some Reflection Questions:

- Who has surprised me with a visit to say hello?
- Whom might I visit or contact to find out how they are doing?
- Do I appreciate that Mary came to La Salette to bring her concerns for us, her children?
- What do her tears mean to me?

Tuesday, June 7 (#360)
Tenth Week in Ordinary Time

Matthew 5:13-16: *"You are the salt of the earth. You are the light of the world."*

Meditation:

Jesus tells us what he really thinks of us! The judge of all is plainly calling us *"the salt of the earth"* and *"the light of the world."* Normally, we would attribute such titles to Jesus alone, praising him as the light that shines in our darkness, or the living Bread that sustains us. But today Jesus holds us up to view and asks that we look at ourselves as our God in heaven sees us – as gifts to be dearly valued and unsparingly shared with others. *"Your light must shine before others, that they may see your good deeds and glorify your heavenly Father."* Imagine what the world would be like if we lived out the truth of who we are, the image and likeness of God, and the astonishing fact that God saw fit to call the entire creation *"very good"* (Genesis 1:31).

ON THE HOLY MOUNTAIN, Mary appears to Melanie and Maximin in a globe of bright light. She invites them to *"come closer"* and share in that brightness. Echoing her Son, she reminds us that we are the light of the world, and that if we could see ourselves in the light of God's love for us, we would obtain heaven. As she vanishes into the light, she urges us to relay that message to all her people, a reaffirmation of what her Son told us long ago: *"You are the light of the world"!*

- Do you find it easy or difficult to accept the praise Jesus speaks of you in today's gospel?
- Are you sharing God's gifts of "salt" and "light" with others?

Wednesday, June 8 (#361)
Tenth Week in Ordinary Time

Matthew 5:17-19: *"I have not come to abolish, but to fulfill."*

Meditation:

Jesus affirms that what he is about is doing the will of his Father. It is not God's will that the earth should be destroyed, but redeemed. It is not the will of God that we should be cast out of heaven, but that we should draw ever closer to our eternal happiness. *"For God so loved the world that he gave his only Son, so that everyone who believes in him might not perish but might have eternal life. For God did not send his Son into the world to condemn the world, but that the world might be saved through him"* (John 3:16-17). Jesus fulfills the law by restating the greatest commandment, the commandment that sums up the entire law and the prophets: *"You shall love the Lord, your God, with all your heart, with all your soul, and with all your mind... You shall love your neighbor as yourself"* (Matthew 22:37,39).

The Beautiful Lady of La Salette asks us to *"come near and not be afraid."* The question is why are we so terrified of this good news? What is it that holds us back from the saving arm of Mary's Son? Maybe it is that, in order to renew the world of God's creation, we have to give up the world that we ourselves have created and are quite complacent in – even if it is filled with false hopes and empty promises. Maybe we are dulled by our routines, schedules and duties, so much so that the good news of a better world interferes with those things that have taken on tremendous importance to us. Like Jesus, Mary confronts us with a choice: to stay in our own little world and suffer the consequences, or be converted, believe in the good news of salvation and fulfillment, and get a healthy taste of "the real world!"

Reflection Questions:

- Are you living in "the real world"?
- Can you come nearer to God and manage not to be afraid?

Thursday, June 9 (#362)
Tenth Week in Ordinary Time

Matthew 5:20-26: *"Go first and be reconciled with your brother or sister, and then come and offer your gift."*

Meditation:

Mother Teresa of Calcutta said, "Give until it hurts," and Jesus seems to say "Forgive until it doesn't hurt anymore!" Forgiveness is a basic attitude, a calling, a vocation. Reconciliation is not simply a one-time occurrence. We cannot simply forgive and forget, as the saying goes. Forgiveness is like a surgeon's scalpel that reopens old wounds in order to clear out the infections of anger, bitterness and resentment. At the same time, forgiveness is a soothing ointment, liberally applied, to cleanse and heal old or new wounds. Jesus bids us to *"forgive seventy times seven times"* (Matthew 18:22). Forgive even though everyone does not request it. Forgive even though everyone does not deserve it. This gift Jesus offers as a key to heaven; our eternal happiness can begin now if we so choose.

THE OLDEST AND BEST KNOWN TITLE OF OUR LADY OF LA SALETTE is Reconciler of sinners. In her apparition she assures us that she *"prays without ceasing for us,"* thereby affirming that forgiveness – rather than an occasional act of kindness or isolated instance of bigheartedness – is a lifelong vocation for the Christian. *"And this is from God who reconciled us to himself in Christ, and has entrusted to us the ministry of reconciliation... God was in Christ not counting our trespasses against us"* (2 Corinthians 5:18-19).

Reflection Questions:

- Have you ever been the one to take the first step in bringing about reconciliation with a friend, a neighbor, a relative?
- Is there someone in your life you cannot bring yourself to forgive?

170

Friday, June 10 (#363)
Tenth Week in Ordinary Time

Matthew 5:27-32: *"it will do you less harm to lose one part of yourself than to have your whole body thrown into hell."*

Meditation:

Jesus uses strong language here. The reality of the kingdom of God compels us to search our innermost impulses and to uproot all those longings that could hinder its growth within us. Jesus is applying the greatest commandment, the command that we should love God, our neighbor and ourselves in such a way that whatever violates it or could lead to its violation be seen as evil. The human heart, he knew well, is capable of the basest and the noblest of instincts and deeds (see John 2:24-25). He condemned the inner thought even unaccompanied by outward effect. Internal anger is already murderous, he warned, because once ignited they can intensify and become murderous. Lustful looks are already unfaithful because they can inflame passion and lead to infidelity. The Savior's heart addresses the original goodness of our hearts. *"For where your treasure is, there your heart will be also"* (Matthew 6:21).

MARY AT LA SALETTE makes use of strong language. She speaks in plain terms: *"How long I have suffered for you... If the harvest is ruined, it is only on account of yourselves... A great famine is coming... Children under seven will be seized with trembling and die in the arms of those holding them."* The bitter consequences of our refusal to change our ways and convert are painfully evident in our own days, the most violent in recorded human history. May the seeds of destruction and violence never find fertile soil in our hearts.

Reflection Questions:

- What dark impulses and reflexes within you need to be cast off?
- In what ways is the kingdom of God coming into your heart and life?

Saturday, June 11 (#364)
Tenth Week in Ordinary Time

Matthew 5:33-37: *"Say 'Yes' when you mean 'Yes' and 'No' when you mean 'No'."*

Meditation:

We learn to lie at a very early age. Although we were taught that "honesty is the best policy," telling the truth is what usually gets us into the most trouble. Lying offers an easy way of escaping the truth's harsh consequences and eventually becomes a way of life. So much so that we become addicted to reflexes that blind us to the truth. As we well know, this induces a state of constant denial. What Jesus tells us is what men and women of wisdom have been telling us for ages: "Be true to yourself." However painful truth may be, facing it, owning up to it, is redemptive. The truthful person doesn't have to take oaths or swear to God or anyone else. Truthful people are taken at their word. Truth leads to trust and the trustworthy earn valued respect.

IT IS THE WOMAN OF THE WORD, honored as the Seat of Wisdom, who speaks to us from that stone bench high in the French Alps. Her reassuring *"Don't be afraid"* to the children, was similar to the words the angel Gabriel had first spoken to her. *"Be it done to me as you say,"* she had replied. A 'Yes' she ratified all her life until its culmination at the foot of the cross. She pondered the word constantly and it bore fruit in the generous soil of her Immaculate Heart. Founded to make her apparition known to all her people, the La Salette Missionaries are to preach Mary's message "more so by the example of their own lives than by their words."

Reflection Questions:

- What keeps you from facing the truth?
- What keeps you from telling the truth?

Sunday, June 12 (#166)
The Most Holy Trinity

(Proverbs 8:22-31; Romans 5:1-5; John 16:12-15)

Meditation: *Access*

The Holy Trinity by **Nicolò Semitecolo circa 1370**

In the worlds of politics and art it is often said that who you know is more important than what you know. The point is that through influential people, we have access to other, more important, persons and to opportunities we otherwise might not have had. In the past one relied on patronage; in the modern world one relies on agents.

St. Paul writes that through faith in Christ we have gained "access" to grace, that is,. to God's favor. Christ is the mediator between us and God.

Catholics rely also on the patronage of other mediators—"patron" saints—especially for specific needs associated with specific saints. This is reflected in the Third Eucharistic Prayer where the celebrant refers to "the Saints, on whose constant intercession in your presence we rely for unfailing help."

Among the Saints Mary stands as the greatest. We rely on her intercession in a special way. At La Salette she twice makes reference to this: "How long a time I have suffered for you," and "However much you pray, you will never recompense the pains I have taken for you." Note that she indicates that she has taken the initiative in interceding for us.

Today we celebrate the Solemnity of the Trinity. Fr. Joe Ross, M.S., likes to call the Trinity "a communitarian God," meaning that Father, Son and Spirit are in a deeply intimate relationship with each other, so intimate that they are One God. This kind of relationship is intimated in today's first reading, from the Book of Proverbs.

The "communion of saints" mentioned in the Apostle's Creed reflects a similar bond uniting believers. We are one with all believers of every time and place, sharing "spiritual goods," as we read in the Catechism of the Catholic Church.

When we neglect spiritual goods, we do harm to ourselves and damage the bond of unity. Repairing that damage is the work of Reconciliation, which Jesus accomplished. Our Lady of La Salette is invoked as "Reconciler of Sinners." She gives us "access" to THE Reconciler, who reunites us to the Father and to one another.

Monday, June 13 (#365)
Eleventh Week in Ordinary Time

Matthew 5:38-42: *"Offer no resistance to (the wicked)."*

Meditation:

The word "injury" calls up all sorts of mental images, from a cut on a finger to injuries sustained in a serious accident. Wouldn't a person want to offer resistance to injury? Isn't that the normal thing to do? It is the pain and suffering that come with injuries that people shun? This goes to the core of our being. Jesus, however, did not shun injury or suffering. He embraced it for the good of all. The inconvenience and bother of reaching out and attending to a fellow human being in need draws us out of ourselves.

EARNING A MODEST LIVING AS A FARMER in the mountain villages around La Salette was an ungrateful task. It was very hard work with precious little to show for it. Mary urges these poor people to return to the practice of their faith, promising them newfound closeness to God, consolation and hope.

Reflection Questions:

• How can the injury you embrace and the suffering associated with it bring you closer to God?

• In what way can embracing injury and its attendant suffering bring you closer to others?

Tuesday, June 14 (#366)
Eleventh Week in Ordinary Time

Matthew 5:43-48: *"... be perfect, just as your heavenly Father is perfect."*

Meditation:

We may think that Jesus' call to "perfection" in today's gospel is almost impossible. How can we be as perfect as our heavenly Father is perfect? The command that Jesus gives us is a continuous action. It is something that we continually work toward. Our human nature is always in need of conversion and healing. Jesus offers us healing that can bring us closer and closer to our goal of perfection. We are not saints, but we are striving for the wholeness that only Jesus can give.

AT LA SALETTE Mary sought to encourage Maximin and Melanie and us to seek wholeness. This can be found in her Son alone. When we pray for our enemies, we are working toward that wholeness. Running in circles is certainly not the answer; changing the subject is not the answer; neither is blaming others. Unless we change our hearts, wholeness will elude us. And how do we change our hearts? By praying. Prayer can change our hearts.

Reflection Questions:

• What area of reconciliation do you need to work on in your life?

• Is there any healing that you need to attempt – perhaps with an estranged family member, coworker and friend?

Wednesday, June 15 (#367)
Eleventh Week in Ordinary Time

Matthew 6:1-6,16-18: *"Be careful not to parade your uprightness in public to attract attention."*

Meditation:

We are probably very familiar with our gospel today. As part of its annual instruction on the proper observance of Lent, the church proclaims this gospel on Ash Wednesday. Jesus tells us it is not the exterior action that matters most but the innermost intention of the person performing the act of fasting, penitence, or prayer. Our heavenly Father not only sees our actions but the intentions and motives behind them.

Mary at La Salette grieved that the people of the day at times only practiced their faith to mock religion. Their hearts and souls were not really in it. They spoke Jesus' name not in prayer but in swearing when they were angry or upset. By keeping inward their sentiments of adoration, love and trust from their worship, it was only a grudging and reluctant service they offered to their Maker.

Reflection Questions:

• When doing a good deed for someone, or giving to a charity, or participating at Mass, are you doing so with a truly sincere intention or are you performing the action with an ulterior motive in mind – perhaps your own gain?
• Who are you called to serve in your life? Your family, friends, neighbors, or co-workers?

Thursday, June 16 (#368)
Eleventh Week of the Year

Gospel: Matthew 6:7-15: *"This is how you are to pray."*

Meditation:

Jesus' emphasis is on the quality of prayer rather than its quantity: "Your Father knows what you need before you ask him." Matthew, in his gospel, gives us the ideal example of Christian prayer which is ascribed to the Lord himself and which has always been a prominent feature of the Christian liturgy. There is probably no other prayer in the church that has been so often and extensively commented on, meditated on and written about than the Lord's Prayer. It contains every type of prayer: praise, adoration, petition, supplication, confession and forgiveness of sins. It asks for the strength and the grace to forgive others. Finally it is a prayer for deliverance from the oppression of evil.

Mary at La Salette told Melanie and Maximin to pray this specific prayer. Mary encourages us to pray using the words her Son himself taught his followers. This is a timely reminder that, first and foremost, we are his disciples, called to share in his spirit and carry his mission forward. Isn't it most appropriate that we would also use his words to pray to "*Our Father.*"

Reflection Questions:

• When you pray the Lord's Prayer how aware are you of the various forms of prayer it contains?
• Are you moved to forgive others as you ask your Father in heaven to forgive you?

Friday, June 17 (#369)
Eleventh Week in Ordinary Time

Matthew 6:19-23: "*Where your treasure is, there your heart is also.*"

For Your Reflection:

How often we have heard this phrase! But do we really understand its meaning? It means keeping material things in their proper place and spiritual things at the center of our concerns and lives. The material treasures we store up bring us a fleeting satisfaction and enjoyment. It is usually in the striving for the material treasure that we find the most pleasure. Once we have obtained it, we become bored and seek yet another treasure. Spiritual treasures, at the center of our lives, serve to anchor us. They bring us serenity and stability amid the distractions and annoyances of everyday living.

THE DISTRACTIONS AND EVILS OF CONTEMPORARY SOCIETY can lead us to dejection and disheartenment. They can cause us to lose our inner peace and serenity. Mary encouraged Melanie and Maximin to become well-anchored in prayer, so that the enticements of the world would not blind them to the true and lasting values. Prayer and spiritual realities at the heart of our lives can give us welcome light and hope.

Reflection Questions:

- Have you heard Our Lady of La Salette's call to cultivate your inner life?
- Do you really see spiritual goods – such as love, prayer, gratitude and the like – as the most valuable "possessions" in your own life?

Saturday, June 18 (#370)
Eleventh Week in Ordinary Time

Matthew 6:24-34: *"Do not worry about tomorrow…"*

For Your Reflection:

The AA (Alcoholics Anonymous) program is centered on two days of the week that one should not worry about: yesterday and tomorrow. One is already over – its hopes and joys, its gains and failures are gone. Tomorrow is not yet here – neither are the joys or disappointments it can bring. In today's gospel Jesus gives us a similar message: "Which of you by worrying can add a moment to your life span?" Jesus tells us to remain anchored in the present moment. That is the only place where we can seek God's will for us and endeavor to carry it out. Attempting to do God's will today should be all that we are concerned about.

"COME NEAR, MY CHILDREN, DON'T BE AFRAID." These were the opening words of Mary at La Salette to Maximin and Melanie. Once these children's fear and worry had vanished, they were able to be present to that graced moment in their lives. Mary as an ambassador for her Son urges us to be fully present to the graced moments in our own lives.

Reflection Questions:

- Have you allowed your anxiety and fear to be dispelled so that you can hear God's word more clearly?
- What might God's will be for you today?

Sunday, June 19 (#169)
The Most Holy Body and Blood of Christ

(Genesis 14:18-20; 1 Corinthians 11:23-26; Luke 9:11b-17)

Meditation: *Food in a Deserted Place*

La Salette is a remote place in the lower French Alps. Compared to the millions of pilgrims visiting Lourdes each year, maybe 250,000 come to this mountain Shrine, and then mostly in the spring and summer. Otherwise, it is a deserted place.

That was certainly the case on September 19, 1846. A handful of persons, including the two children, Maximin Giraud and Mélanie Calvat were minding cattle or mowing hay. From where they had their simple meal of bread and cheese, Maximin and Mélanie could see no one else.

Then, suddenly, a Beautiful Lady was there!

She spoke, among other things, of other deserted places—the churches. During the French Revolution roughly 50 years earlier, France had become fiercely anti-Catholic. Times had changed since then, but the effects were still felt, and the nominally Catholic population retained some hostility toward religion.

Every now and then people leave the Catholic Church because of a conflict, or scandals, or rejection of Church teaching, etc. In so doing, they deprive themselves of the Eucharist. Today's readings make it very clear how essential the Eucharist is to our Catholic Christian way of life. In both theory and practice, it is hard to imagine one without the other. Without the Eucharist, we find ourselves truly in a deserted place.

Psalm 107 describes a similar scenario:

> Some wandered in the desert, in the wilderness,
> finding no way to a city they could dwell in.
> Hungry they were and thirsty;
> their soul was fainting within them.
>
> Then they cried to the Lord in their need
> and he rescued them from their distress
> and he led them along the right way,
> to reach a city they could dwell in.

Let them thank the Lord for his love,
for the wonders he does for men:
for he satisfies the thirsty soul;
he fills the hungry with good things.

In the Mass, Christ blesses us and fills us with very good things indeed. Why should anyone prefer the deserted place?

Monday, June 20 (#371)
Twelfth Week in Ordinary Time

Matthew 7:1-5: "*... the standard you use will be the standard used for you.*"

Meditation:

How often we like to think our way of seeing or doing things is the right way. Others are wrong. We like to make ourselves superior to others because this boosts our own ego. In the Christian way of life things are quite different. The way for us to avoid judgment, Jesus tells us, is not to judge others. We find this mandate very difficult because seeing the faults in our brothers and sisters is easier than seeing them in ourselves. An unknown author once wrote: "There is so much good in the worst of us, and so much bad in the best of us, that it ill behooves any of us, to find fault with the rest of us."

At La Salette Mary, whose entire life was devoted to the person and mission of Christ, speaks to the two children about conversion, conversion to the person and mission of her Son. Those who follow him share their Lord's mind and do his deeds. They look upon others with understanding and show them compassion.

Reflection Questions:

- What plank in my eye is now obstructing my view of certain other people?
- What plank in my eye is blocking my vision of my mission in Christ?

Tuesday, June 21 (#372)
Twelfth Week in Ordinary Time

Matthew 7:6,12-14: *"So always treat others as you would like them to treat you."*

Meditation:

Often, we may try to live by two separate standards: the way we like to be treated and the way we treat others. There is usually a great difference between the two. Jesus tells his disciples to be calculating and discerning. What is worthwhile should not be wasted on lesser opportunities or with the reckless. The road that leads to perdition is indeed enticing and inviting. It can easily attract. But it inevitably leads to a dry and arid wasteland. The road to what is life-giving is often difficult and presents many obstacles. However when we invest our best talents and gifts in this effort, the outcome is life-giving for ourselves and for others as well.

MARY CHOSE TO LEAVE A MEMORIAL of her visit to La Salette. The spring that sprang forth following her visit to that privileged site, and which has not ceased flowing since the day of the apparition, remains a sign and symbol of all that is life-giving, of all that sustains life. The life Mary refers to is eternal life in her Son. Following him in faithful discipleship is the road that leads to abundant and full life.

Reflection Questions:

- What gifts and talents has God given you as a special means to eternal life?
- Are you aware of double standards in yourself when you relate to others?

Wednesday, June 22 (#373)
Twelfth Week in Ordinary Time

Matthew 7:15-20: *"...you will be able to tell them by their fruits."*

For Your Reflection:

Jesus gives us a warning: "Be vigilant where the behavior and actions of others are concerned." Again, if we are discerning, we will recognize the goodness and genuineness of people by their behavior, by what they do. Jesus used the ordinary experiences familiar to the people of his day to illustrate his teachings, comparing the kingdom of God with nature and agricultural realities. A healthy plant or tree, for example, will yield healthy fruit. The essence of goodness within the plant or tree manifests itself in the fruit it bears. Decay, too, is telltale.

So too did Mary at La Salette graphically call the attention of Melanie and Maximin to spoiled wheat, worm-eaten walnuts and rotted grapes, reflections in nature of what was happening in their day, in the lives of the people around them. The evils of today's society: crime, drugs, and murder are indicators that the core of our society is in need of conversion and healing.

Reflection Questions:

- What good fruits do you recognize in your life that help in the building of the Kingdom of God?
- How much care and prayer do you bring to the choices and decisions you are called upon to make?

Thursday, June 23 (#587)
The Nativity of St. John the Baptist

Luke 1: 57-66,80: *"All their neighbors were filled with awe and the whole affair was talked about throughout the hill country of Judaea."*

Meditation:

In the lives of most people, there are certain moments that family members and neighbors will never forget. Perhaps it is the successful outcome of a medically difficult birth. Or it may be someone surviving an accident which could easily have been resulted in a fatal outcome. Or perhaps it is an simple as a birth of a child or the celebration of a wedding. Special moments can affect people for the rest of their lives! The situation around the birth of John the Baptist was accompanied by several such events. One was that Elizabeth in her older years would have conceived at all! Another was the naming of her newborn son being affirmed by Zechariah and, of course, Zachariah's being able to speak once more. And lastly, due to all these special events that led up to his birth, his friends and family had reason to wonder: "What will this child turn out to be?" As we already know, *"the child grew up and his spirit grew strong."* His was a very special life and vocation, to *"prepare the way"* for the Savior.

AT LA SALETTE another very special event happened: Our Lady appeared, bringing a message and giving "her people" a mission: *"You will make this message known to all my people."* Although many years have passed since that special Saturday morning on the top of a mountain in the Alps of Southeastern France, the effects of that event still ring through those beautiful mountains and ring forth for the entire world to hear: Mary's Son wants us to follow him closely and faithfully, praying, celebrating and living the message of her Son.

Reflection Questions:

- What words of Mary (or her Son) do you need to reflect on? What area of your life needs a spiritual boost or strengthening?
- Whom should you share the La Salette message with in the near future?

Friday, June 24 (#172)
The Most Sacred Heart of Jesus
(Ezekiel 34:11-16; Romans 5:5b-11; Luke 15:3-7)

Pope Francis at Mass in St. Peter's Square said: "This celebration of... the Solemnity of the Sacred Heart of Jesus invites us all to turn to the heart, the deepest root and foundation of every person, the focus of our affective life and, in a word, his or her very core... The Heart of the Good Shepherd is not only the Heart that shows us mercy, but is itself mercy. There the Father's love shines forth; there I know I am welcomed and understood as I am; there, with all my sins and limitations, I know the certainty that I am chosen and loved...

"The Heart of the Good Shepherd tells us that his love is limitless; it is never exhausted and it never gives up. There we see his infinite and boundless self-giving; there we find the source of that faithful and meek love which sets free and makes others free; there we constantly discover anew that Jesus loves us "even to the end" (John 13:1), to the very end, without ever imposing.

"The Heart of the Good Shepherd reaches out to us, above all to those who are most distant. There the needle of his compass inevitably points, there we see a particular "weakness" of his love, which desires to embrace all and lose none. Contemplating the Heart of Christ, we are faced with the fundamental question... : Where is my heart directed? It is a question we need to keep asking, daily, weekly... Where is my heart directed? ... What is my heart set on? ...For as Jesus says: "Where your treasure is, there will your heart be also" (Matthew 6:21)...

At La Salette, Mary would not have been in tears if her deep love for her own Son and his Sacred Heart were not so intense. As Fr. Normand Theroux, M.S., stated: "The tears of Our Lady at La Salette are meant to be understood according to the common assumptions of ordinary people: they express profound sadness. They are a sign that the weeping person has reached the limit of his or her capacity to conceal pain. The flood of distress has reached the point of overflow and affliction becomes 'flesh' spilling down the face in streams of liquid heartache."

Reflection Questions:

• Did you ever see your parent (or family member) cry? Do you know what event or feeling brought them to tears?
• 'When have you wept at some event or feeling? What brought you to tears?

Saturday, June 25 (#573)
The Immaculate Heart of Mary

Luke 2:41-51: *"His mother stored up all these things in her heart."*

Meditation:

There are many profound lessons in this gospel passage for young and old, married or single, parents or childless. Just one piece of wisdom is that we all need to be open to learning more each and every day. Even in the Holy Family of Nazareth, the parents of Jesus were not perfect or all-knowing. They needed to appreciate that their Son indeed had a very special calling. Their obvious and reasonable upset was justified on the one hand but also needed to be tempered with a deepened appreciation of who their Son was and what he was called to do. This event was just one example of how loving and accepting these parents needed to be as they did their best to surround their Son with love as he grew up. In a sense, as all parents realize at one time or another, parents truly need to "grow up" along with their children. That Mary did by *"(storing) up all these things in her heart."* We should do the same, whether we are parents or not. God has much more to teach us

AT LA SALETTE, Mary came to bring the message of her Son to *"her people."* Her words and actions give us much to ponder. *Her invitation* to *"Come near, (and) do not fear"* should calm our hearts no matter what our concerns. Her warnings could initially seem severe but certainly came from a loving and compassionate heart. She needed to get our absolute attention. *Her promises* were to encourage "her children" not to lose hope but instead be faithful to our vocation as baptized followers of her Son. *Her mission* was one that every follower of her Son should be willing to do – to be an evangelizer and *"make her message known".*

Reflection Questions:

• How well have you "pondered in your heart" the message and mission of Mary at La Salette? Have you allowed her words to touch and renew your faith in her Son?

• When have you shared her powerful message with others?

Sunday, June 26 (#099)
Thirteenth Sunday in Ordinary Time
(1 Kings 19:16b, 19-21; Galatians 5:1,13-18; Luke 9:51-62)

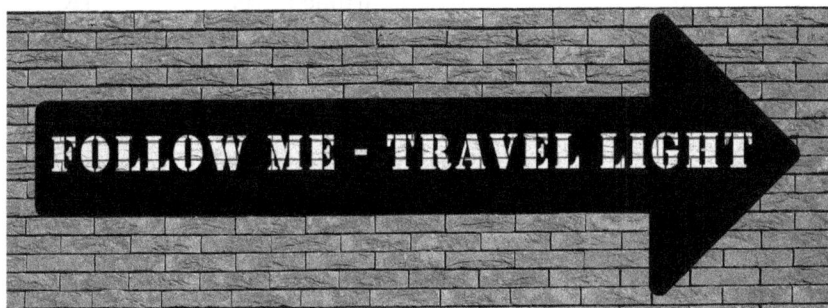

FOLLOW ME - TRAVEL LIGHT

Meditation: *Hello, Goodbye*

Most people have had experiences of making friends and then later, for various reasons—not necessarily bad—going their separate ways.

It doesn't often happen, however, that meeting one person requires us to say goodbye to another. That is the scene in today's first reading and in the Gospel. Elisha knows that his encounter with Elijah means he must leave his family behind. Jesus demands the same, even somewhat harshly, of those who wish to follow him.

We might be surprised at Jesus' manner. We expect him to be welcoming and encouraging. But we would also expect his honesty, not sugar-coating the demands of discipleship. It isn't a question of saying goodbye just to family and friends, but to a way of life. St. Paul makes this eminently clear in the second reading: "Live by the Spirit and you will certainly not gratify the desire of the flesh."

As we sometimes drift away from relationships, so we can also gradually drift away from living by the Spirit, from the sensed need of religious faith and practice in our day-to-day existence. That certainly was the situation for the two children to whom Mary appeared at La Salette. The little world they were born in had drifted away from God; they had received no religious instruction. Without the experience of September 19, 1846, they would very likely have remained in that state.

Obviously the Blessed Virgin didn't come just for them, but she came for them, too. They, and many others who "encountered" Our Lady of La Salette through them,—including Maximin's father—bade farewell to their old way of life and embraced once again the faith that was their true heritage.

The story and message of La Salette continue to speak to us today. The same drifting away from faith has occurred (New Hampshire and Vermont are prime examples). We need to help our world say goodbye to an increasingly pointless life. La Salette is a call to renewed encounter with Christ and the Christian community: a new hello of sorts.

Monday, June 27 (#377)
Thirteenth Week in Ordinary Time

Matthew 8:18-22: *"Follow me."*

For Your Reflection:

Multiple choice test... On the surface it would seem easy to follow Jesus. Anyone who counts himself or herself a true believer would readily and gladly do whatever Jesus might ask if he came down and spoke his request directly. But he doesn't do that. Instead he invites us in today's world to discern among multiple possible actions what we must accomplish to follow him faithfully. For guidance as we make our choices we look to prayer, our own inner light, and especially the input of our sisters and brothers in the faith.

THE CHILDREN OF LA SALETTE WERE GIVEN A MISSION – to make Mary's message of reconciliation known. On that first day, no doubt, the mission was glowingly clear for them. Each day afterward they had to decide over and over again to be true to her mission. Many times they were offered excruciatingly difficult choices – to betray their calling or even face the threat of death or imprisonment. The first miracle of La Salette was the apparition itself. The second was the fidelity with which the children followed their calling.

Reflection Questions:

• Do you understand your own calling with great clarity?
• If not, are you reaching out to others for help in discerning what it could be?

Tuesday, June 28, (#378)
Thirteenth Week in Ordinary Time

Matthew 8:23-27: *"(Then disciples said,) What kind of man is this?"*

Meditation:

That Titanic feeling: the apostles were not quite out in the middle of the ocean about to be struck by an iceberg but for them the situation no doubt seemed just as desperate. Fear gripped their bodies and terrified their souls. Would their lives be snuffed out by this rampag-

187

ing power of this freakish storm? Suddenly Christ, answering their alarmed plea for help rebuked the winds and the sea. All became calm. *"(Then disciples said,) What kind of man is this?"* In the simplest terms, he was the kind of man who answered those who called out to him. Similarly he does that for us in the midst of the most terrifying hours of our lives. How could he not? After all, did he not call us his friends (see John 15:15)?

THE WORLD THAT MAXIMIN AND MELANIE INHERITED was one that was being torn by violence at the dawn of industrialization and in the lingering twilight of the French Revolution. Society had been torn from its three-thousand-year-old moorings and an agrarian way of life was experiencing violent upheavals. Jesus sent his Mother to calm us, to reassure us, to tell us "not to be afraid, for she had great news to tell." It was simply that her Son remains deeply present to suffering humanity. *"What kind of man is this?"* In ways that our theology cannot explain he is the one who suffers with us even in eternal glory.

Reflection Questions:

•At the darkest times of your life, how did your faith in Jesus sustain you? Reflect on how frightened you were, how reassuring Jesus was for you?

•Do you know of any person who seems troubled in their faith? Why not at least say a prayer for them today.

Wednesday, June 29 (#591)
Sts. Peter and Paul, Apostles

Matthew 16:13-19: *"But you,"* he said, *"who do you say I am?"*

Meditation:

In speaking of the new evangelization, the Church is reminding us that we must stand on our own two feet and be able to respond to Jesus' question posed in the gospel for today: *"But you,"* he said, *"who do you say I am?"* Nobody else can answer that for us. We must have reflected deeply on this subject and sought to answer it for ourselves. We must have taken seriously our Baptismal call to follow Christ personally, daily, faithfully.

OUR LADY OF LA SALETTE brought us a message that is truly one of evangelization – for ourselves and for the other members of the Church. Since the essence of the Church which Saints Peter and Paul helped establish is evangelization – that is, supporting in ourselves a lively faith and reaching out to others to help them to live their Baptismal commitment – Our Lady could bring no other message except the message of her loving Son. She mentioned many helps to faith when she commented on daily prayer, the Eucharist, reverence for God's name, the use of Lenten faith habits and sharing her message with "all her people."

Reflection Questions:

- How well have you listened to Mary's words at La Salette?
- Have you examined your life to see how you are doing with regard to daily prayer, the Eucharist, reverence for God's name, the use of Lenten faith habits and sharing her message with "all her people"?

Thursday, June 30 (#380)
Thirteenth Week in Ordinary Time

Matthew 9:1-8: *"A feeling of awe came over the crowd."*

Meditation:

The people were simply awestruck. That would have blown us away too. This paralytic was healed not only of his infirmity, but also, and more importantly, he was forgiven his sins. There was universal applause from the crowd for the healing… but concerning his act of forgiving sins, some scribes mumbled, calling this blasphemy. Jesus, in effect, was making himself the equal of God. That was certainly too much to accept.

OUR LADY AT LA SALETTE talked about humanity's sins (read: yours and mine). Our sins are to be forgiven if we but ask. That is a miracle in itself, but in addition, she promised that *"rocks and stones will turn into mounds of wheat."* In the Sacrament of Reconciliation (and certain other sacramental moments) we are cleansed and made whole. And when we get in touch with the deepest part of ourselves, we are in touch with that deep-down, hidden part that touches God and is touched by God. In those rare but gifted moments of great spiritual insight, we cannot but be in awe of the wondrous work the Almighty does in us. Those graced moments fill us with the deepest feelings of awe and wonder.

Reflection Questions:

- How open are you to experiencing (and giving thanks for) those graced moments described above?
- At any time in your life have you been deeply awed by God's work in you, perhaps even to the point of tears?

Friday, July 1 (#381)
Thirteenth Week in Ordinary Time

Matthew 9:9-13: *"And indeed I came to call not the upright, but sinners."*

Meditation:

Jesus didn't come mostly for the upright, but especially for sinners. If ever there were words in Scripture that are both shocking and comforting, they are the ones cited above. First, the virtuous need some help and support. But realistically, since they are already doing so well, they weren't Jesus' prime target audience. Second, it is a great comfort that Jesus does in fact seek out sinners. It should be comforting that we can look forward to getting serious help in our efforts toward goodness, for Jesus says we are number one in his book. How about that!

AT LA SALETTE, VERY MUCH IN HER SON'S MODE, Our Lady came to seek out sinners, just as Jesus so generously offers help and forgiveness to his more needy people. She speaks powerfully about her suffering and prays for all who are far from being virtuous. Many people may have thought that the church was the exclusive home of only the holy and Eucharist was our reward for good behavior. However a more accurate view is that Eucharist is also food and drink for the wayfarers, the ever-needy people who sometimes falter along the way. Indeed the Church includes both saints and sinners.

Some Reflection Questions:

- Are you thankful that the Church welcomes both saints and

sinners?
• Whom do you know who is a very strong person of faith?

Saturday, July 2, (#382)
Thirteenth Week in Ordinary Time

Gospel: Matthew 9:14-17: *"Nor do people put new wine into old wineskins."*

Meditation:

Wine making, anyone? Although precious few of us know much about wine making, and even less about wineskins, all of us have a fairly good idea what point Jesus was making. If we are to make any type of progress on our spiritual journey, we have to understand the interior transformation that is called for. The new wine of Jesus' love and forgiveness cannot be poured into the old skin (container) of our obdurate and hardheaded selves. If our gas tank is leaking, constantly refilling it will not fix things. The hole is bound to get bigger. Unless we radically change our focus, pouring God's love into our self-centered selves will never lead us to embrace our world.

AT LA SALETTE Our Lady invited us to conversion. As we know, conversion does not simply mean making minor adjustments. It often means a radical shift away from the way we operated in the past – a 180 degree turn. What does it take for this to happen? Oftentimes it could be triggered by a major setback in our health, plans, financial fortunes; often, it could be brought to the fore by challenges or even failures in our most valued relationships. Our hearts are broken. We are deeply hurt and perhaps even feel abandoned. Since God's ways are not our ways, a heart broken is often a heart already open to anything that can help. The Living God might find in them a welcome mat not found previously. Radical setbacks, paradoxically, can make close encounters with our God more likely.

Reflection Questions:

• How has God helped you through challenges in relationships whether within your own or other's families?
• What person has helped you through some difficulties?

Sunday, July 3 (#102)
Fourteenth Sunday In Ordinary Time
(Isaiah 66:10-14c; Galatians 6:14-18; Luke 10:1-12, 17-20)

Meditation: *Peace, Mercy*

He Sent them out Two by Two **by James Tissot (1836–1902)**

"Peace to this household," are the words Jesus tells his disciples to begin with as they go off to preach the Kingdom.

At La Salette, Mary's first words are essentially words of peace: "Don't be afraid, my children." When I am with people who know La Salette well, I sometimes ask what their favorite part of the message is. Many quote those opening words.

We tend to think of peace as a goal. In fact, it is a starting point. Just as conflict begets conflict, so also peace begets peace. It is the "peaceful person" in the gospel on whom the preacher's peace will rest.

The old saying says you can't give what you haven't got. St. Paul, at the end of a letter marked by controversy, invokes "peace and mercy" on the Christians of Galatia. Now there is plenty of evidence to show that Paul was by no means a placid individual. He dealt with conflict almost everywhere he went. He had a famous confrontation with Peter, and a falling out with Barnabas. We might be tempted to wonder, Who is he to talk about peace and mercy?

The Beautiful Lady of La Salette said not to be afraid, and then went on to speak of frightening realities. Again we could wonder, What is really being communicated here?

The spirit of peace and mercy is no guarantee that there will never be troubles or even conflicts, but it makes a huge difference in how we deal with them. The key lies in that manifestation of peace and mercy which is called Reconciliation.

Every now and then I encounter people who seem addicted to indignation. But even the most righteous indignation has to be at the service of Reconciliation. "Peace to this household" and "Don't be afraid" are not greetings that can be shouted in anger.

St. James reminds us that human wrath does not accomplish God's righteousness. St. Paul writes to the Ephesians, "Do not let the sun set upon your anger." In other words, we should let the sun set—and rise—always on peace and mercy.

Monday, July 4 (#383)
Fourteenth Week in Ordinary Time

Matthew 9:18-26: *"She touched the fringe of his cloak."*

Meditation:

Pay attention. These two miracles offer us great insight as to Jesus the man. An important religious official came to see him imploring that Jesus do something about his daughter. She had just died, yet the man stated his first belief that she was not beyond Jesus' power to save. Jesus and his disciples were on their way to another mission of mercy. Jesus certainly was single-minded, but not so focused that he could not sense power leaving him as a person touched his cloak in a confident bid for healing. What amazing presence to people Jesus had even in times of personal stress!

MARY AT LA SALETTE tells us that God has not lost that desire to be present to us in all the moments of our lives. Although taken up with the providential guidance and maintenance of the ongoing miracle of creation – an expanding universe whose size is beyond calculation, this same God notices a father and child discussing spoiled wheat in the corner of a remote field. Mary communicates this concern for Maximin's father and his anxiety about being able to provide for his family. God (and Mary) truly care for the "little ones" of this world. That is most comforting.

Reflection Questions:

• When have you felt anxious about a person or event in the circle of your family or friends?

• When has God (perhaps through the assistance of a friend or family member) helped you through an anxious time or challenging event? How have you expressed your thankfulness to them for their help or their love?

Tuesday, July 5 (#384)
Fourteenth Week in Ordinary Time

Matthew 9:32-38: *"They were... like sheep without a shepherd."*

Meditation:

Jesus is looking for a few good men (and women). Jesus had a special love for the poor. Surely most of those who followed him were such. Life for them undoubtedly was one of harassment by the rich and powerful and of burnout from the constant struggle just to survive. Jesus felt very sorry for them. He saw how great their need was and realized that he as a person could not meet them all. And how he wished that more people were available to give him a hand. He himself was in great demand as he went about curing and healing, listening and sustaining, encouraging and challenging.

THE TEARS OF OUR LADY OF LA SALETTE speak of an endless love for her people. She saw the crowds of a Europe at the threshold of the industrial age. She could not help but see how harassed and dejected they were. It is true they were sinners and yet, as once was said, they were more sinned against than sinning. Mary, like Jesus, in his name, took pity on them. Her tears spoke most eloquently and she missioned two new young disciples, Melanie and Maximin, to spread the message of God's concern for her often harassed and dejected people.

Reflection Questions:

• Today's communications revolution makes us immediately aware of the evils being perpetrated against the innocent around the

world. How do you do your part to help those most in need?
•At times, do you use "limited resources or personal obligations" as an excuse for your inaction?

Wednesday, July 6 (#385)
Fourteenth Week in Ordinary Time

Matthew 10:1-7: *"Do not make your way to gentile territory ... go instead to the lost sheep of the House of Israel."*

Meditation:

Scripture contradicting itself? Reading the above passage brings to mind a number of contradictions found in Scripture. In this case Jesus prohibits his disciples from going to evangelize people outside the Jewish faith. And yet toward the end of this same Gospel according to Matthew he tells us to "go and make disciples of all nations" (Matthew 28:19). Well, which is it? Both, actually. Some are called to be missionaries in faraway lands. Others are called to stay put and work among and with their own. In God's eyes, disciples are making disciples in both instances.

MARY AT LA SALETTE speaks especially to those who are of the faith, in need of conversion or a change of heart – of metanoia, to use the fancy word. Is she against preaching the gospel message in distant lands? Of course not! She simply makes it clear that those sheep within the fold are in need of continuous conversion. And the La Salette Missionaries have historically expended a great deal of their energies staffing shrines, spiritual life centers, as well as preaching parish missions in that very same spirit.

Reflection Questions:

•St. Therese of Lisieux was designated Patroness of the Missions, despite the fact that she never stepped out of her cloister. Have you ever met missionaries who serve in foreign lands, perhaps even some La Salette Missionaries?
•Have you personally exercised your call to evangelize (from your Baptism) by reaching out to inactive Catholics in your own circle of friends or acquaintances?

Thursday, July 7, (#386)
Fourteenth Week in Ordinary Time

Matthew 10:7-15: *"Provide yourselves with no gold nor silver, not even with coppers for your purses."*

Meditation:

We are called to travel light. Perhaps some of the image of Jesus on which we were fed as youngsters was a bit saccharine, syrupy. Jesus seemed anything but a forceful leader. Very different from the picture we get in listening to his words in the gospel for today. In staccato fashion he tells us what disciples should and should not do in carrying out their mission: *"Cure the sick, raise the dead, cleanse those suffering from virulent skin-diseases, drive out devils."* And for good measure, *"give without charge."* Then just in case we have failed to notice how exacting and demanding a taskmaster he is, he bids us leave on our apostolic journeys with nothing in support, except other people's willingness to share with us. His demands are quite radical. Norman Vincent Peale's classic work on how to win friends and influence people was obviously not on his reading list.

WE NOW TURN TO MARY in her apparition at La Salette. The message that she entrusted to Melanie and Maximin was a commissioning that went beyond belief. Not only were they lacking gold, silver, or copper to fulfill their journey, they were also bereft of basic human qualifications, such as charisma, education, an outgoing personality or being articulate – to say nothing of prayerfulness, theological grounding, or pastoral know-how. They had to get out there and "tell everyone" what their Beautiful Lady had told them "to make known."

Reflection Questions:

- As odd as it may seems, are you aware that it is precisely because of what you lack, and not what you have, that makes it possible for God to work through you?
- Do you ever get fooled by a messenger's high-class appearance, bearing, and considerable credentials which influence your acceptance of their message or can you see "to the heart"?

Friday, July 8, (#387)
Fourteenth Week in Ordinary Time

Matthew 10:16-23: *"I am sending you out as sheep among wolves."*

Meditation:

From Jesus, we don't hear the most compelling slogan for a recruitment poster for his followers. He doesn't offer people to "be all they can be." He doesn't entice them by promising them an endless stream of benefits that grow with the passing of the years. No – quite the contrary. He offers persecution (if the job is done right). And then he says that we will be guaranteed protection from death. Of course, he is not referring to physical death. If we should get in harm's way in his service we may even die. But he does promise that under questioning you will be given by the Spirit what you should say. He promises that we will escape death only in the sense that we are promised a final resurrection. Can it be surprising that so few choose to follow him in any radical way?

AGAIN WE FOCUS ON THE CHILDREN OF LA SALETTE, on the message they had to impart, their lack of human, material or spiritual resources, on the opposition with which they frequently met. If the apparition at La Salette is miraculous, the faithfulness of the witnesses in spreading the message comes in a close second in terms of the miraculous. Undaunted, they went out in true gospel fashion, *"as sheep among wolves"*. They were offered bribes, ridiculed, and even threatened. Secular and church officials subjected them to grueling and seemingly interminable interrogations. Though humanly unprepared for the task, they were given what to say under very difficult questioning. Amazing!

Reflection Questions:

• Do you rejoice that the Lord has decided to foil the crafty and the clever and reveal the mysteries of the kingdom to the humble?
• Whom do you know who are seen by the world as less than impressive but whom you feel are actually filled with the wisdom of God? What attitude should this divine partiality toward the lowly inspire in you?

Saturday, July 9, (#388)
Fourteenth Week in Ordinary Time

Matthew 10:24-33: *"So if anyone declares himself for me in the presence of human beings, I will declare myself for him in the presence of my Father in heaven."*

Meditation:

All hands on deck! This is a call to witnessing. As Catholics many of us are not very good at it. We weren't trained for it as children. Probably it was not part of our religious upbringing. Religion for us was pretty much a private affair, except of course for those who are supposed to be doing it professionally: religious brothers, sisters, deacons, and priests. However the vast majority of us are simply satisfied to approach the Sacraments as spectators, and give a minimum in the collection. And in our consumerist society, finding a church that "feeds us" amounts to saying: a church that says what we want to hear, and will not challenge us beyond our comfort zone. All Jehovah's Witnesses, all Mormons, among others, are expected to witness. Witnessing is an integral part of living their faith. Most of us are just not aware of our call to evangelize which comes from our Baptism.

At La Salette Mary, Mother of the Church, the first and most eminent of all Christians, does precisely what "witnessing to the faith" calls for. She tells us about the privileged place her Son holds in her own life. She shows what her Son means to her. She proclaims this for all the world to hear. At La Salette she not only does witness to her Son and his Gospel message, she is the prophet who speaks his words to us in his name, indicating how deeply she has absorbed him and his Word. She witnesses boldly, straightforwardly, and without equivocation. She also responds to her children with untold compassion, understanding and love.

Reflection Questions:

- When was the last time you fearlessly let you faith convictions become known when the circumstances demanded it?
- In social or work-related settings, how often have you expressed your Christian beliefs and values when the need arose?

Sunday, July 10 (#105)
Fifteenth Sunday in Ordinary Time

(Deuteronomy 30: 10-14; Colossians 1:15-20; Luke 10:25-37)

Meditation: *Do This, Do Likewise*

The Good Samaritan **by David Teniers the Younger (1610–1690)**

The question, "Which commandment is the greatest?" was apparently regularly debated in Jewish religious circles of Jesus' time. Luke, however, frames the question differently: "What must I do to inherit eternal life?" And we are told that the scholar who asks it is in fact testing Jesus. Jesus simply invites the scholar to answer the question himself, then says, "You have answered correctly. Do this and you will live."

Then the exchange continues, and Luke gives us the wonderful story of the Good Samaritan. In one respect it's a little like Romeo and Juliet. Not a love story, but the story of an act of love involving persons from two hostile worlds, a story told to show the meaning of the commandment, "You shall love your neighbor as yourself." And Jesus concludes, "Go and do likewise."

The message of La Salette is also about what we should do to have eternal life. In her own way Mary echoes the words of Moses in today's first reading: "If only you would heed the voice of the Lord, your God, and keep his commandments and statutes."

The echo continues into the second reading, where we read of Jesus "making peace by the blood of his cross." This is precisely the source of eternal life, and the reason why Mary appeared bearing a crucifix on her breast.

When we take her words to heart we cannot fail to hear, "Do this and you will live." God's commandments are not for his sake but for ours, to guide us to him along a sure path.

And we hear, "Go and do likewise" in the words, "Made this known to all my people." As we are reconciled, as we witness reconciliation, we are invited to become reconcilers ourselves. There is no single way to carry out this mission, but there is one spirit that underlies all the efforts made to promote reconciliation. Opportunities will not be lacking, for many are the nations, cultures and even families that keep traditional hostilities alive.

Each of us has unique gifts. How can they best be placed at the service of this great cause?

Monday, July 11, (#389)
Fifteenth Week in Ordinary Time

Matthew 10:34 to 11:1: *"Anyone who welcomes a prophet because he is a prophet will have a prophet's reward."*

Meditation:

Prophets are those who, having experienced conversion themselves, carry that message of our need for conversion to the people of God. Maximin Giraud, the younger of the two cowherds to witness the apparition at La Salette, did not have a happy home life. His mother died when he was young and his stepmother mistreated him. His father, a wheelwright by trade, spent much of his time in the village tavern. Shortly after the apparition, when Maximin was repeating the story, Mr. Giraud interrupted him. The little boy protested, "But, Father, that is not all; let me tell you what concerns you. The Beautiful Lady also spoke about you." His father was aghast as Maximin repeated the incident of the field at Coin. As a consequence of their discussion, Mr. Giraud assisted at Mass daily until his death three years later.

ONE OF THE MANY GRACES OF LA SALETTE is that of conversion. The

Beautiful Lady undoubtedly appeared as a prophet at La Salette; she, whose life was formed by bearing the Word of God, proclaimed that word faithfully to the people of God. Her simple words and loving gestures touched the heart of the two children and have done so for many thousands of pilgrims who have followed in their steps to the site of the apparition on the Holy Mountain in France.

Reflection Questions:

- What do you hear in the message of La Salette that speaks to you personally?
- What conversion is needed by you; what part of your life needs to be changed? Have you brought the message of conversion to others whom you know?

Tuesday, July 12 (#390)
Fifteenth Week in Ordinary Time

Matthew 11:20-24: *"You shall go down to the realm of death!"*

Meditation:

There is only one means of transit from this life to the next, and none of us gets out of this world alive! We are all destined to die. And we believe that the passage from death to life involves some sort of judgment. Looking at our own lives, we are quick to realize that we have sinned and that our love is genuine but imperfect. Moreover we realize that the way we choose to live in this life helps to determine the way we will experience eternal life. So we continue to throw ourselves upon the mercy of God, trusting that God knows us better than we know ourselves.

It was out of love for us that God sent the Beautiful Lady to La Salette to call all people away from sin. The "great news" the Beautiful Lady came to proclaim is that of God's forgiveness. There is no such thing as an unforgivable sin, or else God's call is in vain. Instead, the Beautiful Lady draws us to God with a wonderful picture of what forgiveness effects: "If they are converted, the stones and rocks will change into mounds of wheat, and the potatoes will be self-sown in the land."

Some Reflection Questions:

• Are you willing to accept God's gift of forgiveness?
• Do you recognize that your latent desire to "do it your own way" is actually a temptation to refuse to live your life God's way?

Wednesday, July 13, (#391)
Fifteenth Week in Ordinary Time

Matthew 11:25-27: *"I bless you, Father, Lord of heaven and of earth, for hiding these things from the learned and the clever and revealing them to little children."*

Meditation:

God respects the dignity of every human person. God loves every human person. Thanks be to God, that love does not depend on our intelligence or goodness, age or strength. We are literally expected to "do the best we can with what we have." God wants us to strive for perfection, knowing full well that we aren't and never will be *"perfect as my heavenly Father is perfect"* (Matthew 5: 48).

As we reflect on the La Salette apparition, there is something that genuinely alarms us; namely, the character of Maximin and Melanie, the witnesses of the apparition. They were uneducated: neither spoke formal French neither could read or write. The boy was a regular chatterbox and a constant fidget. The girl was moody, stubborn, sulky, withdrawn, and was known to have a temper. Yet it was to these two that the Beautiful Lady was sent to convey her message of great news. We may judge the witnesses of the apparition to be of less-than-sterling character but that is not judging by God's standards. God could only look upon Maximin and Melanie the way he looks upon us all: with deep love and acceptance of us as we are – with our faults and our good qualities.

Reflection Questions:

• Do you treat every person with the God-given dignity that is due them? Do you sometimes allow externals to prevent you from seeing others (or yourself) as God does?
• Who is a person who accepts you as you are – in other words, like God does? Have you thanked God for them lately?

Thursday, July 14, (#392)
Fifteenth Week in Ordinary Time

Matthew 11:28-30: *"Come to me, all you who labor and are overburdened, and I will give your rest."*

Meditation:

This Gospel passage, proclaimed at today's Eucharist, is also read during the celebration of the Sacrament of the Anointing of the Sick. When we are beset by illness, whether of mind or body, the Church reminds us of this invitation of Jesus to come to him and be refreshed. Even when we are not sick, the world has a way of wearing us down. Sometimes life seems quite overwhelming. The good news is that we are not alone! God is always with us to help lift our burdens and brings us the peace that only God can give.

At La Salette the Blessed Virgin in her words and actions reminded us that we are not alone. No matter how far people felt separated from God, she reminded them that they simply needed to turn away from those things that separate us from God. This is always the case. Jesus said, *"Come to me..."* The Blessed Mother said, *"Come near, my children..."* Every time we notice the weight of the world on our shoulders, God seems to send someone to call us back. God loves us that much!

Reflection Questions:

•Do you pause to listen to the voice or inner yearning which is calling you back to God? Have you become so busy that you forget to pray?
•Do you take the time regularly to thank God for his unending invitation to draw closer to him?

Friday, July 15, (#393)
Fifteenth Week in Ordinary Time

Matthew 12:1-8: *"For the Son of Man is master of the Sabbath."*

Meditation:

The rules and practices of our faith are important. They help form our identity as a people; they help guide us along the way. They put us in touch with deeper truths about our life with God. In the Old Testament, special attention is given to the Sabbath because of its place in the scheme of creation and the focus on God's activity above all else. In the New Testament, special attention is given to the first day of the week as the day on which Jesus rose from the dead and those known as Christians met to break bread in memory of him. But even the regular practice of our faith and its rituals can sometimes become empty of their original meaning. We need to remind ourselves of the deeper meaning of what we do and celebrate. Jesus is doing exactly that for his hearers in today's gospel.

At La Salette, Mary came to remind us of the religious practices that were being neglected, especially noting that people chose to work on Sundays, rather than participate in the Mass, the Eucharistic Celebration. But Mary's point could not simply have been to fill the churches. Her people had forgotten God and the primacy of the call to love God, our neighbor and ourselves. She simply listed some elements of our faith that her people needed to once again pay attention to, as followers of her Son. One such valuable habit was participating in weekly Eucharist. This "Sabbath habit" was central to who they were and what they regularly needed in order to live a life of love and service as Jesus has shown them.

Reflection Questions:

- Are you aware of the deeper truths behind the religious practices that are a part of your Christian life?
- How can or should you make the Sabbath holy?

Saturday, July 16, (#394)
Fifteenth Week in Ordinary Time

Matthew 12:14-21: *"In (my servant whom I have chosen) the nations will put their hope."*

Meditation:

This passage from Matthew's Gospel reminds us how greatly the name of Jesus came to be prized. In the Acts of the Apostles, we see that converts to the New Way (Christianity) are baptized in Jesus' name; people are healed in Jesus' name; his name is the way to salvation. In Philippians 2:9-11, Saint Paul quotes an early hymn that states that God is glorified in giving Jesus the *"name which is above all other names, so that all beings ... should bends the knee at the name of Jesus."*

IT IS WITH THIS BIBLICAL BACKGROUND that we can appreciate the importance of Mary's complaint at La Salette about misusing the name of her Son. *"Those who drive the carts cannot swear without introducing the name of my Son!"* How easy it can be to allow her Son's name to be irreverently included in our crude exclamations. How trivial we make this holy name, using it for precisely the opposite purpose for which it was revealed to us. Yet how quickly we get upset when someone trivializes our name or that of our family. We readily take this as a personal insult. It is so easy to use Jesus' name irreverently without thinking. Hopefully our efforts at disciplining our own speech is one way to respond to Mary's tearful pleas at La Salette.

Reflection Questions:

•Do you give the name of the Lord Jesus the respect it truly deserves?

•Also do you readily go out of your way to give compliments to those around you who deserve a "thank you"?

Sunday, July 17 (#108)
Sixteenth Sunday in Ordinary Time

(Genesis 18:1-10; Colossians 1:24-28; Luke 10:38-42)

Meditation: *Listen, or Serve?*

Martha's complaint about her sister Mary reminds me of words that have been heard in many a family: "Well, it would be nice if somebody around here helped out once in a while!" In clubs, committees, parishes, etc., the same people are called upon to take on more and more responsibilities because no one else is willing to come forward. It's a far cry from Isaiah's "Here I am, Lord, send me!"

At La Salette, Mary has a similar complaint. "How long a time I have suffered for you,... and you pay no heed. However much you do, however much you pray, you will never be able to repay the pains I have taken for you."

While she stood at the foot of the cross, Jesus gave his mother to us, and gave us to her. The disciple took her not only into his home, but into his heart. No doubt their individual and personal vocations in some way merged during Mary's remaining years on earth.

Christ at the house of Martha **and Mary by Alessandro Allori (1535–1607)**

So too for us. In the Catholic tradition (like the Orthodox), as we follow Christ we are accompanied by his mother, our mother.

The Beautiful Lady of La Salette reminded us of this fact, most especially when she recalled the touching episode, which she alone witnessed, of Maximin's father wondering how he would be able to feed his family as famine approached.

In her message Our Lady is more like Martha than Mary in the Gospel story. She has a special concern about food, but only because it is a deep and alarming concern for her people. But at the same time she actually invites us to be more like Martha's sister Mary. Insisting on daily prayer and weekly Mass, she is encouraging us to "sit at the Lord's feet and listen to him speak." The Blessed Virgin herself, we are told twice in Luke's Gospel, "kept these things in her heart."

The Apparition shows that she kept not only "things" in her heart, but most especially "her people." We can collaborate with her by imitating both of the sisters in today's gospel. Like Mary, we are fed by the Lord's word. Like Martha, we respond in a spirit of service.

Monday, July 18, (#395)
Sixteenth Week in Ordinary Time

Matthew 12:38-42: *"On Judgment Day the men of Nineveh will appear against this generation and they will be its condemnation."*

Meditation:

In the time of Jonah, the nation of Assyria, whose capital was Nineveh, was the most powerful nation in the world. The Assyrians had invented the chariot and were able to conquer their neighbors. They were without equal. The story of the conversion of Nineveh is, then, a great and important one. That such a mighty people heard and took to heart the word of God shows what power that word has. They knew that all their achievements were worth nothing if they had strayed from God. No wonder Jesus invokes them as judges to condemn those who don't recognize the revelation of God in their midst.

THE VIRGIN OF LA SALETTE is reminiscent of Jonah. She comes into the midst of a people indifferent to God's presence among them, indifferent to the truth of the Gospel. She calls them (and us) to repentance and conversion. God never gives up on us but uses every means to call us back. In God's eyes, none of us is a lost cause. He considers us worth *"the pains"* Our Blessed Mother has taken on our behalf.

Reflection Questions:

• Just as the Ninevites repented, are we willing to (or need to) repent? What needs forgiving in your life?
• Do you listen to homilies at Mass with your full attention? At Mass do you wait for God to speak to you through the words or prayers of the priest or deacon?

Tuesday, July 19, (#396)
Sixteenth Week in Ordinary Time

Matthew 12:46-50: *"Anyone who does the will of my Father in heaven is my brother and sister and mother."*

Meditation:

The most sublime and profound title bestowed upon the Virgin Mary is certainly the "Mother of God." The Word was made flesh and made his dwelling among us, taking his human nature from his mother in her womb. It is indeed a great honor. But Jesus is not speaking about mere biological connections when he refers to his "brother and sister and mother." Jesus is speaking about the "kinship" or connection that is based on discipleship

MARY IS CONSIDERED BY MANY BELIEVERS as the first disciple of Jesus. Her response of "fiat" to the angel at her Annunciation was the official beginning of her discipleship. We also recall her fidelity at the foot of the Cross, when most of the disciples fled in fear. At La Salette, she comes again as the faithful disciple. Where the others have forgotten, she has remembered how her Son has brought salvation and how his name continues to save. Our Tearful Mother, the first disciple, is calling us back to the ways and message of her Son. She can speak with genuine pride about him since she has been faithful to him from his cradle to his grave and beyond. We should listen well to her words, her gestures and her mission given to us all.

Reflection Questions:

•As true disciples and sisters and brothers of Jesus from our Baptism, how do you share your faith with others?
•Do you look like and sound like his disciple? What have you sacrificed in order to remain faithful to her Son, Jesus, your Brother?

Wednesday, July 20 (#397)
Sixteenth Week in Ordinary Time

Matthew 13:1-9: *"Anyone who has ears should listen!"*

For Your Reflection:

In the parable of the sower, Jesus addresses different reactions to the word of God. Not all the seed fell on fertile soil. One question this raises is whether we allow our own faith to bear fruit in our lives. Or is the faith we profess somehow cut off from the lives we lead? Is Sunday so separate from the rest of the week that it has no bearing on how we act? By its very nature, our faith should be all-encompassing. Buried in the innermost recesses of our hearts, it has the ability to affect every aspect of our lives. Not allowing it to do so assures that we will produce no fruit, no good works, no legacy of love in our lives.

AT LA SALETTE THE BLESSED VIRGIN COMES TO NOURISH THE SEEDS OF OUR FAITH. It is as if she is saying that it's never too late: there is still time for the seed to fall on fertile ground and bear much fruit. When we hear the promise of stones being turned into wheat, does the picture of that happening in fields and on mountain slopes move us? Or is it more of a miracle to know that our stony hearts, our rock-hard minds, can yet yield a harvest for ourselves and others – even a hundredfold!

Reflection Questions:

- Do you consider your daily choices and actions as necessarily flowing from the faith you profess?
- What part of the parable of the seeds matches your own life at this time?
- What concrete action can you take today to express your own faith and trust in God's love and mercy?

Thursday, July 21, (#398)
Sixteenth Week in Ordinary Time

Matthew 13:10-17: *"Anyone who has will be given more and will have more than enough; but anyone who has not be deprived even of what he has."*

Meditation:

At first this Gospel passage strikes me as unfair. Does God really intend that the rich get richer and the poor poorer? Upon reflection, I realize that Jesus is speaking about faith. If we do not practice our faith, it will wither, become dry. Prayer is one way to nourish our faith. The one who prays finds faith growing stronger and stronger. One who does not pray finds faith growing weaker, until it ends by being discounted altogether.

At La Salette, Our Lady calls us to the life of prayer. She beseeches us to participate in Sunday Mass. She asks us to pray at morning and evening. She reminds us to observe the practices of Lent. She does all this for the simple reason that these things put us in touch with God, deepening the relationship of faith that has been given to us as gift, and drawing us to the springs of life which always make us strong.

Reflection Questions:

- "Do you pray well, my children?"

• Have you experienced growing "richer" as a result of remaining faithful?

Friday, July 22, (#603)
St. Mary Magdalene

John 20: 1-2,11-18: *"So Mary of Magdala told the disciples, 'I have seen the Lord,' and that he had said these things to her."*

Meditation:

The word "witness" in the bible does not mean being passively present to an event; rather it has an active connotation, an obligation to share what we have witnessed. Such is the case of Mary of Magdala in the gospel of John. After she met the person whom she thought was the gardener at the tomb of Jesus, and once the risen Jesus had revealed himself to her, she couldn't contain her excitement and wanted to embrace Jesus with love, she quickly returned to the disciples with the news that she had seen the Lord! She is a wonderful example to us of what it means to spread the "gospel", that is, the "good news." Mary of Magdala was a dedicated and quite genuine evangelizer.

At La Salette, Our Lady told the two witnesses of her apparition, Melanie and Maximin, to do what Mary of Magdala had done so well, *"make the message known"* to all her people. This task of witnessing or making the message known is now passed onto us who have also heard her words and hopefully taken them to heart. We are the contemporary "Mary Magdalenes, Melanies and Maximins" who are urged to share what we have witnessed – that God's love and forgiveness are alive and well and ready for the taking.

Reflection Questions:

• Do you remember who told you first about the message of La Salette?
• In turn, with whom have you shared the message of La Salette?

Saturday, July 23 (#400)
Sixteenth Week in Ordinary Time

Matthew 13:24-30: *"But he said, 'No, because when you weed out the dar-*

nel you might pull up the wheat with it.'"

For Your Reflection:

It is the sower of the seed that will not allow the weeds to be uprooted. He is afraid of damaging, and thereby losing good plants. We also wonder whether the sower is hoping that the weeds will turn into good plants. After all, if we identify with the harvest, how do we know whether we are weed or wheat? The conclusion of the story of our life remains yet untold. God is slow to condemn us; we are given every chance to change our lives. God will employ any means to win us back. The fate of the weeds is postponed.

THE WEEPING MOTHER WAS SENT TO LA SALETTE TO REMIND US of the salvation already won for us in Christ, her Son but how easily we forget. However God uses every means to remind us. Perhaps God was hoping that Mary's words would turn the weeds into good plants. After all, if he can turn rocks into wheat, why not weeds into good plants! And if Mary's words can't make it happen, maybe her abundant tears will. God uses every means possible to turn our hearts and minds back to God.

Reflection Questions:

• When have you seen how Christ can turn people's lives back to God?
• Has there been a point in your life when God helped you in some unexpected or wonderful way?

Sunday, July 24 (#111)
Seventeenth Sunday in Ordinary Time

(Genesis 18:20-32; Colossians 2:12-14; Luke 11:1-13)

Meditation: *Ask, Seek, Knock*

Mary at La Salette observed that her people were doing just the opposite of what Jesus tells his disciples in today's Gospel. Finding the potato harvest blighted, instead of asking, seeking and knocking in a spirit of faith, "you swore, you threw in the name of my Son."

In the *Catechism of the Catholic* Church the first part of the definition of blasphemy states that it "consists in uttering against God—inwardly or outwardly—words of hatred, reproach, or defiance." That is precisely what Mary was speaking about. Fortunately it is, I think, totally foreign to the experience of most of us.

This doesn't mean we can't ever complain to God. The Psalms show us that all our emotions have their place in our prayer. We can talk to God about anything.

Look at Abraham in today's first reading, bargaining with God. He even goes so far as to say, "Far be it from you to make the innocent die with the guilty." He speaks to him persuasively, as to a friend, on behalf of the just.

Jesus went beyond that. St. Paul writes: "[Jesus] brought you to life along with him, having forgiven us all our transgressions."

Our Lady of La Salette adopts, naturally, the same attitude: "If I want my Son not to abandon you, I am obliged to pray to him without ceasing." She is asking, seeking, knocking, all the time, not on behalf of the just but the unjust.

She comes to us, too, asking, seeking, knocking on our door. She teaches us simple ways in which we ourselves can ask, seek, knock. And she promises us that, as a result. our lives can be transformed.

Here again she resembles her Son, this time as he speaks in the book of Revelation. "Behold, I stand at the door and knock. If anyone hears my voice and opens the door, I will enter his house and dine with him, and he with me."

What a wonderful prospect! The same invitation echoes loudly at La Salette. Why would anyone not respond?

Monday, July 25, (#605)
St. James, Apostle

Matthew 20:20-28: *"The Son of man came not to be served but to serve,*

and to give his life as a ransom for many."

Meditation:

The never-ending quest for power, prestige and money is not just a contemporary problem. It can even invade the group of twelve disciples. They seem to be confused by their personal attraction to prestige even within that small group. Jesus deals directly and openly with the need of a few of his disciples who want to know who is first, second and third in that special group. In his usual fashion he takes what is considered common knowledge and turns it on its head: *"anyone who wants to become great among you must be your servant, and anyone who wants to be first among you must be your slave."* God's ways are certainly not our ways.

AT LA SALETTE, Our Weeping Mother, like her Son did in selecting his disciples, chose two children that perhaps nobody else would have guessed were "witness material." They were the first two people called by Mary to *"make the message known"* and so they did. They succeeded where perhaps more talented people would have failed. Their task was to transmit her message faithfully and often. This they did with remarkable candor and forthrightness, in the face of challenges from bishops and clergy of all stripes and motivations. With minimal education they managed, somewhat remarkably, to narrate and remember what the Beautiful Lady said and did on the Saturday morning in September on that remote hillside. Maximin and Melanie served well their Weeping Mother and her wishes until they met their God face to face.

Reflection Questions:

- Who are the people you serve most often in your life? Do you ever pray for them, thanking God for them?
- Who do you know whom you consider a very good "servant of the Lord"?

Tuesday, July 26, (#402)
Seventeenth Week in Ordinary Time

Matthew 13:36-43: *"Then, leaving the crowds, he went to the house; and his disciples came to him and said, 'Explain to us the parable about the darnel* *in the field."*

Meditation:

Life is filled with opportunities for communication. Each day brings moments for us to experience the richness and complexity of the universe, of our fellow human beings and of our own hearts. Listening to each of these "communications" may be very challenging in a world filled with constantly distracting influences. At times it is not easy to understand either others or ourselves. Often understanding demands exceptional attention. Jesus is aware that the disciples do not fully grasp his message, his parable. He takes them to a quiet place and creates an opportunity to listen to their questions and speak directly to them. With loving care he takes the time to explain further the underlying meaning of his parable. After all, his disciples have become truly significant people in his life and mission.

At La Salette, Mary, thankfully attentive to the non-verbal communication of the two children, becomes aware that their understanding of her words is limited. She then begins to speak in the local patois or dialect. She reaches out to communicate in a way that respects the needs of her listeners. She honors clear communication as central to this relationship that she is establishing with these two peasant adolescents. She takes the necessary time to be sure that there is some understanding of the message that she shares with them.

Reflection Questions:

• What is the quality of your communication with the significant people in your life? Are you attentive to the words, questions, gestures and non-verbal messages that are given to you?
• Are you patient and flexible in your efforts to respond to people's questions and concerns?

Wednesday, July 27, (#403)
Seventeenth Week in Ordinary Time

Matthew 13:44-46: *"…the kingdom of Heaven is like a merchant looking for fine pearls; when he finds one of great value he goes and sells everything he owns and buys it."*

Meditation:

We live in a world of abundance. The abundance, however, is not equally distributed. Some people experience abundance as clutter, overwhelming their lives. Others experience abundant needs. We are all merchants in the marketplace of material goods. All that we humanly need to be comfortable may be available to us, yet we may not be at peace. The desire for more may leave us living in an unsatisfied manner. Today's scripture invites us to look at the choices we make and to examine our priorities.

MARY INVITED THE TWO CHILDREN to consider what was important in their lives. Although they lived in a harsh peasant world, their daily lives were filled with simple but profound choices. Did they understand the importance of each choice? Were they able to pay attention to the God who loved them? Did they appreciate the actions of their parents?

Reflection Questions:

• In what way is your life cluttered? Are you able to pay attention to what is truly important and central? Are "first things first" for you in your life?
• How does your faith rank in importance in your daily life? What about prayer and worship?

Thursday, July 28, (#404)
Seventeenth Week in Ordinary Time

Matthew 13:47-53: *"Again, the kingdom of Heaven is like a dragnet that is cast in the sea and brings in a haul of all kinds of fish. When it is full, the fishermen bring it ashore; then, sitting down, they collect the good ones in baskets and throw away those that are no use."*

Meditation:

Each day brings opportunities to choose. Usually, we attend first to our survival needs. Then, other demands and expectations for the use of our time enter the fabric of our days. What choices will I make for quality relationships, for responsible work, for acting with integrity within the community of human beings where I find myself this day? How clear are my intentions? Am I able to sort out that which strangles and limits creativity, responsiveness to the good, holy and sacred? Jesus invites, by way of parable, his disciples to daily be attentive to their choices.

At La Salette, Mary calls attention to Maximin's experience of dried wheat in the fields. Starkly, she notes the difference between that which gives life and nourishment and what is unable to sustain life. In this, she invites her young hearers to be attentive to the choices they make. "Choose life that you and your descendants may live" (Deut 30:19).

Reflection Questions:

- Life offers us a plethora of choices. Can you be attentive today to sorting through the options?
- Do you continually ask yourself: Is this a life-giving choice?

Friday, July 29, (#607)
Saints Martha, Mary and Lazarus

John 11:19-27: *"Jesus said: I am the resurrection... Do you believe this?"*

Meditation:

There is a clue imbedded in these lines that gives to this entire passage a life of its own. John the writer knows he has to tell us this: "Now Jesus loved Martha and her sister and Lazarus." Martha was well aware of this and does not hesitate to make her friendly but straightforward reproach to Jesus: "Lord, if you had been here, my brother would never have died." Earlier, Jesus had said: "Our beloved Lazarus has fallen asleep, but I am going to wake him." Later when the crowds saw Jesus approaching the cave where Lazarus lay and saw him weep, they remarked: "See how much he loved him!"

John the gospel-writer knows that some things are too important to be left to chance. By referring three times to Christ's love for his family and for his friend, he makes the magnificent claim that Jesus raised Lazarus from the dead because he loved him and would not be separated from him. The miracle is accomplished in an environment of profound affection. The point of it all is that we are given new life not just for the sake of God's power and his urge to create but for the sake of his need to love and to give life to those he loves. At this juncture people might think they have seen all the splendor of this miracle. It gets better still.

Lazarus' return to life was not only a passing miracle, it was an ongoing one. He had become a living, walking, talking, laughing, feasting proof that Christ was indeed who he said he was: the Messiah, Son of God. Jesus' enemies could weather a lesser wonder. But it was difficult to blot out the memory of a man who was dead and had been made to rise from death. The Person who did this must not be allowed to live.

As John tells it, the miracle of Lazarus, the victory of life over death, was to be the very cause of the passion and death of Christ. Lazarus had been the last "straw." The immediate reason for the cross of Christ, then, was the love of a family, the love of a disciple. The miracle was not only an epiphany of power, it was especially the response of the fidelity of God to the faith of a friend. This sign remains to this day the hallmark of the Lord: that in the categories of God death is never the end of love and life is only the beginning. (*by Fr. Normand Theroux, M.S.*)

At La Salette, two reasons for visiting La Salette were not only her love for her Son, Jesus, but also her love for her people. Her tears were a powerful sign of her overwhelming sorrow and her special visit to this mountaintop was an expression of her motherly love for her people who had wandered away from following her Son. The truth is: we need Christ to lift us up and change our hearts. This can only be done if we truly believe that he is the "resurrection and the life."

Saturday, July 30, (#406)
Seventeenth Week in Ordinary Time

Matthew 14:1-12: *"Prompted by her mother…"*

Meditation:

This Gospel may be an opportunity for us to reflect on the influence our own mothers and other significant people have had in our lives.

Herodias suggested to her daughter that she ask for the head of John the Baptist on a dish. Salome, perhaps not yet her own person or out of filial devotion, obliges. An evil act is initiated. Herod does not have the will power to follow his own inner instincts. He succumbs. A chain reaction begins, unstopped because neither Herodias nor Herod is able to break the chain of negative influence.

At La Salette, Mary acknowledges the love and compassion that her Son bears for humankind. She acknowledges the pain of her Son who sees the faithless living of those who call themselves Christian. She has always urged disciples to "do what he tells you.' Here, as mother, she seeks to prompt and influence these two shepherds. She invites them to pray more attentively, She encourages them to be attentive to the gestures of their parents. She urges them to make the message known. The task she gives to the children is simple: within their sphere of influence, their small world, they are to be in communion with God and announce what has happened to them.

Reflection Questions:

• Are you conscious of your opportunities today to influence others?
• Is it possible for you to seize these moments, to initiate positive thinking and action among those with whom you will come in contact?

Sunday, July 31 (#114)
Eighteenth Sunday in Ordinary Time

(Ecclesiastes 1:2; 2:21-23; Colossians 3:1-5, 9-11; Luke 12:13-21)

Meditation: *What Matters*

YOUR POSSESSIONS DO NOT DEFINE YOU!

I like to point out that Our Lady of La Salette spoke about wheat and potatoes, grapes and walnuts, because these things mattered to her people, and what mattered to them mattered to her. At first glance today's readings seem to take us in the opposite direction, to say that such things don't really matter after all.

Well, yes and no. They do matter. The readings just make the point that some things matter more than others.

This is true also of La Salette. In fact, Mary makes a clear connection between what matters most—our relationship with her Son—and the other concerns that matter in our life. "If they are converted, the rocks and stones will be turned into heaps of wheat." We hear the echo of Jesus' words, "Seek first the Kingdom of God, and all the rest will be given you besides."

In yet another Gospel text, the Parable of the Sower, speaking of the seed sown among thorns, Jesus cautions us against letting certain needs and desires suffocate faith. St. Paul today writes much the same, contrasting faith with a list of evil desires.

The Beautiful Lady, however, doesn't find fault with her people's desires. Their needs are real, their fears well founded. Unlike the rich man of today's Gospel, they are keenly aware of the prospect of death. No doubt it seemed obvious to them, as to many still today, that "All is vanity."

In the face of such despair, Mary did not come to the Holy Mountain merely to lay blame. That would have been "vanity" indeed. Yes, she wanted us to take responsibility for our failure to practice our faith, but in view of a change. As we read in today's Psalm, "If today you hear his voice, harden not your hearts."

La Salette reminds us that faith and hope are intimately linked. We are called to live by God's word and to place our trust in his promise. In this way we become "rich in what matters to God."

What matters to God is the relationship he wants to have with us. Mary wants to help restore that relationship.

Monday, August 1, (#407)
Eighteenth Week in Ordinary Time

Matthew 14:13-21: *"They collected the scraps left over, twelve baskets full."*

Meditation:

Jesus goes with his disciples to a secluded place and reflects with them on the death of John the Baptist. They take time in prayer. When the crowd finally finds them, they immediately begin ministering to these needy people, and also wonder how all these people could find something to eat. When they bring the problem to Jesus, he first says: *"There is no need for them to go: give them something to eat yourselves."* The disciples are startled at Jesus' response that they simply provide food for the crowd themselves. Yet Jesus then provides food for all present. Then the gospel simply states that twelve baskets of food were left over. The sign for all who would look and listen was that God provide us with more than we need in life.

Mary, the Queen of Heaven, was described by the children simply as the "Beautiful Lady". Her approachability and compassionate presence were obvious to the two initially scared children. Her sincere interest in the plight of Maximin's father was a touching gesture indeed. She even attended to those who were not standing in front of her! The fears of Maximin's father was important to Mary and she felt that she needed to respond to it. Just as her Son responded to the hungry "cast of thousands," Mary was similarly concerned about the fate of those parents who had the responsibility to feed their family.

Reflection Questions:

- How aware are you of those in your own neighborhood or city which have little or no food each day?
- Have you ever donated to or participated in serving food to the hungry? If not, why not volunteer to do so?

Tuesday, August 2, (#408)
Eighteenth Week in Ordinary Time

Matthew 15:1-2,10-14: *"(Jesus) called the people to him and said, 'What goes into the mouth does not make anyone unclean; it is what comes out of the* *mouth that makes someone unclean.'"*

Meditation:

Jesus invites his listeners to be attentive to the sentiments and values of their hearts. He wants to be clear in his teaching. The core values that influence how a person lives, makes decisions and acts are the very values with which Jesus invites us to be concerned. We are not to be distracted by the superficial, the external, the secondary. Jesus challenges us to be clearly focused on what is re-ally important in our lives.

At La Salette, Mary raises the question of language. Sacred language is being used carelessly, betraying an underlying attitude of disrespect. Speech is one way to express the sentiments of the heart It is a distinct way to reveal who we are, what is important to us and how we shape our lives. Attentive to our speech, we may become more attentive to the core values that govern our lives, motivate as and influence the way we live.

Reflection Questions:

- Do I consider that what comes spontaneously to my mouth may help me to reflect on the values I have adopted?
- How attentive am I to the way that I express myself? Am I aware that my words are a mirror of my soul?

Wednesday, August 3, (#409)
Eighteenth Week in Ordinary Time

Matthew 15:21-28: *"the (Canaanite) woman had come up and was bowing low before him. 'Lord,' she said, 'help me.' He replied, 'It is not fair to take the children's food and throw it to little dogs.' She retorted, 'Ah yes, Lord; but even little dogs eat the scraps that fall from their masters' table.'"*

Meditation:

It is a humble, peasant, gentile woman who challenges Jesus to extend his compassion beyond the house of Israel, beyond the boundaries of family and tribal clan with whom Jesus had become initially identified. Jesus boldly responds to someone, who might be considered an outcast in the eyes of his society, with compassion and love and healing.

Is it possible to imagine that Mary could have chosen others to be the witnesses at La Salette? In the eyes and opinions of the residents of the hamlets located around La Salette, the response would be a resounding yes. The credibility of the witnesses challenges the credibility of the message. The fact is that these two illiterate, unknown and little appreciated adolescents were chosen and entrusted with a profound message and a daunting mission. The good news is certainly not restricted to the well to do or to any exclusive club founded on ethnic origin, skin color or cultural tradition. It is addressed to all people.

Reflection Questions:

- If this day you encounter someone different from yourself – whether unemployed, homeless, speaking a language other than your own, with a different skin color, what attitude will guide your words and deeds?
- Will you share the good news of God's love by your presence?

Thursday, August 4 (#410)
Eighteenth Week in Ordinary Time

Matthew 16:13-23: *"But (Jesus) turned and said to Peter, 'Get behind me, Satan! You are an obstacle in my path, because you are thinking not as God thinks but as human beings do."*

For Your Reflection:

What a challenge! To think as God thinks and not in the terms of human perspective and vision. Paul urges us "to put on the mind of Christ." Jesus lets it be known that following him will challenge us to look at life in a new way. There is no such thing as "cheap grace." This is a Savior willing to pay the price himself first. This is a Savior willing to love us first. And as beloved sons and daughters, we are called to follow in his footsteps, to understand the transitory nature of human life in this world and to share in paying the price of humankind's redemption.

At La Salette, Mary clearly states that a business-as-usual or a lax attitude toward the sacred is unacceptable behavior for the disciples of Jesus. Whether it is one's language, prayer, attendance at Mass or respect for Lenten regulations, these matters are serious because they reflect what is in the heart. Mary's communion with her Son is so profound that she longs for each of "her people" to share that intimacy with the Holy One. Our words and deeds are valued not because of a prevailing fad or custom but because of their intrinsic worth and merit.

Reflection Questions:

- What control do the opinions of others have upon the decisions you may make this day?
- Do you listen most attentively to the prompting of your heart or the whispers of your friends?

Friday, August 5 (#411)
Eighteenth Week in Ordinary Time

Matthew 16:24-28: *"Anyone who wants to save his life will lose it; but anyone who loses his life for my sake will find it. What, then, will anyone gain by winning the whole world and forfeiting his life? Or what can anyone offer in exchange for his life?"*

Meditation:

All of Scripture speaks the Word of God and the message of Jesus in proclaiming the reign of God. Some passages, however, cut to the heart of the matter, to the quick of the subject. Here Jesus touches what is central to his whole message and preaching. Life exists beyond the observable that we encounter daily. Life indeed has many layers of meaning. External success, achievement, honor, prestige, wealth, and all that might accompany these, ultimately will pass. In fact, they may stifle real life. Winning and gaining, accomplishing and achieving for itself alone is really losing and costing one's life. What a paradox!

MARY'S INTERVENTION AT LA SALETTE speaks a similar message. Life is a precious gift, not to be taken for granted. Our lives are sacred. Creation is sacred. We honor the sacredness of our lives and of creation by a deep inner connection with the divine presence made manifest in Jesus, in other human beings and in creation. This is an invitation to go beneath the surface and to live life more deeply. It is an invitation to see life as much more than a series of social interactions. It is an invitation to read the events of our lives with a respectful heart.

Reflection Questions:

- Do you take time each day to examine the motives of your choices?
- How important is the good opinion of others in your decision-making? Are you willing to take unpopular positions?

Saturday, August 6, (#614) The Transfiguration of the Lord

Luke 9:28b-36: *"(Peter) did not know what he was saying."*

Meditation:

The event of the Transfiguration was certainly a spectacular event and it is quite understandable that Peter got caught up in the glory of the moment as he suggested that they make three shelters for Jesus and the two extraordinary guests. Jesus dismissed the idea but did not scold Peter. As we know, Peter had a lot to learn and Jesus was patiently preparing his disciples for his Passion and Resurrection. He taught them by who he was, what he said and what they themselves experienced of his stories and acts of love.

MARY AT LA SALETTE is also a wonderful, patient teacher, a Weeping Mother whose loving concern shows through her every word, gesture and tear. The two children, although they had no idea who she really was, were completely taken in by her radiant presence and listened well to this woman in tears. Their dialogue was geared directly to the two children and her concern that they understand was of paramount importance to Mary. After her initial prophet words of warning, she spoke directly to the minds and hearts of her simple, poor cowherds.

Reflection Questions:

- How patient and understanding are you to those around you, young and old alike?

•Do you take the time to be present and listen well or do you think that you are the expert and everyone should listen to you for your pearls of wisdom?

Sunday, August 7 (#117)
Nineteenth Sunday in Ordinary Time

(Wisdom 18:6-9; Hebrews 11:1-2, 8-19; Luke 12:32-48)

Meditation: *Faith and Treasure*

No one is obliged to believe that the Blessed Virgin Mary appeared at La Salette. And even though Our Lady of Lourdes and Our Lady of Fatima are included in the universal liturgical calendar of the Church, we are free to believe in them or not.

In the Catechism of the Catholic Church we read: "Throughout the ages, there have been so-called 'private' revelations, some of which have been recognized by the authority of the Church. They do not belong, however, to the deposit of faith. It is not their role to improve or complete Christ's definitive Revelation, but to help live more fully by it in a certain period of history." (CCC, #67)

This does not mean the Church is indifferent to the Apparitions of Mary. They have been carefully examined; the witnesses interrogated. Some, like Bayside, have been officially declared not to be authentic. In many cases no formal judgment has been made. Relatively few have been approved, fewer than 25 in the last 200 years. Approval comes not from Rome, but the local Bishop.

La Salette was approved in 1851, five years after the Apparition. The Bishop wrote that "the faithful are justified in believing it to be beyond doubt." The point of having "faith" in La Salette is this: the treasure of our Christian faith is at the heart of Mary's message.

Jesus tells us, "Where your treasure is, there also will your heart be." There is no doubt where the Beautiful Lady's treasure is. "My people... My Son" In her every word and gesture and in her tears, she reveals her love for both.

Today's second reading is taken from Hebrews 12 where some twenty names are evoked from the Old Testament, each preceded by the phrase, "by faith." It is a record of the fundamental, transforming power of faith in human life.

La Salette is precisely about the transforming power of faith, of living faith. That is why, although the Apparition occurred in "a certain period of history" it is by no means restricted to that period. Wherever the treasure of faith is, Mary's heart will ever be.

Monday, August 8 (#413)
Nineteenth Week in Ordinary Time

Matthew 17:22-27: *"...a great sadness came over them."*

For Your Reflection:

We live in a society that seems to operate on stress. It seems like no matter where we look or in whatever work we are engaged, stress is part of our everyday life. Many books are written on how to deal with our tensions and how to learn to relax. But so often we forget that the best way to deal with our stress was given to us by Jesus. He often told his disciples to come to a deserted place where they could pray. Jesus himself did this many times throughout his ministry.

Mary at La Salette understood the stress that people were dealing with at that time with their wheat spoiling, the grapes and the walnuts rotting, children dying in the arms of those who held them. But she also reminds us how to deal with stressful situations. "Do you pray well, my children?" She invites us to recreate ourselves by going to the source of life — her Son, Jesus Christ. Mary wants us to understand that through prayer we become united with her Son who gives us true rest. "Come to me all you who are overburdened and I will give you rest," he says.

Reflection Questions:

•How do you deal with stress?
•Is your prayer life a cause of stress or is it life-giving?

Tuesday, August 9, (#414)
Nineteenth Week in Ordinary Time

Matthew 18:1-5,10,12-14: *"...unless you change and become like little children you will never enter the kingdom of Heaven."*

Meditation:

What is it like to be a child? Does it mean that we must act childishly? Actually, to be a child means to be full of wonder. Children like to explore and learn about the world around them. Children are also innocent and open to new possibilities in their life. Children are dependent on others. Jesus came to teach us that God is *our Father* and that we are God's children. He invites us to be in relationship with this God who truly loves us. We are invited to explore this relationship with God every day of our lives. We must also realize that we are dependent upon God and that he is the source of our life. Jesus tells us that we must become like little children so that we may be open to the many possibilities and wonders that a relationship with God provides for us.

MARY CAME TO LA SALETTE and calls us her children. She does not call the two shepherds by their names but she calls them, *"my children."* Her message was not just for Maximin and Melanie but it is also for us, her children. Mary comes to remind her children that we have turned away from her Son and have lost our innocence because of our choosing to sin. She challenges and invites us to again enter into a relationship with God. She herself is a mother who suffers because of her children. But she is also a mother who deeply loves her children and wants the best for them.

Reflection Questions:

• How open are you to the presence of God in your life?
• Do you allow yourself to be God's little child? Mary's child as well?

Wednesday, August 10, (#618)
St. Lawrence, Deacon and Martyr

John 12: 24-26: *"Anyone who loves his life loses it; anyone who hates his life in this world will keep it for eternal life."*

Meditation:

Jesus spent his three years of public ministry on earth teaching by word and example. His was a fully integrated life. Jesus life and "day job" were intimately united in his mission, given to him by the Father. He was called to do the Father's will in all things. His was a basically simple message: God loves you; therefore share that love with others. Yet there are seeming contradictions in his message as evidence in the "sayings" Jesus used in the gospel for today: *"Anyone who loves his life loses it; anyone who hates his life in this world will keep it for eternal life."* These are not conundrums given to us to confuse us but rather truths that seem contradictory but are actually visions of life that we must appreciate, absorb and live. On this feast of St. Lawrence, we remember the absolute dedication of Lawrence who, in the most difficult circumstances, remains true to the vision and message of Jesus.

ON THE MOUNTAIN OF LA SALETTE, Mary mentioned – in the most prophetic language and in the most simple of words – that Jesus wants us to follow him each and every day. We are to strengthen and increase our faith by feeding it with God's Word and Sacrament and by doing those things that will keep our faith alive; that is, daily prayer, regular Sunday Eucharist, Lenten habits of faith and making the message of Jesus (and Mary) known. This is our basic Baptismal call, our mission in this life. If we do this, then, we will lose our life in order to save it; we will keep our life eternally if we "hate (or look beyond)" our life in this world.

Reflection Questions:

• When have you said or done things of which the Lord would be proud?
• In what ways have you lived out the vision of Jesus words: "Anyone who loves his life loses it"?

Thursday, August 11, (#416)
Nineteenth Week in Ordinary Time

Matthew 18:21 to 19:1: *"Lord, how often must I forgive my brother if he wrongs me? As often as seven times?"*

Meditation:

To forgive is not easy. It is difficult in two ways. We find it hard at times to ask for forgiveness because we do not want to be reminded that we do things that need to be forgiven. It is often embarrassing to admit that we did something wrong. Sometimes pride will also get in the way of our seeing the need to be forgiven. And there are times when we justify what we have done and so do not see the need to ask for forgiveness. On the other hand it is also difficult to forgive people, especially if they have hurt us deeply or if they seem to continuously hurt us. Peter's question seems very logical to us: How many times should I forgive someone who sins against me? There are times when we find it hard to forgive because we believe an injustice has been done to us and we want the offender to pay the price. If we do not like the person who is asking for forgiveness, we tend not to be very merciful. But why should we forgive or ask for forgiveness? Jesus teaches that forgiveness is an integral part of our spiritual life. We find the strength to forgive because God has forgiven us so much. When we receive forgiveness it helps us grow as persons.

THE LA SALETTE EVENT reminds us that we are in need of forgiveness. Mary mentions the way that we have chosen not to be in union with her Son. The result of all this is various hardships, even death. The Beautiful Lady reminds us that this does not have to be the case. *"If they are converted, the stones and rocks will become mounds of wheat, and the potatoes will be self-sown in the fields."* By admitting our need for forgiveness and reconciliation, we open ourselves to the peace and joy that God's forgiveness and mercy bring us.

Reflection Questions:

- How forgiving are you?
- Do you see the act of forgiving as something that is life giving?

Friday, August 12, (#417)
Nineteenth Week in Ordinary Time

Matthew 19:3-12: *"Let anyone accept this (teaching) who can."*

Meditation:

If we are to be true followers of Christ we must be open to the whole Gospel message. We cannot pick and choose what we think is important and disregard the rest. To accept a teaching requires openness to someone else's point of view. We must be good listeners so that we can focus on what is being presented to us. The Pharisees were not open to Christ and his teaching because they were too absorbed in their own point of view and were thus unaccepting of what Christ was presenting. To accept Christ's teaching means that we must put it into practice in our lives. It must become a part of who we are. It is not enough to say that we believe what Christ teaches, but it is necessary to witness to that teaching by living it in our lives.

THE WEEPING MOTHER AT LA SALETTE reminds us that many times we fall short of being a listener or follower of Christ. *"If I would not have my Son abandon you, I am compelled to pray to him without ceasing; and as for you, you take no heed of it."* Mary underscores the importance of listening to the Word of God in our lives. We are asked to take heed of what is being proclaimed to us, to share that Word with others, and to allow that Word to live in our own hearts. We may choose to be deaf at times, but it is hard to be blind to the tears of a mother who loves us and her Son so deeply.

Reflection Questions:

- How open are you to the Word of God?
- How do you live the Word of God in your daily life?

Saturday, August 13 (#418)
Nineteenth Week in Ordinary Time

Matthew 19:13-15: *"Let the little children alone, and do not stop them from coming to me; for it is to such as these that the kingdom of Heaven belongs."*

For Your Reflection:

The Gospels portray Jesus as being a very approachable person. He had a way of making people feel at ease and was able to make people feel very welcomed. Jesus not only treated children that way but anyone with whom he came in contact. He wanted nothing to hinder people from being touched by the presence of God made human. Everyone was able to approach him, even the dreaded and hated Roman Centurion. Jesus gives us a very good example of how we should be open to our brothers and sisters with whom we come in contact every day. It is through our openness to the presence of Jesus in our brothers and sisters that we become more aware of the kingdom of God growing in our midst.

"**COME NEAR, MY CHILDREN, DO NOT BE AFRAID.**" These were the first words spoken by Mary at La Salette. It was more than an invitation. Mary was letting us know that she too was approachable just like her Son. She wants to be with us and encourages us to spend some time with her and her Son in prayer. Mary's first concern for Maximin and Melanie was to remove their startled reaction at seeing the bright light, "as though the sun had fallen there in the ravine." One of the charisms of La Salette is hospitality. We are asked to follow the example of Mary in inviting the poor, the marginalized of society, the refugees, the sinners, and the unwanted to "come near" in order that they may experience God's love and mercy.

Reflection Questions:

- How open are you to other people?
- Do you allow people to approach you?

Sunday, August 14 (#120)
Twentieth Week in Ordinary Time

(Jeremiah 38:4-6, 8-10; Hebrews 12:1-4; Luke 12:49-53)

Meditation: *Oh, the Shame!*

When you think about it, it's odd that Mary at La Salette should have worn a crucifix. The cross was an instrument not only of torture but of shame, as the letter to the Hebrews acknowledges very clearly: "Jesus endured the cross, despising its shame."

Crucified with real criminals near an entrance to the city, helpless, mocked, naked to the eyes of every passerby, Jesus suffered such humiliation as we can scarcely imagine. This was part of the "baptism with which I must be baptized," as we read in the gospel.

The crucifix is, however, central to the Apparition. Six times the Beautiful Lady speaks of "My Son." That Son is the crucified Christ, here as close to her heart as when he was laid in her arms after his death. She weeps as she did then.

Mary visits Elizabeth

The shame now is that her People seem no longer to care about the suffering and indignity he endured for their sake. His name has so little importance that it is used as a swear word. The Eucharist of his Body and Blood is treated with neglect or as an object of mockery.

The image of Jesus crucified is the most powerful symbol of God's love for us. But Jesus himself recognized that many would reject him, and that faith in him would lead to division. This is no less true today than it was then.

There is no shame in being a disciple of Jesus. People are naturally shocked by any scandal in the community of believers that is the Church, and at times one might even be embarrassed to "admit" to being Christian.

Maybe this is one of the reasons why many Christians wear a cross, "the emblem of suffering and shame," as the song goes. We know we are not worthy of the great gift Jesus won for us. He endured the cross "for the sake of the joy that lay before him," a joy that surely includes us.

Mary wept over us at La Salette. Let us so live as to console her afflicted heart. That is the best way to respond to the shame her words might otherwise inspire.

Monday, August 15, (#622)
The Assumption
of the Blessed Virgin Mary

Luke 1:39-56: *"My soul proclaims the greatness of the Lord... because he has looked upon the humiliation of his servant... the Almighty has done great things for me. Holy is his name, and his faithful love extends age after age..."*

Meditation:

Erasmus, priest, great teacher and theologian once said "Humility is truth." Further expounding on the saying, St. Vincent de Paul added: "Humility is nothing but truth, and pride is nothing but lying." There is a basic worth in being humble, in knowing yourself so well that you need no external façade to hide who you really are. Mary seemed to be a truly humble person. The words of her *Magnificat* seem to say as much. *"My soul proclaims the greatness of the Lord ...because he has looked upon the humiliation of his servant... the Almighty has done great things for me. Holy is his name, and his faithful love extends age after age..."* Her words belied her inner attitude: I thank God for all that God has done for me. I have simply followed God's will and God has blessed me abundantly. On this Feast of Mary's Assumption, isn't it most fitting that she "was taken up body and soul into heavenly glory" (*Catechism of the Catholic Church*, #966), so sinless was she.

MARY AT LA SALETTE shows who she truly is in her attitude of compassion, graciousness and patience. She welcomes the children and dispels their fear. She changes her dialect when she realizes that the children have trouble understanding her. Her connection to their families and their plight (concerning food for the winter) is so touching and tender. She is truly the humble Mother of the Church, caring for us and praying for us "without ceasing."

Reflection Questions:

• How honest and forthright are you in expressing your thankfulness to God and others for what they have done for you?

•Who for you is a truly humble person in your family and acquaintances?

Tuesday, August 16, (#420)
Twentieth Week in Ordinary Time

Matthew 19:23-30: *"Who can be saved, then?"*

Meditation:

The disciples put a very interesting question to Jesus. They seemed to think that a person could be able to do something that would help them to be saved. Jesus answer is that, by and of ourselves, we will find it impossible to be saved; but for God all things are possible. It is when we are willing to open ourselves to the salvific power of Christ that we realize that our salvation is a gift from him. It is Jesus himself who saves and there is nothing we can do for our salvation unless we are united with him. Christ offers this salvation to all people. We have the choice to cooperate with him in working out our personal salvation and that of the world. When we choose to unite ourselves with Christ, it is then that we accomplish the most good.

MARY CAME TO LA SALETTE to ask us to return to her Son because he is the source of our salvation. She points out to us that when we tried to accomplish things on our own, we did not succeed too well. Only if we are converted will we experience the new life. It is in this conversion that we discover the presence of God in our lives and in that of others. It is in our union with her Son through prayer and in following his way of life that we are able to realize that we are a People saved by Christ.

Reflection Questions:

•Are you aware of the presence of Christ working in you?

•How are you an ambassador of Christ's reconciliation in today's world?

Wednesday, August 17, (#421)
Twentieth Week in Ordinary Time

Matthew 20:1-16a: *"Why should you be envious because I am generous?"*

Meditation:

The workmen in the parable seem to have a legitimate complaint against the owner of the vineyard. After all, they worked all day long and received the same pay as the man who only worked for an hour. But that was the agreed wage. The owner has a right to do with his money as he pleases. And so if he chooses to be generous to one person, why should the other man complain? Jealousy and envy are often caused by a preconceived idea of an injustice or unfairness being done to us. If someone else has been blessed this way, then I should be blessed that way also. By looking at others' blessings, we can sometimes overlook God's graciousness. And, in reality, God has blessed us all with different gifts and talents.

Mary's message at La Salette attempts to take us from our own little world to an awareness of a world that has hunger, injustice, the death of children and alienation from God. Mary challenges us to use the gifts and talents with which God has blessed us to change this world. When we become aware of the suffering around us, how can we be envious of others? How can we not be generous and share the blessings we have received in our lives? Mary's tears are an indicator of not only her own suffering but of the suffering of our brothers and sisters as well. It is our own generosity that can help to dry these tears.

Reflection Questions:

- Are you grateful for the blessings that God gives you?
- How generous are you with your time and talent?

Thursday, August 18, (#422)
Twentieth Week in Ordinary Time

Matthew 22:1-14: *"For many are invited but not all are chosen."*

Meditation:

God's invitation to the kingdom is extended to everyone. God does not choose the elect. They are those people who decide to accept the invitation to build the kingdom of God. It is not enough to say that I believe in God, but we must put our faith into action. Jesus said that not everyone who says, *"Lord, Lord"* will enter the kingdom of God. But the one who does the will of God will enter hoe us to be an active participant in the kingdom of God we must seek to do the will of God and not our will. Each and every one who decides to be a part of the kingdom must use the talents and gifts God has given them to help build up the kingdom of God on earth. Through our lives we must witness to the presence of God's kingdom among us. Let our prayer be, *"Your kingdom come. Your will be done."*

THE INVITATION to be part of the kingdom is offered again at La Salette. The invitation is to draw near to Jesus and his mother, Mary. Mary, as taught by the Second Vatican Council, is the model of the Church and she teaches us how we are to build the kingdom of God. Her appearance on the Holy Mountain gives witness to her concern for her children. She intercedes for us *"without ceasing"* so that we may willingly accept her Son's invitation to the kingdom. She hands on the work of reconciliation to us, **"Well, my children, you will make this known to all my people."** What a beautiful invitation for us to participate actively in the building of the kingdom of God.

Reflection Questions:

- What gifts and talents has God given you to use in the building of his kingdom?
- How do you use them?

Friday, August 19, (#423)
Twentieth Week in Ordinary Time

Matthew 22:34-40: *"Master, which is the greatest commandment of the Law?"*

Meditation:

What a question to ask if you are trying to trip someone up! It is a good question to ask if you are looking for an argument. But Jesus gives the only answer that leaves no room for argument, *"You shall love the Lord your God with your whole heart, with your whole soul, and with all your mind ... You shall love your neighbor as yourself.*" To this very day, this response of Jesus is the basis of our religion and our faith. If we can truly live these two commandments then we will be fulfilling the law and the prophets as well. Jesus, in his own life, demonstrated how we should live these commandments. At the Last Supper he told us to love one other as he has loved us. We have much to learn from the way that Jesus loves us. Once we can accept his love in our lives, it becomes easier for us to love others.

MARY'S SOLICITUDE FOR HER PEOPLE when she appeared at La Salette is a wonderful example of how she loves us. She came pleading for us to return to her Son so that we may again open our hearts to the love that Christ has for us. She also encourages us to grow in our love for her Son. We are asked to turn away from sin, to be converted and to experience the life found in being in union with Christ. Her love for her people remains operative today. We invoke her as Our Lady of La Salette, Reconciler of sinners and she, without ceasing, continues to intercede for us.

Reflection Questions:

• How do you express for your commitment to the first commandment (to love the Lord your God)?
• How do you act on and live out the second commandment (love your neighbor as yourself)?

Saturday, August 20, (#424)
Twentieth Week in Ordinary Time

Matthew 23:1-12: *"Anyone who raises himself up will be humbled, and anyone who humbles himself will be raised up."*

Meditation:

We don't hear much about humility these days. Maybe it is because there seems to be a negative connotation connected with the word. A humble person is often seen as someone who has no backbone and lets other people walk over him. Humility is sometimes seen as degrading who we are. But the true meaning of humility is quite the opposite. To be a humble person requires that we accept ourselves as we are and like who we are. It means that we stop pretending to be someone we are not. We stop wishing to become someone cannot become. Humility demands a lot of honesty from us. Jesus had difficulty with the Scribes and Pharisees because they were presenting themselves as other than they really were. They were hypocrites. What Jesus is asking of us is to see ourselves as he sees us. That is true humility.

AT LA SALETTE Mary does not come looking for a place of honor but rather she comes to lead us to her Son. She is dressed as a working homemaker of the day — a woman who is desperately trying to keep her family together. She knows and understands that her Son is the source of our salvation and the fullness of our life. She understands that her role is to serve us by showing the way that leads to her Son. Mary encourages us to be true to the calling that we have received from God. She shows that we are badly mistaken in thinking that we do not need God. It is Mary's humility that gives her the place of exaltation as Queen of Heaven, *"If my people…"*

Reflection Questions:

- How do you live out these two commandments in your life?
- Do you accept yourself for who you are? Or would you rather pretend to be someone you are not?

Sunday, August 21 (#123)
Twenty-First Sunday in Ordinary Time

(Isaiah 66:18-21; Hebrews 12:5-7; 11-13; Luke 13:22-30)

Meditation: *Holy Mountains*

The phrase "Holy Mountain" occurs some twenty times in the Old Testament. It always means Mount Zion, site of the Temple and, by extension, Jerusalem (the "Holy City.")

In the New Testament we find it only once, in 2 Peter 1:18, referring not to Jerusalem at

all but the mount where the Transfiguration of Jesus took place.

For La Salette Missionaries, the "Holy Mountain" invariable refers to the place in the Lower French Alps where Mary appeared. The children first saw the Beautiful Lady in a small ravine between two mountains: Planeau and Gargas. After finishing her discourse, she climbed the slope of Planeau and disappeared. La Salette is the name of the nearest village, where the parish church was.

Isaiah prophesied the return of the exiles to God's Holy Mountain. On her Holy Mountain the Blessed Virgin invites a different sort of exiles to return, not to any particular place but to the Lord who makes holy any place of his choosing.

During his ascent to Jerusalem, Jesus uses the image of a "narrow gate" that we should "strive" to enter. This verb is much stronger than "try." It means making a strenuous effort, as in a contest of some kind. That the Christian life is just such a contest should come as no surprise.

Mary did not ask people to come to the Mountain where she appeared. They came spontaneously. What she did ask was for her people to return to her Son, to the practice of their faith. They were not, for the most part, atheists, but the return would require, for some at least, a certain "striving" against old habits and prejudice, an "uphill battle," we might say.

No narrow gate leads to La Salette, but a winding, narrow road. Once you get there, though, the effort is rewarded with a spectacular view that reinforces the sense that this Holy Mountain calls us to a higher life through a deeper faith.

The life of faith is often described as an ascent. The way can be steep and difficult, but that mountain is no less holy than Zion or La Salette.

Monday, August 22 (#425)
Twenty-First Week in Ordinary Time

Matthew 23:13-22: *"Alas for you, scribes and Pharisees, you hypocrites! You shut up the kingdom of Heaven in people's faces."*

For Your Reflection:

The verses in the gospel of today form the most terrible and most sustained denunciation in the New Testament. Here Jesus directs a series of Woes against the Scribes and Pharisees. Here we see the righteous anger that burns in the heart of love, a heart broken by the stubborn blindness of men. The word hypocrite occurs here again and again. It came to mean an actor in the worse sense of the term, "a pretender." A hypocrite is one who wears a mask to cover his or her true feelings, one who puts on an external show while inwardly their thoughts and feelings are quite different. To Jesus, the Scribes and Pharisees were men who were acting a part. He understood that their whole idea of religion consisted in outward and meticulous observance of the rules and regulations of the law but in their hearts, there was bitterness, envy, pride and arrogance. Jesus accused these men of being missionaries of evil. The abusive attitude of the Pharisees and Scribes was strongly criticized by Jesus. It is very clear that this list of indictments is not directed solely to Israel's leaders of generations past but is leveled at any false leadership in the Christian community of today.

"...AND AS TO YOU, YOU TAKE NO HEED OF IT." Even many years after the apparition at La Salette, blasphemy and hypocrisy still thrive in and around our homes and families. Many still do not believe in God. Many Catholics and Christians do not care to go to Mass or to pray. There is rejection of God and stubbornness everywhere. Many still abuse the name of God and scorn religion. We need to listen again to the message of the Blessed Mother and accept the challenge of bringing our society back to God and to his Son, Jesus,

Reflection Questions:

• Can you see any forms of blasphemy, hypocrisy or stubbornness in your life?
• How are you responding to Mary's call to conversion in your daily life?

Tuesday, August 23, (#426)
Twenty-First Week in Ordinary Time

Matthew 23:23-26: *"Alas for you, scribes and Pharisees, you hypocrites! You pay your tithe of mint and dill and cumin and have neglected the weightier matters of the Law – justice, mercy, good faith!"*

Meditation:

The Pharisees were so absolutely meticulous about tithes that they would tithe even for a little thing. And yet, these same men could be guilty of injustice. They could be hard, arrogant and cruel, denying the claims of mercy. They could take oaths and pledges and promises with the deliberate intention of forgetting them, violating all concept of fidelity. In other words, many of them kept the doctrines of the law and forgot the things that really matter. That spirit of duplicity is not dead and it won't be until Christ rules in people's hearts. There are many people who wear the right clothes to church, carefully place their offering in the collection basket and would not think of missing Mass. These same folks often do not do an honest day's work, are irritable and bad-tempered and can be cruel in their use of money. It is rather easy to observe all the outward signs of religion and yet be completely irreligious. Jesus tells us that these leaders greatest fault is a totally misplaced sense of priorities. Jesus vehemently condemns the disparity between one's heart and one's action – a challenge common to us to this very day.

"HOWEVER MUCH YOU PRAY, *however much you do, you will never recompense the pains I have taken for you."* Mary's call at La Salette is a call of agony, the call of heartbreaking pain of a loving mother. The lack of true faith, of a sense of sin, of the abhorrence of evil is pervasive in our world today. Those in power and authority perpetrate many abuses of justice and fidelity. The true sense of prayer is far from the hearts of many people. We need to pray. We need to become humble. We need to see that all authority and power come from God for the service and preservation of life. God is watching us and giving us the time to turn to him in humility and faith.

Reflection Questions:

- How sincere are you in your prayer?
- Are you sincere and humble in your dealings with others?

Wednesday, August 24, (#629)
St. Bartholomew, Apostle

John 1:45-51: *"You are going to see greater things than that."*

Meditation:

Is this still the age of miracles? Indeed, if we belief that Jesus can do great things, we should only be pleasantly surprised when prayers are answered and hearts are changed and healings happen, people come back to the sacraments. But we shouldn't allow our faith to rely on such wonderful graces from God. We should be faithful in both the green wood and the dry (Luke 23: 31). Jesus invited us to step out in faith and not depend on miracles for us to continue believing. Our vision should be that of "Taking up our cross", not "sitting at the right or left hand of God." Dedication and self-sacrifice is our motto for living. St. Bartholomew was martyred but little else in known of him. But his giving of his life for the faith is a model we can certainly follow as we meet the gifts and challenges of believing in today's world and urging others to follow our example of faith.

OUR LADY OF LA SALETTE brings to her children a mission of reconciliation and evangelization. She speaks of the importance of coming back to faith in her Son as central to daily living (reconciliation). She also leaves the children and us a mandate to "make her message known." Her simple words summarized well the gospel message of her Son: "love God, neighbor and self; baptize all people in the name of the Father, and of the Son and of the Holy Spirit."

Reflection Questions:

- What wonderful works of God (miracles or graces) have you witnessed in your life (or that of others)?
- What do you do to keep your faith alive?

Thursday, August 25, (#428)
Twenty-First Week in Ordinary Time

Matthew 24:42-51: "*... you too must stand ready because the Son of man is coming at an hour you do not expect.*"

Meditation:

We, the People of God, are responsible for the gift of life. We are called to make the best of it at each moment. There is no time to waste. We are reminded by Jesus to make good use of our treasure, time and talent in accor-dance with the golden rule and to be ready to render an account of our stewardship. Each hour of life here on earth is a gift from God and we could profitably see it as our last since no one of us is guaranteed the next. All of this is a call to fidelity and trustworthiness. An uncertain future holds no real terror if, as faithful and trustworthy servants, we care for our household with compassion, love and forgiveness.

Mary's message at La Salette is call to life, a call to make the best of life, with God's help. Mary was very much aware of the presence of evil in our world. At La Salette she points to the tragedies of infant mortality, famine and pestilence as a starting point on the road to conversion and reconciliation.

Reflection Questions:

• How can you show the Lord that you are trying to live for faith in the here and now?
• What have you done within your family or friends to encourage their life of faith or to strengthen their hope?

Friday, August 26, (#429)
Twenty-First Week in Ordinary Time

Matthew 25:1-13: "*So stay awake, because you do not know either the day or the hour.*"

Meditation:

The parable of the ten virgins is found only in the Gospel according to Matthew. Its story of two very different types of wedding attendants is an allegory on the need for alertness during the indefinite period of time before the end. Lack of vigilance costs the foolish bridesmaids entrance to the wedding celebration. There is some evidence in Jewish writings of the day that "oil" was a symbol of good deeds. If Matthew intended that symbolism here, then he would have neatly blended the two dominant themes of this section. Five of the virgins are wise because they have filled their lives with good deeds, the product of the wise use of the gifts of God. The lives of the foolish are empty and thus they are "unknown" to the Bridegroom. This parable is a call to make good use of our talents, blessings and gifts. Jesus reminds us to make the best of our lives even in the ordinariness of our day-to-day activities.

MARY'S CALL TO DO GOOD AND TO BE VIGILANT is very evident in her message at La Salette and in her life. Mary was always active in the service of others: for Jesus and Joseph, for the elderly Elizabeth, for the newlyweds at Cana. Mary was particularly active by her willing assent to events, to God's hand in her life. And Mary is still very active "spending her heaven doing good on earth."

Reflection Questions:

• Do you cherish the gift and the blessing of time given to you here on earth?
• Who has been a true blessing to you in your times of challenge or difficulty? Why not pray for them today.

Saturday, August 27 (#430)
Twenty-First Week in Ordinary Time

Matthew 25:14-30: *"Well done, good and trustworthy servant; you have shown you are trustworthy in small things; I will trust you with greater..."*

Meditation:

The parable of the talents continues the emphasis on the good use of time while shuttling back to the theme of fidelity. The good and faithful servants are those who are willing to risk their own security in using their gifts well. All are given generous gifts (even one talent is an enormous sum) but not all are willing to use them. The servant with the one talent lets fear smother his initiative and he must, therefore, stand accountable before his master. Fear had crippled the fate of the disciples in the boat in Mt. 8:26 and fear caused Peter to sink into the waves in 14:30-31. Here again, Matthew cites fear as the enemy of generous discipleship. Initiative and trustworthiness are very much expected from each one of us. In this parable of the talents, Jesus questions the stand of the Scribes' and Pharisees. Like the man with the one talent, they desired to keep things exactly as they were and for that they are condemned. It is not a person's talent that matters. What matters is how one makes use of it.

MARY RISKED HER OWN SECURITY in speaking her fiat, making it possible for the Incarnation to grace human history. Mary is a supreme model of responsible stewardship of her gifts and talents, of her life itself. This generosity permitted her to become the Mother of God and the Mother of all generations. Mary's call at La Salette to submission to the will of God is a call to risk our life for the sake of God's kingdom.

Reflection Questions:

- How is a person with fewer gifts able to avoid being jealous of the person with many?
- Who is a very gifted person whom you know personally?

Sunday, August 28, (#126)
Twenty-Second Sunday in Ordinary Time
(Sirach 3: 17-29; Hebrews 12:18-24; Luke 14:7-14)

Meditation: *Lowest Place*

Appearing in the French Alps, Mary did not choose the "lowest place," at least geographically speaking. She did, however, associate herself with lowly people—not just two ignorant children, but generally speaking with the people of the locality.

Life in the mountains has never been easy, That year, 1846, had been harder than usual. With

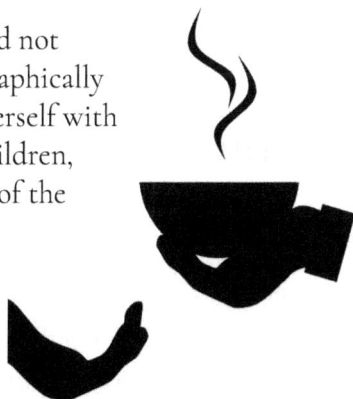

both the wheat and potato harvests blighted, the locals were rightly alarmed. Meanwhile, farmers in other areas with good crops began to hoard them, raising the prices beyond the means of the poor. Even Mr. Giraud, Maximin's father, who was relatively well off, was worried.

Our standard of living is important to us. As much as we admire St. Francis of Assisi or Dorothy Day for deliberately embracing poverty as a way of life, few of us are drawn to imitate them.

We might, under certain circumstances, be willing to accept some degree of decline in our fortunes. But we would not spontaneously "take the lowest place." Even people who decide to get out of the rate race and live more simply are usually in a position to guarantee that their desires and needs will be met.

Mélanie came from a desperately poor family. Her parents really had no choice when they sent her out. from the age of eight, to work on the farms in the region of Corps, making for one less mouth to feed, at least in the summer. Their house was at the far end of the poorest street in town. In a bigger city, it would have been a slum.

By choosing her, the Blessed Virgin in a sense lifted her out of that world, bestowed a dignity upon her that she could never have achieved. Who could have expected that her name would be remembered over one hundred years after her death?

Mélanie did not become rich. She relied on the kindness of others throughout her life. She could apply to herself the words of the Magnificat:" He has looked with favor on his lowly servant." Had she not been so lowly, she might never have been chosen.

Monday, August 29, (#634)
The Passion of St. John the Baptist

Mark 6:17-29: *"When John's disciples heard about this, they came and took his body and laid it in a tomb."*

Meditation:

John the Baptist is probably not someone we might think of inviting to dinner. He was a desert dweller and "wore a garment made of camel-hair with a leather loin-cloth round his waist, and his food was locusts and wild honey. (Matthew 3:4). In fact, he was a relative of Jesus, a prophetic figure, and had a great following of his own disciples.

One laudable quality of St. John the Baptist was that he knew God had called him to preach repentance for sin and he knew that he himself was not the Messiah. He is famously quoted as saying, *"I am not the Christ; I am the one who has been sent to go in front of him.".... (Jesus) must grow greater, I must grow less."* (John 3: 28,30) In our first reading, St. Paul's reflection applies well to the Baptist: *"God chose those who by human standards are fools to shame the wise; he chose those who by human standards are weak to shame the strong, . . . so that no human being might feel boastful before God."*

This feast itself, the Passion (or Beheading) of St. John the Baptist, is one of the oldest feasts in the early Christian church commemorating a saint. And the actual date of this event was probably in the years 28-29AD in Herod's fortified hilltop fortress at Machaerus, located in preset-day Jordan on the eastern side of the Dead Sea.

AT LA SALETTE, Mary was sent to share her Son's words of correction and mercy. Her unmistakable concern for us, her wayward children, is evident is her tears, her words and actions at La Salette. This feast of St. John the Baptist should stir within us a desire to be remind ourselves first, that we are called to make her message known, and second, to share her message of reconciliation with those around us with the deep compassion reflected by our Weeping Mother at La Salette.

Reflection Questions:

- Why not explore the facts (and perhaps the pictures) of our own baptism day?
- What celebration of Baptism did I most enjoy? And why?

Tuesday, August 30, (#432)
Twenty-Second Week in Ordinary Time

Luke 4:31-37: *"He gives orders to unclean spirits with authority and power and they come out."*

Meditation:

Each of Jesus' miracles should be seen as a sign that the kingdom had come in his own person. According to the popular belief of the day, mental illness was attributable to possession by evil spirits. The coming of Jesus' kingdom means that these evil spirits no longer have any power in the human domain. Luke draws on the Old Testament image of God's kingdom – a rule where God's will establishes peace, health, justice and forgiveness, a rule that will reign supreme in the Incarnate Word himself. God's rule is present in the deeds and teaching of Jesus. He acts with the authority of God to overcome the evil spirit. In Jesus, we claim victory over all and any evil spirits that exist in this world.

MARY IS VERY MUCH AWARE of the evil existing on earth. She recognizes the evil of oppression and hunger, social injustice, environmental disaster, the lack of faith in God, the lack of a sense of sin and much more. Our Blessed Mother is very much concerned about these evil situations. The call of Mary at La Salette urges us to turn away from evil and to reconcile with God through her Son, Jesus.

Reflection Questions:

• Are you sincerely working at making God's rule alive and present today?
• When have you (or someone you know) experienced an event of reconciliation?

Wednesday, August 31, (#433)
Twenty-Second Week in Ordinary Time

Luke 4:38-44: "... At sunset all those who had friends suffering from diseases of one kind or another brought them to him, and laying his hands on each he cured them."

Meditation:

Jesus was always ready to serve. Healing all kinds of illness and vanquishing all existing evil was the heart of his mission. Jesus had come to overcome the power of the devil and lead humankind towards the coming of the kingdom. Jesus is the Anointed One of the Father bringing peace, health, justice and new life on earth. Jesus has given that healing power to his apostles. In fact each one of us is given the power to heal to the extent that we believe and trust in Jesus, our master, and see him as the source of healing, justice and victory. In Jesus we find liberation from the sway of evil. In Jesus' ministry, the power of God undermines the power of evil that holds people captive.

MARY IS VERY MUCH AWARE of the evil in today's world. Actually her apparitions at La Salette, Lourdes and Fatima reveal her preoccupation with the spiritual blindness of her people. Her call to prayer and conversion is an appeal to use the power of Jesus in doing battle with the powers of evil.

Reflection Questions:

•How can you make God's presence and power real today?
•Are you aware of the challenges that will touch your life today?

Thursday, September 1, (#434)
Twenty-Second Week in Ordinary Time

Luke 5:1-11: *"Put out into deep water and lay out your nets for a catch."*

Meditation:

We see here a turning point in the career of Jesus. He leaves the synagogue and goes to the lakeside. Jesus went to places where people would listen to him. Fish and fishermen, fishing net and the shoreline are to become commonplace in the mission and ministry of Jesus. The call of Peter and his companions brings the focus of the Lord's ministry to the simple and ordinary folk. They in turn put much trust in this Nazarene. They observed him closely, asked their questions, followed his orders and advice and came to know the success of their new tide, *"fishers of men."* All those who are called to be his disciples and missionaries are likewise asked to risk their very selves for the sake of the Master. With Jesus around the catch is sure. Without the touch of the Master the mission is impossible. We are asked to evaluate the motives of our ministerial service. If it is rooted in our love for the Lord, energized by our trusting and risking in his name, then it will indeed bring forth fruit.

MARY WAS VERY MUCH AWARE of the mission of Jesus. From the time of her fiat response to the angel, she was never very far from his projects and concerns. She stood firm in her mission. She pleads at La Salette for the sake of her Son, Jesus. At Pentecost she rightfully assumes the focal point of the gathered apostles because she did everything for the sake of her Son and she trusted in him.

Reflection Questions:

- Whom do you know who has put out into the deep – that is, has taken chances in their life and succeeded well?
- When was the last time you did something nice "just for the love of it"?

Friday, September 2, (#435)
Twenty-Second Week in Ordinary Time

Luke 5:33-39: *"Surely you cannot make the bridegroom's attendants fast while the bridegroom is still with them?"*

Meditation:

Jesus was radically opposed to religion based on rules and the dutiful observance of them. He challenged this stand of the Scribes and Pharisees at every turn. They prided themselves on the strictest observance of the Law but Jesus could see that their hearts were far from the love of God. This pharisaic attitude still exists today. There seems to be in many religious people a passion for what is old. It is said that, in her wisdom and experience, nothing moves more slowly than the Church. However, the Good News proclaimed by Jesus was indeed news and the Pharisees could not adjust to this radically new approach of Jesus. This whole passage is Jesus' condemnation of the shut mind and a plea that people should not reject new ideas. We should never be afraid of adventurous thought. God is ever leading us into a deeper and wider appreciation of the truth in the power of the Holy Spirit. We should never be afraid of new methods in our approach to mission and ministry. In our own generation, Vatican II has given us new (not novel) approaches in understanding and living in the Church in the modem world. What might we expect from Vatican III?

MARY WAS A WOMAN who was aware of the situation, of the signs of the times. She fully supported the vision of Jesus. Mary was always open to the inspiration of the Holy Spirit. Her call at La Salette is a call to change, an opening to liberation, a call to new life in Jesus.

Reflection Questions:

- What is your attitude towards the changes in the community and the parish, in the mission and ministry?
- Are you open to change for the better?

Saturday, September 3, (#436) Twenty-Second Week in Ordinary Time

Luke 6:1-5: *"The Son of man is master of the Sabbath."*

Meditation:

The Pharisees and leaders were really after Jesus. The opposition was emerging very strongly. The immediate charge against Jesus, they found, was that he violated the law of the Sabbath. The Jewish law states that on the Sabbath it is forbidden to reap, to thresh, to winnow and to prepare food. We see that technically the disciples had broken each of these. To us the whole thing seems fantastic; but we must remember that to a strict Pharisee this was deadly sin. Rules and regulations had been broken. For them this was a matter of life and death. This passage contains a great general truth. Jesus said to the Pharisees, "Have you not read what David did?" The answer was of course "yes." But they had never understood what it meant. It is possible to read Scripture meticulously, to know the Bible inside out from cover to cover, and yet miss its real meaning. They did not bring to the reading of their Scripture an open mind and a needy heart.

JESUS VERY CLEARLY EMPHASIZES the fact that his mission of doing good and saving life is more important than mere Sabbath observance. Mary comes at La Salette to teach and instruct, to beckon with tears and to cajole with maternal love that we open our minds to a new understanding of our Faith and let our hearts be touched and healed. Her entire life was dedicated to making the saving plan of God come true. She is still at work in manifold ways to bring humankind back to the love, mercy and salvation made available to us in and through

Jesus Christ.

Reflection Questions:

- Why did the Pharisees "miss the forest for the trees"?
- Do you know any people who seem to get caught up in the little things of life (or maybe even you) and miss the important events?

Sunday, September 4 (#129)
Twenty-Third Sunday in Ordinary Time

(Wisdom 9:13-18b; Philemon 9-10,12-17; Luke 14:25-33)

Meditation: *Terms of Peace*

The first part of today's Gospel is confusing. The Commandments tell us to honor our parents. How can Jesus tell us to hate them?

The second part, which at first may seem to have little to do with the first, actually affords a clue. We can rephrase the entire text in this way: How willing are we to live our faith to the full? That same question is raised at La Salette. Mary saw that her people were very far from living their faith, and so she wept.

The image of the king who "sends a delegation to ask for peace terms" is enlightening. In the prophets there is a similar image, not of war but of a legal action. There are passages where God confronts his people as in a court of law.

Micah 6, for example, famous for the invitation to "walk humbly with your God," presents just a setting in the preceding verses. "The Lord has a case against his people, he enters into trial with Israel."

Verses 9-12 express God's sentence, and we find astonishing echoes of it in the Message of La Salette. One example: Mary says, "If you have wheat you must not sow it. Anything you sow the vermin will eat, and whatever does grow will fall into dust when you thresh it." Micah says, "You shall sow yet not reap, tread out the olive yet pour no oil, crush the grapes yet drink no wine."

Fortunately that is not the final word. In Isaiah 1:18-19 we read: "Come, let us set things right, says the Lord: though your sins be like scarlet, they may become white as snow... If you are willing and obey, you shall eat the good things of the land."

Now we may return to the first part of the Gospel, Jesus is saying that our faith in him comes first, above everything—and everyone—else. But for those who live faith to the full, there is no either-or. By its very nature, faith is inclusive.

Reconciliation, at the heart of La Salette, is the ultimate goal of God's "legal action" and of our decision to "ask for peace terms." Nothing is to be gained by fighting against God (Cf. Acts 5:39).

Monday, September 5, (#437) Twenty-Third Week in Ordinary Time

Luke 6:6-11: *"Is it permitted on the Sabbath to do good, or to do evil; to save life, or to destroy it?"*

Meditation:

In today's Gospel, opposition to Jesus has become quite open. The Scribes and Pharisees are looking for something to use against him. Jesus might just as well have cured the man with the withered hand the next day; but he broke the Sabbath law to teach us something very important: namely, that it is always permitted to do good on the Sabbath. *"Is it lawful to do good on the Sabbath – or to do evil?"* This question must have struck home to his listeners: while Jesus was seeking to restore life, the scribes and Pharisees were doing all they could to destroy Jesus.

AT LA SALETTE, Mary wept because her children had gone astray and no longer sought to follow the ways of her Son. Her very presence on that mountain in the French Alps makes us realize that she always sought to carry out her Son's wishes. Mary knew what Jesus was about and she pleaded with her children to return to him. Her tears conveyed to Melanie and Maximin how serious her message was. Her gentle voice told them of her deep love for them.

Reflection Questions:

• In moments of indecision, do you stop and ask, "What would Jesus do?"
• Do you seek to do good in every aspect of your life?

Tuesday, September 6, (#438)
Twenty-Third Week in Ordinary Time

Luke 6:12-19: *"Jesus went onto the mountain to pray; and he spent the whole night in prayer to God."*

Meditation:

Jesus was about to make a very important decision, one that would have consequences even to our day. He was about to choose twelve men to be his intimate followers. Much would be asked of them: to give up families and work, their personal desires and goals, to follow a man none of them fully understood. It would require a tremendous leap of faith. Before inviting them, Jesus spent the night in conversation with his Father. Together they would decide whom to invite.

At La Salette, Mary asked the two children if they prayed well. Immediately they responded, "Not very well, Madam." Mary must have smiled at their complete honesty. Perhaps that is why they were chosen. Mary then told them, "But you must pray well, my children." Mary knew the power of prayer. She knew how conversing with the Father gave her Son courage and strength in the darkest moments of his life. Mary knew there would be dark moments in the lives of Maximin and Melanie. There will be dark moments in our lives as well. Whether dark or light, prayer seeks to put us in touch with God at every moment.

Reflection Questions:

- "Do you pray well, my children?"
- When is it hardest for you to pray?

Wednesday, September 9, (#439)
Twenty-Third Week in Ordinary Time

Luke 6:20-26: *"Blessed are you who are poor..."*

Meditation:

Jesus knew that we all have a craving for things. And if we set our hearts on obtaining the things our society values most, we might get them – but it might be all we get. On the other hand, if we set our hearts on being loyal to God, we may run into all kinds of difficulties, but Jesus calls us blessed. Will we concentrate on the world's rewards or will we concentrate on Jesus? In taking the world's way, we will have to abandon the values of Jesus. And if we take Jesus's way, we will have to abandon the values of the world. We can't have it both ways.

AT LA SALETTE, Mary chose to appear to two humble cowherds. Melanie lived in a one-room house with her grandmother, while Maximin lived a very simple life with his father. They had acquired very little in life. Perhaps Maximin's most prized possession was his dog, Lulu. When Mary appeared to them, it was like nothing else that had ever happened in their lives. It was certainly not something they expected, and certainly not something they "earned." It was grace. It was blessing – the kind of blessing God bestows on the poor.

Reflection Questions:

- Do you ever find yourself believing that a certain amount of money would solve all your problems - or all society's problems?
- How have you experienced beatitude blessing in your life?

Tuesday, September 8, (#636)
The Nativity of the Blessed Virgin Mary

Matthew 1-16,18-23: *"... the Lord had spoken through the prophet (Isaiah): Look! the virgin is with child and will give birth to a son whom they will call Immanuel, a name which means 'God-is-with-us'."*

Meditation:

Pope St. John Paul II, in the introduction to the Vatican's 2001 *Directory on Popular Piety and the Liturgy: Principles and Guidelines*, explains that "Popular piety is an expression of faith which avails of certain cultural elements proper to a specific environment... Genuine forms of popular piety, expressed in a multitude of different ways, derives from the faith and, therefore, must be valued and promoted. Such authentic expressions of popular piety ... predispose the people for the celebration of the Sacred Mysteries."

Indeed, popular piety is seen as "a true treasure of the People of God"

(*Directory*, #59). The Directory, in chapter five, discusses extensively "the veneration of the Holy Mother of God, which occupies a singular position both in the Liturgy and popular devotion."

At La Salette, Mary showed how much she loved her Son and how closely she expressed his wishes for us to follow him. On this celebration of the birth of Mary, we are reminded among other things that, as William Wordsworth wrote in 1822 in a sonnet entitled "The Virgin", Mary is "our tainted nature's solitary boast." She is Mother of Jesus and, as St. John the evangelist described about Jesus on the cross, he gave his mother to us all and she is indeed Mother of the Church.

Reflection Questions:

- What do we especially admire about Mary at La Salette?
- What is our favorite Marian prayer or devotion?

Friday, September 9, (#441) Twenty-Third Week in Ordinary Time

Luke 6:39-42: *"Why do you observe the splinter in your brother's eye and never notice the great log in your own?"*

Meditation:

Jesus's message here seems blunt and unmistakable. We have no right to criticize since we are not free of faults. How quick we are to notice the faults of those around us. They seem so obvious. A poet once said, "There is so much bad in the best of us and so much good in the worst of us that it ill becomes any of us to find fault with the rest of us." These are surely good words to live by, for in the *Our Father* we ask God to forgive us our failings in the same way that we forgive the failings of others. We need to leave judgment to our heavenly Father, for he sees the complete picture while we often see only a small part of the reason behind another's actions.

At La Salette, Mary shed tears of sorrow. Melanie would later state, "She wept all the while she spoke to us." Our Blessed Mother told Melanie and Maximin, *"If my people do not obey, I shall be compelled to let go of the arm of my Son. It is so heavy that I can no longer restrain* *it.*" It is our own lives she asks us to reflect on and not the faults of others.

Reflection Questions:

- Do you often judge others?
- How often do you criticize your neighbor while failing to see your own shortcomings?

Saturday, September 10, (#442)
Twenty-Third Week in Ordinary Time

Luke 6:43-49: *"Good people draw what is good from the store of goodness in their hearts; bad people draw what is bad from the store of badness. For the words of the mouth flow out of what fills the heart."*

Meditation:

We cannot be judged in any way but through our deeds. Our actions indeed speak louder than our words and leave impressions long after our words are forgotten.

On January 23, 1998, a fence which for 163 years divided graves in a city cemetery in Jasper, Texas, was taken down. The ministers in that town had often spoken of racial harmony, but when loved ones were buried, the blacks were always on one side of the fence and whites were on the other side. That fence made sure that even in death blacks and whites would be separated.

But on that chilly January morning, as members of the town gathered in prayer, that fence was torn down. Perhaps the tearing down of an old iron fence in a small cemetery seems insignificant in this country's battle with racism and segregation; but to the people of that community, it was an important symbol of good people producing goodness from the good in their hearts.

THE MESSAGE OF LA SALETTE was not merely for the people living in that small hamlet high in the French Alps. It was a message of God's deep love and Mary's great concern for all people in all places. Mary spoke of "a great famine coming," in which "people would pay for their sins through hunger." There seems to be such a hunger today for genuine equality in our society where all people, regardless of race or religion, have the same opportunities and the same freedoms. And that hunger seems to be of God.

Reflection Questions:

- By your actions, do you speak words of peace or of discord, of equality or of racism, of justice or of injustice?
- Which is "abundant" in your heart?

Sunday, September 11 (#132)
Twenty-Fourth Sunday in Ordinary Time

(Exodus 32:7-11,13-14; 1 Timothy 1:12-17; Luke 15:1-32)

Meditation: *The Art of Persuasion*

Verse 12 of today's reading from Exodus is omitted in the Lectionary. It reads: "Why should the Egyptians say, 'With evil intent he brought them out, that he might kill them in the mountains and wipe them off the face of the earth'? Turn from your burning wrath; change your mind about punishing your people."

Moses was not above saying to God, "What will people think?" implying that God had his reputation to worry about. This was not all Moses said, as the whole reading shows, but in his attempt to persuade God not to destroy his people, no tactic was ignored.

The Prodigal Son

We do the same thing, both in the public forum and in private. We try to show others the rightness of a course of action and the wrongness or danger of it opposite. It's not surprising that we find the same approach in the Message of La Salette.

Mary begins each of the two major sections of her discourse with "If." The first part focuses on the dreadful consequences "If my people refuse to submit." In the second she offers a vision of hope, "If they are converted."

In her own way she echoes the theme of today's Gospel, particularly the parable of the Prodigal Son. In effect she says, "See what happens when you turn away from God?—and when you return to him?" Or, to paraphrase Paul's words in the second reading: "Stop being blasphemers, respond to God's mercy."

Mary uses every means at her disposal: tears, complaints, promises, warnings, encouragement. As Moses did not hesitate to speak certain truths to God in order to save his people from God's wrath, so Mary did not hold back in her efforts to save us. The difference is that Mary is speaking to us. But she does say she has been "pleading constantly with her Son" for us, doesn't she?

No wonder our invocation to her reads: "Our Lady of La Salette, Reconciler of sinners, Pray without ceasing for us who have recourse to you."

That's us persuading her not to give up.

Monday, September 12, (#443) Twenty-Fourth Week in Ordinary Time

Luke 7:1-10: "*I tell you, not even in Israel have I found faith as great as this.*"

For Your Reflection:

Some years ago some Jewish refugees in Mexico expressed a desire for German pastries. The pastries were not essential, but they would be a treat. Rev. Oswald Goiter, a missionary to Mexico, went through extra trouble and expense to obtain these pastries. "But why did you do that?" someone protested. "They don't even believe in Jesus." Rev. Goiter responded, "But I do!" We do what we do because of our faith, a special gift from God. We are called to be people of faith.

THE LA SALETTE MESSAGE IS A CALL TO BE FAITHFUL AND FAITH-FILLED.

We are called to make the message known to the entire world. At all times we will need that special faith to carry out this message of La Salette.

Reflection Questions:

- Reflect on an example of where and how your faith has sustained you.
- Can you remember a time you performed an act of kindness because you are a Christian, regardless of the belief of the recipient?

Tuesday, September 13, (#444) Twenty-Fourth Week in Ordinary Time

Luke 7:11-17: *"The Lord said … to her, 'Don't cry.'"*

Meditation:

A little girl was late coming home from school. Her mother said, "Why are you late?" She said she met little Mary, and Mary was sad because she broke her favorite toy. The daughter said to her mother, "I helped Mary." "How could you help? What did you do?" "I sat next to her and held her hand, and we both cried." There is a time to laugh and a time to cry. Both are good. We learn from the Gospels that Jesus also wept. What do we say when someone approaches us and is crying? Our suggestion is to offer this prayer: "I wish I could change things for you. I wish I could do things. I can't. God never promised that I could. God only promised that I could love you and I do."

MARY WEEPING is that trademark of the apparition at La Salette. She weeps because she loves us. Mary invites us to weep – but more especially communicates the same message as Jesus – that is, to love.

Reflection Questions:

- When have you been touched to heart and began shedding a tear?
- When have you comforted someone in their time of sorrow?
- hands?

Wednesday, September 14, (#638)
The Exaltation of the Holy Cross

John 3:13-17: *"God (so) loved the world: he gave his only Son..."*

Meditation:

Often while watching a baseball or football game on television, we may see some scripture passages on signs that people hold up for all to see. Many see these as acts of a religious fanatic but we may be missing something good if we do that. In fact, "John 3:16", an oftenused bible citation is certainly a central passage of the New Testament. In fact, no other verse in the scriptures summarizes God's relationship with humanity in such a succinct way. First, God loves us abundantly. Second, the unimaginable extent of God's love is that God sent his only Son to live, and die, and rise – all for love of us! Thirdly, anyone who does believe in Jesus will be saved – and will be welcomed into heaven "for ever and ever." All this comes from this one remarkably short verse and gives us a great revelation and immense hope. In other words, the cross of Jesus does save us.

MARY AT LA SALETTE wore a crucifix on her breast during the apparition. The children stated that, during the entire apparition, the crucifix gave off tremendous light which almost overpowered everything else. The light from the crucifix was so bright that it was even difficult to see Mary. This unique La Salette crucifix was not only the central focus of the apparition. It was also the summary of the purpose of our lives. People later commented on the possible meaning of the symbols of the hammer and pincers that "floated" under the right and left arms of the crucifix on which the living and moving body of Jesus could be seen! The hammer seems to be symbolic of our sins, which hammer the nails into Jesus' hands. The pincers can be seen as our good and loving acts which mercifully remove the nails from the Lord's bloody hands.

Reflection Questions:

- What words or actions of yours have put the nails into Jesus' hands?
- What good actions of yours have removed the nails from his holy hands?

Thursday, September 15, (#639)
Our Lady of Sorrows

Luke 2: 33-35 (second option): *What the Old Man, Simeon, saw*

Meditation:

He was quite a man this "certain man" named Simeon. He as not only just, he was also pious, awaiting "the consolation of Israel and the Holy Spirit was upon him." He was so just and pious that the Holy Spirit had revealed something quite special to him: he would not die until he had seen the Messiah. The Holy Spirit, in fact, seems quite partial to Simeon. This is the only time Simeon is mentioned in the New Testament and three times in this passage he is associated with the Holy Spirit.

The Holy Spirit was upon Simeon, that is, the Spirit of God had come from above as a free gift to rest on Simeon, and his presence, recognized and heeded, made Simeon just and pious. There is a great deal of light for you and me in these verses. The revelation to Simeon is not of his own composition; it comes from the Spirit and it is this Spirit who is speaking to me through this old man. He is telling me that the Child he is holding in his arms is, in fact, the Lord and Savior...

It is good to recall that the Holy Spirit that gave old Simeon the power to believe is the very same Spirit that allows us to believe that Christ is alive within us. It is this same Spirit that gives us the strength to hope and cope and to live in fidelity to the word of God in our lives...

And so it is that an old man believed and ..prophesied about the Christ before Christ himself could walk and talk. Simeon... may have appeared only once in the New Testament but it was quite a walk-on.

At La Salette, the Spirit was at work in the two unsuspecting young witnesses. At first, Melanie said to Maximin: "...look at the pretty light over there!" Then they both approached the globe of light. He described: "At the beginning we saw nobody in that light. And then it lowered and we saw it part. And all of a sudden we saw a Lady in it. "We were both afraid", said Maximin, and Melanie dropped her walking stick in surprise. He assured Melanie, saying "Keep your stick, now! I hold onto mine and if she does us any harm, I'll give her a good whack!" But once Mary stood and welcomed them, their fear simply dissolved. They had a change of attitude, a change of heart.

The Spirit was now helping them listen to this Heavenly Messenger. And certainly, following the Apparition, their new ministry of "of making (Mary's) message known" they did with heartfelt sincerity, dedication and consistency. (Writers: Frs. Normand Theroux, M.S. and Ron Gagne, M.S.)

Reflection Questions:

• When have you been graced with the ability to deal with a surprising or challenging situation?
• Can you remember a situation where God's grace was evidently present in your own life or that of others?

Friday, September 16, (#447) Twenty-Fourth Week in Ordinary Time

Luke 8:1-3: *"(Jesus) made his way through towns and villages preaching and proclaiming the good news of the kingdom of God."*

Meditation:

Brother Juniper once asked St. Francis, "Teach me to preach as eloquently as you. I am not good with words." Francis replied, "I will teach you to preach more eloquently than I. Meet me tomorrow morning." Brother Juniper dutifully met Francis early the next morning. To Juniper's surprise, they began walking. They walked through the marketplace, smiling at the laborers, the merchants, the children. They helped an old woman carry her wash up a set of stairs. They walked and walked. Finally, an exasperated Brother Juniper asked, "Francis, when will you teach me to preach?" Replied the Saint, "Why, we *are* preaching but sometimes we may even need words!"

IN TODAY'S GOSPEL, Jesus invites us to practice what we preach – and to preach what we practice. What did Mary preach at La Salette? Prayer, reconciliation, penance; come to the Lord's table; don't abuse Jesus' name. Mary's homily at La Salette was an "action parable" – a mother weeping over the sins of her children. Action parables are positive gestures without words. Often our actions shine forth better than our spoken words.

Reflection Questions:

- What do you "preach" by the way you live your daily life?
- Do you remember any words or phrases in a sermon or in the scripture that got your attention?

Saturday, September 17, (#448) Twenty-Fourth Week in Ordinary Time

Luke 8:4-15: *"As for the (seed) in the rich soil, this is people... who... yield a harvest through their perseverance."*

Meditation:

The fact is, in Jesus's depictions of the Kingdom of God, a little goes a long way. A little yeast makes the whole dough rise; a little seed grows into a big tree; a few loaves feed thousands. If we catch onto this dynamic of the way things work with God, we understand the call to perseverance. The lack of signs of success often tempt us to give up. "What's the use? Look at the way the world is! Nothing changes; nothing does any good." But over and over Jesus calls his disciples to persevere. "It was never the big things," he seems to say. "It was never what you were doing; but what God is doing. Hang in there; keep your eyes fixed on God."

Mary's promises at La Salette sound very much like the promise of seed on good ground: stones turned into heaps of wheat and potatoes self-sown in the fields. That sounds a lot like the "hundredfold." So I think, "Maybe submission isn't so different from perseverance." Perhaps we will hear the call to conversion and perseverance throughout our lives. Perhaps that's "all it takes" to be disciples of Jesus!

Some Reflection Questions:

- What helps you "hang in there" when things look dark or useless?
- Have you noticed how God uses small things to bring about great results?

Sunday, September 18 (#135)
Twenty-Fifth Sunday in Ordinary Time

(Amos 8:4-7; 1 Timothy 2:1-8; Luke 16:1-13)

Meditation: *God or Mammon*

"Mammon" was not a god, but simply an expression meaning wealth or gain. To "serve mammon" means to be obsessed with wealth. Amos describes people putting profit ahead of religious duty.

The people who lived in the vicinity of La Salette in 1846 were neglecting their faith, too, but their obsession was not with wealth. It was with survival. Famine and infant mortality were foremost on their minds.

"No one can serve two masters"

Why, then, did the people neglect their faith? Recall that the French Revolution was still a living memory. Bishop de Bruillard, who approved the Apparition of Our Lady of La Salette as authentic, had been a "priest of the guillotine," secretly absolving the condemned as they mounted the scaffold. He knew first-hand the hostility of the revolutionaries toward religion.

Anticlericalism became dominant. Religion was for "elderly women," to use Mary's words. When men spoke of God, it was to abuse his name and mock the Church. No surprise, then, that neither Maximin nor Mélanie had had any religious education.

In such a world, the prevailing culture, combined with peer pressure, must have made it hard even to be a believer, let alone a practicing Catholic.

That is why Mary, while speaking at times in a boldly prophetic manner, is so gentle with the two children and opens up a prospect of hope for those who will return to the faith. Reconciliation is the goal.

As we read in St. Paul today, "There is one God. There is also one mediator between God and men, the man Christ Jesus, who gave himself as a ransom for all."

The tragedy is that, for a variety of reasons, including so much human suffering, many people are resisting, if not rejecting, that gift of redemption. They turn a deaf ear to the invitation to be reconciled with God and the Church. Still, there is hope. Otherwise, why would Mary have come to La Salette?

Monday, September 19, (#449) Twenty-Fifth Week in Ordinary Time

Luke 8:16-18: *"No one lights a lamp to cover it with a bowl or to put it under a bed. No, it is put on a lamp stand so that people may see the light when they come in."*

For Your Reflection:

In the "great commissioning" before his Ascension, Jesus told the disciples to "go forth, to teach and to baptize." In order to do that they had to be prepared and so do we. Jesus tells us that we are to be salt and light and leaven. We need the Lord's help in order to actualize that. "Apart from me you can do nothing." Our work is to reflect Christ, the "light of the world."

MARY AT LA SALETTE REMINDS US of our Christian duties. She deeply lamented the lack of enthusiasm for the Gospel that was so prevalent among her people. Prayer and worship are prerequisites for anyone, especially those involved in the Lord's work.

Reflection Questions:

• What type of light are you reflecting to others at this time in your life?
• Are you reflecting or deflecting the light of faith that was enkindled in you in Baptism?

Tuesday, September 20, (#450)
Twenty-Fifth Week in Ordinary Time

Luke 8:19-21: *"Your mother and brothers are standing outside and want to see you."*

Meditation:

We have always heard this passage with some conjecture. Jesus says that *"his mother and brothers and sisters are those who hear the Word of God and act upon it."* Certainly there were never any truer words, though, applied to his holy mother and the band of apostles who walked with him daily. These people were co-founders of the Church. Without their having perceived the reality of God's Word in their midst and proclaiming it, future generations would never have recognized or heard the Word.

FROM THE FOOT OF THE CROSS when Mary was uniquely entrusted to us and we to her, she has been our helper, our advocate and friend, and a true mother in all aspects. It is interesting to note that Mary wasn't asked by her Son to accept this role. But her *fiat* at the Annunciation allowed her to become both Mother of the Savior and Mother of the Church, born from the wounded side of Christ on the cross.

Reflection Questions:

- Do you understand Mary's role as "handmaid" of the Lord?
- Do you see yourself as a Christian who is modeled after her calling?

Wednesday, September 21, (#643)
St. Matthew, Apostle and Evangelist

Matthew 9:9-13: *"I came to call not the upright, but sinners."*

Meditation:

Sometimes we have certain expectations even before we meet someone. If they are millionaires, we might expect a person with obviously expensive clothes, an aloof attitude and an inflated self-image. However some of the richest people in the world in reality dress quite casually and are very affable and approachable. The Pharisees had definite expectations about how Jesus would act, with whom he would relate and eat a meal, and so on. Today we hear Jesus pointing out to the Pharisees that their attitudes needed adjusting. They were looking at some people with their own eyes rather than that of God. Jesus saw people – who were judged by some as "unworthy and to be avoided" – as persons who needed his love and forgiveness, much like the sick who need a doctor. The truth was that Jesus "came to call not the upright but sinners."

Mary at La Salette came, like her Son, to call sinners back to repentance, forgiveness and reconciliation. She was concerned about all her children and their needs, but especially those who had lost their way and needed to be welcomed back into the fold of the Good Shepherd. Her gestures and words were those of a tearful Mother welcoming back her wayward children – and doesn't that include all of us in some way!

Reflection Questions:

• How welcoming are you to those who have fallen away from active faith?
• Do you criticize or look down on them or are you as welcoming and encouraging as Mary at La Salette?

Thursday, September 22, (#452) Twenty-Fifth Week in Ordinary Time

Luke 9:7-9: *"So who is this (person) I hear such reports about?"*

Meditation:

Religion writers speak about a growing disinterest in "denominationalism." That term basically refers to the many brands of Christianity. The problem these days is that increasing numbers of people don't really care what denomination they belong to. Many change from one to another with increasing frequency. Herod, in our Gospel passage today, is interested in Christ because he was unique and not like the others. A generic, "feel good" Christianity is not what Jesus came to announce.

Our Lady of La Salette lamented indifference in religion and especially within the Catholic Church in regard to practices in prayer and worship. When we think of France in the 19th century we see a country where at least a majority of the people were baptized. But even then there were many "unchurched" and lapsed members. Coming to know, love and serve God is a genuine vocation.

Reflection Questions:

- How genuine is your commitment to the Catholic faith?
- Can you speak intelligently about it?

Friday, September 23, (#453)
Twenty-Fifth Week in Ordinary Time

Luke 9:18-22: *"But you,' he said to them, 'who do you say I am?' It was Peter who spoke up. 'The Christ of God,' he said."*

Meditation:

Our lives as believers are a continuous "proclamation of faith." We are expected to witness to Christ whether "convenient or inconvenient." The profession of faith in Jesus as Messiah and Lord on Peter's lips is also our own. We are often challenged by the voices of this world to proclaim our faith. The martyrs do this eloquently. They are beacons of strength for us who can be so weak. Through the Holy Spirit we are taught what to say and how we are to say it. Christ promises us that even our adversaries will not be able to refute us. Remember the most effective Christians are those who are committed to the cause of truth. The Church holds up for us great saints to give us an example of heroic virtue in the face of difficulties.

OUR LADY OF LA SALETTE spoke and wept about the way we miss living out our faith. She lamented our indifference to the life-giving sacraments of salvation. How sad indeed if we forget how to pray to the very Source and Center of our existence.

Reflection Questions:

- Who do you say that Jesus is? How do you show this in the way you live?
- From your life and actions, would anyone suspect that you are a Christians?

Saturday, September 24, (#454)
Twenty-Fifth Week in Ordinary Time

Luke 9:43b-45: *"You must have these words constantly in mind: The Son of man is going to be delivered into the power of men."*

Meditation:

There is something innate in us, which wants to have everything go our way, according to our plans. Simon Peter, for one, had other plans for Christ. Jesus, we are told, "remonstrated" with him. In other words, he showed Simon that he was wrong about his perceived goals. The prophet Isaiah says: *"'...for my thoughts are not your thoughts and your ways are not my ways', declares Yahweh. For the heavens are as high above earth as my ways are above your ways, my thoughts above your thoughts"* (Isaiah 55:8-9). God sees the big picture and His will is always for our continued growth and sanctity. We may not appreciate our own plans not being fulfilled but God's plans always seem to carry a blessing.

Our Lady at La Salette asks us to go a different course. She asks that we be "converted." To leave our former way of life and to seek to live according to God's way is truly revolutionary. To pattern our life after Mary's is a good way to do this. Though Mary cried tears of grief for us at La Salette, they are poignant reminders of how serious and important it is to live according to God's plan.

Reflection Questions:

• Do you resist the Gospel call to repentance?
• How have you come to experience that your greatest good is not necessarily the one you want?

Sunday, September 25 (#138)
Twenty-Sixth Sunday in Ordinary Time

(Amos 6:1a, 4-7; 1 Timothy 6:11-16; Luke 16:19-31)

Meditation: *Complacency*

These days one often hears the expression, "comfort zone." We settle into a set of opinions or way of life that is taken for granted, and we are not happy when it challenged.

The rich man of today's parable, and the rich persons described in the reading from Amos are so comfortable in their wealth and luxury that they care nothing about the misery outside their doors, assuming they are even aware of it. They are secure, complacent.

It is by no means only the rich who can become complacent. Anyone can become "contented to a fault," smug about some aspect of life, ready to let the rest of the world go by.

St. Paul tells Timothy to "compete" for the faith. No complacency there!

Amos and Jesus both use images intended to shake their listeners out of their complacency.

Mary at La Salette is within that same tradition. Her people had settled into a comfort zone where their more or less generic faith did not challenge them, a rationalism which took for granted that religion was for the unenlightened.

Gustave Doré illustrating the parable of *The rich man and Lazarus*

This attitude is reflected in the first reaction of the secular press to news of the Apparition, published in Lyons on November 26, 1846: "Well, here we go again! More stories of apparitions and prophecies!" The article goes on to present a completely trivialized account of the Apparition and the Message.

Even believers can become complacent, faithfully observing the religious practices that the Beautiful Lady specifically mentioned, but not grasping that these are intended to lead us to a deeper awareness, to see the world around us as Mary sees it and respond to it as she does.

Our Lady of La Salette speaks of the minimum daily, weekly and annual requirements of Catholic life, without which our faith cannot grow: prayer, Eucharist, Lent.

She does not even remotely suggest, however, that we complacently settle for the minimum!

Monday, September 26, (#455)
Twenty-Sixth Week in Ordinary Time

Luke 9:46-50: *"Anyone who welcomes this little child in my name welcomes me."*

Meditation:

Jesus had a great love for all people and especially for little ones. This famous scene often read at Baptismal celebrations shows Jesus welcoming the little children and telling the elders not to hinder them in their coming to Christ. As the Lord aligned himself with the lowly and the poor we are called to look upon all life as coming from God. In a world where many deny the very existence of God it takes much courage to proclaim his view of things. To welcome children is a great privilege. How important it is to transmit the faith to our youth!

MARY APPEARED AT LA SALETTE to two children. Of all possible messengers to communicate her words to the world, she chose unlikely candidates, poorly schooled and unconnected. Once again we see God's wisdom as very different from our own.

Reflection Questions:

- What is your attitude towards young people?
- Do you engage them in conversation and good example?

Tuesday, September 27, (#456)
Twenty-Sixth Week in Ordinary Time

Luke 9:51-56: *"They went into a Samaritan village to make preparations for him, but the people would not receive him because he was making for Jerusalem."*

Meditation:

REJECTION IS ONE OF THE MOST PAINFUL HUMAN EXPERIENCES. This can happen in interpersonal relationships; it can happen when one is overlooked for promotion at work. We are told in the Scriptures that the Messiah would be rejected. We should all be appreciative of the fact that "by his stripes we are healed." Through the Lord's sufferings, his passion and death, we are redeemed. He suffered in his own innocent body for us! No greater love has anyone than one who "lays down his life for his friends."

MARY CRIED AT LA SALETTE because the Gospel of her Son was being rejected, in fact, by the way people lived. Indifference and apathy towards religion was the rule of the day. If Christ has laid down his life for us how can we continue to be so unloving toward God?

Some Reflection Questions:

• How does it make you feel when you are rejected in one way or another?
• Can you identify with Christ and his mother who also have seen their love and concern for us rejected?

Wednesday, September 28, (#457) Twenty-Sixth Week in Ordinary Time

Luke 9:57-62: *"As Jesus and his disciples were making their way along, someone said to Jesus, 'I will be your follower wherever you go.'"*

Meditation:

We have to admire the enthusiasm of the "someone" who indicated to Christ his/her desire for discipleship. In today's Gospel passage we recall that others mentioned that they too wanted to follow the Lord but on their terms and according to their personal schedules. A Christianity of ease and convenience is not the faith of Jesus. One of the greatest dangers to the contemporary Church is the temptation to accommodate to the whims of our particular society. This can prove dangerous as the Gospel can he compromised and lose its force.

AT LA SALETTE we see the need to return to Gospel values and living. The practice of the faith as exhibited in the liturgy is made manifest in our living out of the Gospel imperatives. A lukewarm brand of Christianity leads nowhere.

Reflection Questions:

- In what way is my profession of faith "counter-cultural?"
- Have I ever done "the difficult thing," knowing this was where Jesus was calling me?

Thursday, September 29, (#647)
Sts. Michael, Gabriel
and Raphael, Archangels

John 1:47-51: *"Jesus replied (to Nathanael), 'In all truth I tell you, you will see heaven open and the angels of God ascending and descending over the Son of man.'"*

Meditation:

The word, *angel*, is derived from the Latin, *angelus*, meaning "messenger" and is indeed seen as a messenger of God. Our feast of the Archangels, Sts. Michael, Gabriel and Raphael, reminds us of God's protection of us, a mystical presence based on our belief that God oversees and guides us through the journey of life. In fact, many of us can point out people in our lives who, in one way or another, also do exactly that – watch over us lovingly.

In our gospel for this feast, we hear about Nathanael, who is described as "a genuine Israelite". The contemporary etymology of the name *Israel* was "one who sees God." He is promised a vision of heavenly things, and told that he will see "the angels of God ascending and descending over the Son of man."

AT LA SALETTE, Mary was sent to share her message with us. Yet we know that Mary could only be bringing the message of her Son, Jesus, and not her own. She had angelic qualities but was a very real human being who concern was expressed so touchingly in her gentle tears for her wayward and oftentimes ungrateful children. On this feast of the Archangels, we give thanks to God for watching over us on our journey back to the Father. We need to listen to the words of our Heavenly Messenger at La Salette and fulfill her mandate to make know her message of reconciliation to all her people, whenever the opportunity offers itself.

Reflection Questions:

- How has God protected you during your lifetime?
- Who has God placed in your life to watch over you?

Friday, September 30, (#459)
Twenty-Sixth Week in Ordinary Time

Luke 10:13-16: *"Anyone who listens to you listens to me; anyone who rejects you rejects me, and those who reject me reject the one who sent me."*

Reflection:

OUR CONNECTION WITH GOD is called "religion". Its Latin root means "to tie or bind." We are "bound" to God by hearing the Word of God and keeping it. In a world of many voices we have chosen to follow Christ's voice. We do not always reflect that in our daily dealings with people. Remember the Jewish elder in the Old Testament who simply said, "As for me and my house, we will serve the Lord." That should also be our response in the midst of all that the world seems to be saying.

MARY APPEARED IN AN OUT-OF-THE-WAY PLACE AT LA SALETTE. It was more a home to wild flowers, breathtaking scenery, sheep and cattle, than a home to humans. It was there that the Mother of Christ engaged and challenged "her children" to listen to the voice of God. Mary's tears are a result of earthly voices distracting the "other worldly." One of the Psalms in the Bible says, "If today you hear His voice, harden not your hearts." God's voice is all around us. We need to learn to hear it and then listen to it.

Some Reflection Questions:

- How is the voice of the Lord not being heeded in your town or city?
- Can Christ be rejected even by "his own" within the fold?

Saturday, October 1, (#460)
Twenty-Sixth Week in Ordinary Time

Luke 10:17-24: *"I bless you, Father, Lord of heaven and of earth, for hiding* *these things from the learned and the clever and revealing them to little children.”*

God's ways are not our ways. This theme is reiterated often in Scripture. It is also a great blessing. Think if God's ways were our ways! There is a huge difference between Divine Justice and human justice, between Divine Mercy and human mercy. Thankfully!

How interesting that children are often cited for having a perception of God that adults don't have. A priest once said that he thought children from their first moments until about five years old or so have an innate knowledge of God — only to lose it later. According to Jesus, children have a lot to teach us about God.

Mary in her merciful apparition at La Salette spoke to two poor children. They were unlikely candidates for this heavenly visitor. They were ignorant, impoverished, fickle and basically unchurched. They didn't know their prayers and were not known to be the best behaved in their families. Today they would probably be classified as coming from some “dysfunctional” roots.

Reflection Questions:

- What is your attitude towards prophets in your midst?
- Might you look to a child for Divine inspiration?

Sunday, October 2 (#141)
Twenty-Seventh Sunday in Ordinary Time
(Habakkuk 1:2-3; 2:2-4; 2 Timothy 1:6-8, 13-14; Luke 17:5-10)

Meditation: *Big Faith*

One doesn't usually think of faith as a quantity, and yet the Apostles ask Jesus, “Increase our faith.” We might have expected, “Strengthen our faith.”

Be that as it may, the phrase expresses Mary's reason for coming to La Salette. Her people's faith had become too small, puny even, virtually non-existent. How to make it bigger?

Jesus responds with the image of a mustard seed. Even a faith that tiny could accomplish wonders.

St. Paul uses a different image in his letter to Timothy. "Stir into flame the gift of God." In other words, don't let it die out. This too jibes perfectly with the Message of the Beautiful Lady.

Faith is indeed a gift. Some gifts we keep always with us or in plain sight. Others are stored in closets to be taken out for seasonal use. And some end up in boxes waiting for the "someday" when we will get to them.

There is a saying, "Reject the gift, reject the giver." Abuse of the Lord's name is a rejection. So is the failure to worship. It doesn't require much observation to see that we live in a world that, without much serious reasoning, is adopting a kind of rationalism that justifies that rejection. Believers often feel at a loss to respond.

If you have faith as small as a mustard seed, you can say to this mulberry tree, 'Be uprooted and planted in the sea,' and it will obey.

But this is precisely where the faith of those who do believe comes in. A faith response to Our Lady of La Salette goes well beyond simply believing that the Apparition actually took place. We are called to use the means at our disposal, very simple means really, not so much to make others believe as to help ourselves believe more fully, more deeply. Then we can begin to believe also in the power of faith. Then we can "stir into flame" the gift of faith until it becomes a blaze that, as with the burning bush in the book of Exodus, burns within us without consuming us.

Or to return to the image of the Gospel, we can ask the Lord to give us faith at least the size of a mustard seed. And then we can ask him to make it really big.

Monday, October 3, (#461)
Twenty-Seventh Week in Ordinary Time

Luke 10:25-37: *"Master, what must I do to inherit eternal life?"*

Meditation:

Our questions can have many meanings. Sometimes we question (challenge) authority or we question (doubt) another's sincerity or we question (inquire about) a motive. Sometimes a question is a test and really an effort to confuse the other, as the lawyer was attempting to do to Jesus here. And sometimes a question is really a statement, like Jesus's, *"Which of these three was the real neighbor?"* Jesus is saying that true Life is found in loving, and not in accumulating money or knowledge or by observing religious or social regulations. Indeed, prostitutes and tax collectors are among the first to enter the Kingdom. Why? Because they can love by squandering precious ointment or by giving back four-fold what they have stolen. Many of the rest of us just talk about love by asking many questions.

"**DO YOU SAY YOUR PRAYERS WELL, MY CHILDREN?**" A question from Mary at La Salette. Another question, *"Have you ever seen spoilt wheat?"* It's obvious that Mary is not looking for information here. She is trying to direct our attention to the fact that the Everlasting is aware of our life here and now and that Everlasting Life invigorates our earthly existence through prayer. Sharing in the Eucharist, keeping holy the Lord's Day, respecting the name of the Lord, observing the practices of Lent, saying at least an *Our Father* and a *Hail Mary* – these can all be an opportunity to pause and reflect, thereby becoming an invitation to do the loving thing.

Reflection Questions:

- Do you ask your "life questions" to the Lord?
- How can you live as a Christian disciple today?

Tuesday, October 4, (#462)
Twenty-Seventh Week in Ordinary Time

Luke 10:38-42: *"Mary ... sat down at the Lord's feet and listened to him* *speaking."*

We believe that doing the loving thing is the real ticket that gains admission to the Kingdom of God. Martha and Mary have gained Gospel fame over the centuries because they have helped distinguish between active and contemplative prayer, between the apostolic and contemplative consecrated lifestyles, or they have highlighted the legitimacy of different temperaments serving the Lord.

However, the real contrast here is not between activity and inactivity. Both Martha and Mary are doing something. One is busy about the matters of meal preparation and hospitality while the other is busy about the activity of listening and hospitality. And Jesus said that Mary has chosen the better portion. Why? This same Lord said elsewhere that whoever listens to the word of God and keeps it is true mother, brother and sister. Mary is very active in listening to her Lord. She is learning from him. She is doing heart-to-heart hospitality. She is seated at the feet of the Lord learning what "doing the loving thing" might mean for her.

WE KNOW THAT MARY, the mother of the Lord, listened well. She kept the word of her prayer and the word of her experience and *"pondered them in her heart"*. At La Salette, she continues to ponder as she listens to God and listens to the struggles and the suffering of her children. The result is tears and pleading, *"How long a time do I suffer for you... and as to you, you take no heed of it... I am compelled to pray to him without ceasing."* Yes, Mary is "doing the loving thing" for us and, like Martha's sister in the Gospel story, she has a direct connection to the heart of the Lord.

Reflection Questions:

• What are some of the ways that you listen to the word of God?
• What proportion of a typical day do you spend listening to God? What proportion do you spend in "doing things" for him?

Wednesday, October 5, (#463)
Twenty-Seventh Week in Ordinary Time

Luke 11:1-4: *"When Jesus had finished, one of his disciples said, 'Lord, teach us to pray.'"*

Meditation:

I wish I knew which disciple made this request of the Lord. That disciple was obviously close enough to Jesus to observe him at this very special activity. There must have been something attractive and compelling in observing Jesus in prayer. This disciple was moved to want the same thing. This disciple wanted the same peace, courage, strength, conviction, and clarity of vision and mission displayed by Jesus. This disciple was quite sure those gifts were granted in prayer. So, this disciple asks, *"Lord, teach us to pray."* In response, we were given the Lord's Prayer – an inexhaustible, life-long way to approach God in prayer. This disciple should be honored by all generations as the Patron Saint of Prayer.

*"*AH, MY CHILDREN, *you must be sure to (say your prayers) well, evening and morning, even if you say only an Our Father and a Hail Mary."* With this very simple and doable request, our Blessed Mother is giving us a formula for peace that will last a lifetime: God is our Father; his Name and Will are supreme; he is involved in our earthly lives (daily bread); a relationship with him means both giving and receiving forgiveness; and our faith assures our ultimate triumph over any adversity. In saying the *Hail, Mary*, we are taking literally Mary's words at La Salette. *"I am compelled to pray to (my Son) without ceasing."* Yes, she will be supporting us in that prayer at the two most important times of our lives – now, and at the hour of our death.

Reflection Questions:

• Where is your "certain place" to pray?
• Standing with Melanie and Maximin, let yourself hear the question, "Do you say your prayers well, my children?"

Thursday, October 6, (#464)
Twenty-Seventh Week in Ordinary Time

Luke 11:5-13: *"If you then, evil as you are, know how to give your children what is good, how much more will the heavenly Father give the Holy Spirit to those who ask him!"*

Meditation:

Our First World parents indulge their children in the excesses of consumerism such as have never before been seen. Yet we quickly see that such "good things" in themselves do not assure happiness. Certainly the "good things" of food, drink, clothing and shelter are necessary, but not worth the loss of our souls (Luke 12:18-19). For the Rich Man, they became the source of condemnation because he would not share with Lazarus at his door (Luke 16:25). However, we do know of loving and conscientious parents who would willingly sacrifice themselves to assure that their children have the necessities of life. "How much more" will the heavenly Father give? Luke says that he will give the Holy Spirit who assures intimacy with God as Father, a knowledge of his Will, and a desire to see a flourishing of his Kingdom. This Holy Spirit is given to those who ask, seek and knock. This same Holy Spirit is our eternal life.

LIKE MOST OF US, Maximin's father was a good person and a sinner. In the face of famine and deprivation, he would give his son his last piece of bread. Most probably he would have gone on to curse God and the famine when it came. But something happened. His scatterbrained son said that the Beautiful Lady mentioned him. The "farm at Coin" incident spoke of God's presence to a seemingly insignificant expression of fatherly love. This changed Mr. Giraud's life. He was given the Holy Spirit of conversion. He went to confession, went to Mass, and received Holy Communion for the first time in years. He was to do so every day for the rest of his life.

Reflection Questions:

- When and how have you asked for the Holy Spirit?
- How might you do so today?

Friday, October 7, (#465)
Twenty-Seventh Week in Ordinary Time

Luke 11:15-26: *"Anyone who is not with me is against me; and anyone who does not gather in with me throws away."*

Meditation:

Jesus declares himself to be the stronger one, the finger of God who casts out devils, the one in whose Sacred Heart the reign of God is found; and he rejects Beelzebul or any other source of spiritual or material power. And he asks us to choose. It's the choice of discipleship, a choice wherein we hear the words of Saint Paul, *"All things are yours... and you are Christ's and Christ is God's"* (1 Corinthians 3: 21-23). The vast sweep of vision contained in this verse reflects a direct line of order, a sense of possession and ownership that says our true meaning and purpose in life is in Jesus Christ, and no devil, no power for evil, can destroy the unity of that relationship. Vatican II would say it this way: "Jesus Christ is the goal of human history, the focal point of the longings of history and of civilization, the center of the human race, the joy of every heart, and the answer to all its yearnings" [*Gaudium et Spes*, 45].

"**IF MY PEOPLE WILL NOT SUBMIT**" begins Our Lady's plea at La Salette, urging us to seek the Lord while he may be found – in all places, at all times, and in all seasons. We certainly will find him in keeping holy the Lord's Day, in reverencing his Holy Name, and in sharing devoutly in the sacramental life of the Church. And we certainly find him in our sensitive and dutiful citizenship among the People of God, where famine, disease and the abuse of children scream for our attention and our efforts to build social and political structures that are just and equitable for all.

Reflection Questions:

• What problems do you find particularly vexing and challenging in your life of service to God and God's people? What can you do about them?
• Think of someone you know who needs God's help. Can you pray that God may help them today?

Saturday, October 8, (#466)
Twenty-Seventh Week in Ordinary Time

Luke 11:27-28: *"More blessed still are those who hear the word of God and keep it!"*

Meditation:

The quality of our discipleship needs constant attention. Parents are told at the baptism of their child that their word and example are essential for that baby to grow and "bring the dignity" of the new creation, symbolized by the white garment "unstained into the everlasting life of heaven." Similarly, they are given a lighted candle with these words: "Parents, this light is entrusted to you to be kept burning brightly." And so it is that many conscientious and loving parents embark on the grandest of vocations: to make their child's heart a most worthy and fertile receptacle for the seed of God's word. Those of us who have been blessed with such faith-filled parents can exclaim with the woman in today's Gospel passage, *"Blessed is the womb... !"*

But the burden of responsibility one day is passed on to another. Each of us reaches the point where we must discern for ourselves. Blessed as we have been with a Christian upbringing, we must see ourselves as a new creation, clothed in Christ. It is ultimately the daily routine of faithful obedience and the challenge of doing God's word today that deepens the light of Christ shining in our lives.

"**FOR HOW LONG A TIME DO I SUFFER FOR YOU.**" Mary is all too aware that the white garments of our Baptism have been soiled and our candles are often flickering. Thus, her tears flow. She knows that we have the capacity to give love and to receive love. She has seen us do it before. This is the "submission" to which she calls us. She has not given up on us. In fact, the purpose of her visit is to remind us that hearing the word of God and keeping it begins with honoring the Name of God and the Lord's Day. She can't do it for us, but she can remind us of what to do. And she prays for us without ceasing.

Reflection Questions:

- Do you tend to be smug in your religious pedigree, rather than perform the acts proper to discipleship?
- What will hearing the word of God and keeping it mean for you concretely today?

Sunday, October 9 (#144)
Twenty-Eighth Sunday in Ordinary Time

(2 Kings 5:14-17; 2 Timothy 2:8-13; Luke 17:11-19)

Meditation: *Living by Denial*

Today's second reading contains one of the New Testament's scariest thoughts: "If we deny him [Jesus], he will deny us.

Mary used a similar image at La Salette, in different words. "If I want my Son not to abandon you," she says, "I am obliged to plead with him constantly." The prospect of being denied or abandoned by Jesus is truly frightening!

The Gospel, on the other hand, is the famous story of the ten lepers healed by Jesus. At least one of them, a Samaritan, was not in good standing in the Jewish world and, like Naaman the Syrian in the first reading, had no reason to expect a Jewish healer to cure him.

One of the most unpleasant experiences we can have is to lose a friend over a disagreement or an offence. Sometimes, however, there is no dramatic event, just a drifting apart. This was Mary's concern at La Salette. Her people had lapsed into a certain indifference, not exactly denying Jesus, but far from proclaiming themselves his disciples.

In blaming God for their troubles—rotten potatoes in particular— they denied his goodness. In abusing his name, they denied his holiness. In "going to the butcher shops like dogs," they denied the importance of the passion, death and resurrection of Jesus.

The danger in all this denial is that we might be left to our own

Jesus Heals Ten Men With Leprosy

devices, as we read in Psalm 81, where God is so frustrated with his people that he says, in effect, "All right, then, have it your way!"

I left them in their stubbornness of heart to follow their own designs.

This is definitely not a situation we would ever want to find ourselves in. The alternative is not simply to avoid denying God. We want to be as far removed from denial as possible.

Faith and gratitude go hand in hand. Naaman thanks God by expressing faith in the God of Israel as the one God. The grateful Samaritan leper is reminded that his faith saved him. And Mary teaches us to renew our faith in God, whose love we must never deny.

Monday, October 10, (#467)
Twenty-Eighth Week in Ordinary Time

Luke 11:29-32: *"For just as Jonah became a sign to the people of Nineveh … , so will the Son of man be a sign to this generation."*

Meditation:

The Ninevites heard the preaching of Jonah and saw something of God. They believed! The queen of the South heard about the wisdom of Solomon and saw something of God. She believed! Our present generation is given Jesus, the Son of Man. Do we believe? We are told, *"Philip, he who sees me sees the Father"* (John 14:9). We ask, *"Lord, when did we see you, give you to drink, care for you?"* We are told, *"Each time you did it to the least of my brothers and sisters, you did it to me"* (Matthew 25:40). The words quoted from today's Gospel were spoken by Jesus on his way to Jerusalem. Later, he would weep at the sight of the Holy City, because the people did not believe, and his efforts to keep those he loved from destroying themselves went for naught. *"When Jesus had come near, and when he saw the city, he wept over it. 'Would that even today,' he said, 'you recognized the things that would give you peace! But, as it is, they are hidden from your eyes … because you did not recognize the day when God visited you'"* (Luke 19:41-44).

"**Come near, my children.** *Do not be afraid. I am here to tell you Great News.*" Mary, at La Salette, in true discipleship, continues the mission of Jesus. She weeps over our callousness and insensitivity to the things of God. She weeps with powerlessness in preventing the disasters and calamities that our greed and blindness will bring upon us. Yet, she speaks *Shalom (Peace).* She is visiting in the name of God. She is doing her Son's work. She speaks in his name, *"If my people will not submit... Six days have I given you to labor, the seventh I have kept for myself; and they will not give it to me."* The Great News that Mary announces is the glorious, brilliant cross of her Son next to her heart. In paschal power, Christ will save us, not abandon us.

Reflection Questions:

- It is said that the blind and the deaf do not know what they are missing. What can we say of those who are spiritually blind and deaf?
- Do you know someone struggling with their faith or other challenges. Why not pray for them today?

Tuesday, October 11, (#468) Twenty-Eighth Week in Ordinary Time

Luke 11:37-41: *"Give alms from what you have and, look, everything will be clean for you."*

Meditation:

Writing a check can give us a new lease on life. Almsgiving, when it originates within us – close to our hearts – is an act of faith and religion that connects us ever more closely to God. Why? Because it springs from an awareness of the other – outside ourselves – who has less than we: the poor, whom we are called to serve in imitation of Jesus. Almsgiving happens only when we can open hands and hearts and part with the money and material goods to which by nature we tend to cling. Now that's miraculous!

THE BEAUTIFUL LADY OF LA SALETTE seems to offer another route to God. Honor God's name, keep his day holy, live your sacramental and prayer life devoutly and you will see *"the stones and rocks become mounds of wheat and the potatoes... self-sown in the fields."* Then the poor, the sick and dying, and the hungry will be served. But almsgiving achieves the same end. Serve the poor with your heart, share with those who have nothing, and you will be honoring God and blessing his life-giving name. *"The commandment we have heard from him is this: those who love God must love their brothers and sisters also"* (1 John 4:21).

Reflection Questions:

- What causes or needs successfully prompt your almsgiving?
- When was the last time you gave alms to the poor?

Wednesday, October 12, (#469)
Twenty-Eighth Week in Ordinary Time

Luke 11:42-46: *"Alas for you Pharisees! ... Alas for you lawyers as well!"*

Meditation:

"Stop it! Cut it out! Think about what you're doing!" This is what "woe!" means. Jesus is objecting to the neglect of central commands – the heart and meaning of the Law – while the details and externals are being lifted high on the public altar of observance. The term "pharisaic" comes from these verses in Luke. It refers to those who wash their outsides but not their insides, who tithe even a tenth of their garden herbs, but neglect justice, who love praise and attention and who load people down with burdensome religious demands. We act in that way when our service or worship comes from a desire to be seen rather than from a pure heart and out of love for others. People may sometimes be fooled, but God isn't. Our discipleship must be sincere. By bringing our inner life under God's control, our outer life will naturally reflect him.

"IN THE WINTER, WHEN THEY DO NOT KNOW WHAT TO DO, *they go to Mass only to mock at religion."* This is Mary's way of saying, "Stop it!" Have we lost touch so much with the heart and meaning of Eucharist that our very presence at Mass can be construed as mockery at religion? Yet, that can indeed be what is happening if our presence in church is for show or based on externals or if our charity is limited to what we put in the collection basket. Only two persons can answer that question: God and ourselves. We know what discipleship calls us to be: salt, light, leaven. That is the purpose and meaning of our religion and its practices.

Reflection Questions:

- How and why is the Lord asking you to "Stop it!" today?
- How do you express righteous indignation in your ministry, work or relationships?

Thursday, October 13, (#470)
Twenty-Eighth Week in Ordinary Time

Luke 11:47-54: *"And that is why the Wisdom of God said, 'I will send them prophets and apostles; some they will slaughter and persecute.'"*

Meditation:

God sends prophets as mouthpieces into human history to touch our hearts, to shape our thinking, to help us to see the evil of the day, to call us back. Prophets never have an easy time of it. The eternal truth of the gifts of life and grace does not change, while the reality of sin, which separates us from God, has many guises. The mission of the prophet is to call the Word of God to bear upon sin in any age. Prophet and people share a dynamic relationship. Some scribes and lawyers in Jesus's audience prefer a religion of their own making. They prefer to control their people by the manipulations of tenets and regulations that make God's truth hard to understand and practice. Jesus presents himself here as more than just a human prophet. He is the very Word of God and is directly revealing God's message. They reject both him and the message.

MARY COMES AS A PROPHET at La Salette. The first sight of her reveals a woman dressed in the garb of the day, seated, weeping, her face in her hands. Her words of greeting, *"Come near, my children. Do not be afraid. I am here to tell you great news,"* melt any fear in the children and remove any defensiveness in us as we listen. Mary wants to talk to us and *with* us. She engages in dialogue, asks questions, chides gently. As a prophet, she speaks for God with the message that he knows about our life and struggles and that he is closer to us than we realize. It is a message we need to hear.

Reflection Questions:

- How are you called to be a prophet? How are you called to speak up or speak out in various situations?
- Have you (or anyone you know) ever been persecuted for being a

prophet?

Friday, October 14, (#471)
Twenty-Eighth Week in Ordinary Time

Luke 12:1-7: *"To you, my friends, I say: Do not be afraid."*

Meditation:

Today's gospel passage says "a crowd of thousands had gathered, so dense that they were treading on one another." It's easy to imagine that pushing, tugging mob pressing on Jesus as his inspiration for talking about the number of hairs on one's head and flocks of sparrows. In the midst of that scene, Jesus speaks consoling words, *"I say to you who are my friends..."* This is the only time in the synoptic gospels that Jesus uses the term "friends" to address his disciples. He is obviously very adept at identifying his disciples. This Jesus who can identify his friends in the midst of a pressing crowd is talking about his Father, who knows each and every sparrow and excels at counting every hair on our heads. All the more reason to trust that he knows our hearts.

"HAVE YOU EVER SEEN WHEAT THAT IS SPOILED, MY CHILDREN?" Hair, sparrows, grains of wheat – nothing, apparently, escapes the providential care of God and his Mother. Maximin was shocked by the detail of recollection; even more, his heart, that of his father, and those of all believers of the apparition, are awestruck by God's interest and involvement in even the most insignificant events of our lives. Jesus and Mary both tell us, "Do not be afraid." After this display of providential awareness, we feel that there is nowhere else that we would rather be than standing within that globe of light with our Mother, Mary.

Reflection Questions:

• How and when do I experience fear in my life?
• Does my faith help me deal with my fears?

Saturday, October 15, (#472)
Twenty-Eighth Week in Ordinary Time

Luke 12:8-12: *"Everyone who says a word against the Son of man will be forgiven, but no one who blasphemes against the Holy Spirit will be forgiven."*

Meditation:

This sentence has worried many sincere and conscientious Christians, but it does not need to. Jesus is simply saying that any sin, any sin we can think of in our experience, the experience of others, or even our wildest imaginings, can be forgiven by God if that sin is brought to God. The "unforgivable sin" is a deliberate and ongoing rejection of the Holy Spirit's work and even of God himself. More than just a rejection of Christian preaching or the gospel, this sin is the persistent and obstinate opposition to God himself. A person who has committed this sin has shut himself or herself off from God so thoroughly that he or she is unaware of any sin at all. Jesus is not trying to scare us here nor to inflict doubt into sensitive souls.

BESIDES HER TEARS AND HER PLEAS, the chains Mary wore at La Salette point to the fact that God is not the undisputed Master of the Universe. If God were, we could rightly blame him for the evil around us. No, there is one thing that God cannot do – forgive someone who does not know enough to ask for forgiveness. Mary points to our abuse of her Son's holy name and his holy day as the *"two things which make the arm of my Son so heavy."* But she and her Son cannot infringe on our human freedom and responsibility in responding to God's overtures to loving intimacy with him. *"If they are converted…,"* Mary says. If…

Reflection Questions:

- Where do you find an absence of the sense of God among God's people? What forces have caused this alienation?
- Who do you know who feels alienated from God? Pray for them.

Sunday, October 16 (#147)
Twenty-Ninth Sunday in Ordinary Time

(Exodus 17:8-13; 2 Timothy 3:14—4:2; Luke 18:1-8)

Meditation: *Pray Always, Pray Well*

The dishonest judge in the parable today decides to act on the widow's behalf, not out of compassion or out of love for justice, but just to stop her constant appeals. He gives in because she doesn't give up.

St. Luke writes that Jesus told this parable to encourage his disciples to "pray always without becoming weary." Anyone who knows La Salette will hear the echo of those words in Mary's saying *"If I want*

The Parable of the Persistent Widow

my Son not to abandon you, I am obliged to plead with him constantly." (The French verb prier is translated, depending on the context, as pray, plead, beg.)

The fact is, we do grow weary in prayer. In the first reading, Moses did not tire of praying, but his prayer had the very physical aspect of keeping his arms raised. Aaron and Hur found the way to make sure he didn't give up.

We are more likely to think our prayers are not heard if we don't see results as soon as we might wish. After all, it's not so long ago that we heard Jesus say, "Ask, and you shall receive." Today's parable is sort of a footnote to that statement.

Why would God keep us waiting? Perhaps our faith is weak and the discipline of prayer will help to strengthen it. Or maybe we don't take seriously enough the model given to us by Jesus, "Not my will but yours be done." No doubt many such explanations could be devised, but ultimately it is a mystery.

The Beautiful Lady asked the children—and, through them, us— *"Do you say your prayers well?"* Their answer, "Hardly ever," could be taken

as our expression, "Not really," which is just a way of saying "No."

Praying well and praying always are two notions that belong together. What St. Paul writes to Timothy about proclaiming the word could apply equally to what Jesus and Our Lady of La Salette say about prayer: "Be persistent, whether it is convenient or inconvenient."

Monday, October 17, (#473)
Twenty-Ninth Week in Ordinary Time

Luke 12:13-21: *"What am I to do? I have not enough room to store my crops."*

Meditation:

Life always provokes this same question: at every turn, we must decide on a path to take, a life to live. Choices must be made, decisions taken. Many a choice is relatively easy; living with it isn't. That is because when we choose a path to take, a life to live, a commitment to undertake, we cancel out another. Becoming a father or a mother of a family means taking on responsibilities and giving up much freedom. Choosing specialized work means sacrificing time and energy and giving up many luxuries. Commitment to vowed living means sacrificing the joys of married life. Becoming a pianist, or a carpenter or an electrician, excelling in a sport or profession means living with "doing without."

A life committed to Christ entails more than a few changes and adaptations: it means a new way of life in following the one who declared, *"I am the Way, the Truth and the Life."* Such dedication brings on renunciation of much lawful enjoyment. The rich man with the barns in today's gospel seemed to have an easy time with his choices. It appears that he limited his choices to crops and the barns to store them. The man made his choices in keeping with his privileged lifestyle and decided that if some wealth is good, more is better. The fate of the rich man is stark. The warning given to us, out of loving concern, is that we not make crucial choices with crops and barns in mind.

THE BEAUTIFUL LADY'S MESSAGE AT LA SALETTE begins with an if: *"If my people will not submit, I am forced to let go the arm of my Son.*" The people mentioned in her discourse are faced with a choice: whether or not to submit to the will of God. Still, if we examine the stipulations of that choice in the message of La Salette, the commitment is relatively easy to make. Fidelity to prayer, penance during Lent, respect for the Name of the Lord, as well as observance of Sunday rest and worship – none of these is physically overwhelming; all of these rest well within most people's capabilities. Still, the simplicity of these demands veils their importance in the life of the Christian. Their observance leads to a loving knowledge of God, strength in the face of life's temptations and tragedies, as well as a deepened sense of values when faced with difficult choices.

Reflection Questions:

- Why not take time today to review your life's choices and commitments to see the condition they're in?
- Could I begin and/or end my day with a prayer to God?

Tuesday, October 18 (#661)
St. Luke, Evangelist

Luke 10:1-9: "*... send laborers to do his harvesting.*"

Meditation:

It is amazing but true that none of the four gospels were signed. Later the Church and scholars attributed an author to each, but the writers literally wrote the gospels for the glory of God and not for their own notoriety. Their vocation from Christ was to be his follower. When they were chosen, they were sent "to do (Christ's) harvesting", to bring the good news to all nations, to gather more followers, to spread his message of love, forgiveness and peace. Four of his followers were chosen to write what we today call "gospels (good news)". From what we can gather from his writings (the gospel of Luke and the Acts of the Apostles), Luke was a doctor and friend of Theophilus and of Paul of Tarsus.

AT LA SALETTE, MARY CHOSE THE TWO CHILDREN, MAXIMIN AND MELANIE, TO BECOME DISCIPLES OF HER MESSAGE, sharing it with all who would listen. They were very successful and completed their mission. Then this mission was handed on to the Missionaries of Our Lady of La Salette and, eventually, to all who hear her message. The fact that Mary did not hand her message to Church hierarchy or local dignitaries but to these two poor children and that they were most successful is a testament to the trust Mary places in us who have heard her message. We are all called to be evangelizers of her message, and "doers" of her mission of faith and reconciliation.

Some Reflection Questions:

- From whom did you first hear the message of La Salette?
- Have you ever told the story of La Salette to another? If not, perhaps you should.

Wednesday, October 19, (#475) Twenty-Ninth Week in Ordinary Time

Luke 12:39-48: *"Blessed that servant if his master's arrival finds him doing exactly that."*

Meditation:

One would think that the Creator of heaven and earth, as well as of all humankind, might know better than to demand fidelity from those he calls to serve. Doesn't he have the whole history of Israel before him? Doesn't he know that the temptation to slip into the easy way out is endemic and almost irresistible to the human biped? He should know, too, that when the master disappears for the longest while, the second in command would snatch up his perks? There must be something precious in this phenomenon of fidelity for God to demand it so completely.

Ultimately, fidelity bespeaks respect for the other, and respect is the first law of love. Fidelity to God, according to this passage also implies fidelity to neighbor: the servants suffer when the one in charge is unfaithful to the Master. This is not a new law; it has always been so, "God neglected" means "people forgotten", or battered and killed. The final statement of this passage: *"Much will be required of the person entrusted with much…"* is arguably the most ignored sentence in the New Testament. People bless the Lord for their gifts but often forget the people for whom these gifts were granted. It is all part of being faithful.

MARY IS ONE OF THOSE to whom much, very much, was given. At La Salette she reminds her people of that very gift which made her pleasing to God. *"If my people will not submit..."* The cornerstone of Mary's spirituality was a sacred obsession with the will of God. At the Annunciation, her response to God's requests has an "of course" ring to it: *"You see before you the Lord's servant, let it happen to me as you have said"* *(Luke 1:38).* Elizabeth's pregnancy comes as a sign, indeed a summons to Mary, to be by her cousin's side. She goes "in haste." In the gospel of John, at the miracle of Cana, she urges Jesus to perform the miracle, but finally leaves it all to him: *"Do whatever he tells you,"* she advises the servers.

Reflection Questions:

• How has Mary's all-encompassing words, *"Do whatever he tells you,"* been a factor in your life? Do you respond to anyone like that?
• Who is someone who would do *anything* for you? How about giving thanks to God for that wonderful person!

Thursday, October 20, (#476)
Twenty-Ninth Week in Ordinary Time

Luke 12:49-53: *"I have come to bring fire to the earth, and how I wish it were blazing already!"*

Meditation:

The kingdom of God is always spoken of in terms of peace and reconciliation: but that is the kingdom achieved. Meanwhile, there is the question of commitment to Jesus in faith in the Sacrament of Baptism with its promises of life lived concretely in ongoing change and renewal. All this is a bit much for the gravitational pulls of greed and self-interest, with all the forces of consumerism thrown in. There is need for more power in our lives. *"I have come to bring fire to the earth, and how I wish it were blazing already"* says Jesus. This fire could well be the fire of the Holy Spirit, a fire much needed in the soul to live a life of commitment, prayer and self-giving mandated by life in Christ. John the Baptist spoke about *"someone is coming, who is more powerful than me; … he will baptize you with the Holy Spirit and fire." (Luke 3:16).*

Early in the Acts of the Apostles, when all were gathered in one place, *"there appeared to them tongues as of fire; these separated and came to rest on the head of each of them."* (Acts 2:3). The burden of Christ may be light, but it might also be long lasting, and its light weight comes from the love of him who imposes the burden. The trumpet announcing rescue and deliverance is heard only at the coming of the fires of the Spirit, which makes all tasks and all commitments possible. That Spirit is called the Power, the Advocate, the Fire, the Spirit of truth. In many people's lives that Fire makes all the difference.

THE FIRST THING the children saw of the apparition of La Salette was the light. Then, slowly they discerned the figure of a woman seated within the oval of brightness. It was a light like no other they had seen on earth, a light from heaven, the light of the Resurrection and the fires of Pentecost. The Lady herself was wholly light yet with the appearance of humanity. She came to remind us that the fire of the Resurrection and Pentecost is still with us today to strengthen us for the journey.

Reflection Questions:

- You love the ideal of self-giving excellence in serving Christ. Are you taking the means given to you by Jesus to bring it to reality in your life?
- When have you needed to "read the riot act" (say something seriously) to someone who was acting badly? How did you feel? How did they react to your words of correction?

Friday, October 21, (#477)
Twenty-Ninth Week in Ordinary Time

Luke 12:54-59: *"How is it you do not know how to interpret these times?"*

Meditation:

We won't be judged by the past we have not lived or by the future we have not seen. "The present time" here alludes to the actual presence of Christ, his words and his life. If people are able to foretell the weather, to pontificate about events, and paint the future, they can surely note what Jesus is doing and saying in this "present time," or this kairos. Whatever we think and write concerning our life revolves around one question: is Christ alive or dead? Of course, we say he is alive, which is another word for present among us, as present now as he was when he was asking this famous question two thousand years ago.

This "present time" means a crucial time for me. Practically, it means wide awake awareness of Christ in the world and in my own life, present in prayer, in self-giving, in personal change and conversion, in awareness of others. It means avoiding the idea that this is only a "we" situation, a general, impersonal "present time" situation, not really an "I" or "me" issue or a "here and now" condition. All this may seem severe and unbending but, then again, so is love when the beloved asks, "Do you love me?" The answer has to be "yes," which is the same as choosing between black and white. No one would like to hear a "maybe I love you" here.

OUR LADY'S TEARS TELL US that there is suffering and affection in heaven because there is caring for us there. The Lady says, *How long have I suffered for you! If my Son is not to cast you off, I am obliged to entreat him without ceasing.* She doesn't say the words "I love you," but she underscores what love always does for the beloved: suffer to preserve the love. La Salette is a *kairos* moment, a time-right now, to decide to be reconciled, to "turn around" in conversion, and to begin in this moment. We must respond to the Beautiful Lady's caring tears and suffering. It is time for us to give a caring response.

Reflection Questions:

• This is your own "present time." How will you respond to the calls of Christ and of Our Lady to "come near?"
• When an opportunity to help someone in need occurs, what is your usual response? Do you act like Jesus would do?

Saturday, October 22, (#478) Twenty-Ninth Week in Ordinary Time

Luke 13:1-9: *"Sir, ...leave it one more year and give me time to dig round it and manure it."*

Meditation:

A judgment often pronounced on evildoers is that "God will get them for this." We associate God more with punishment than with any measure of leniency. No matter how often Christ may describe himself and the Father as kind and merciful, "filled with everlasting love," as the Psalms endlessly proclaim, still we remember the Christ of the Last Judgment more often than the image of the Good Shepherd. The message in this section is that a sinner should be given more time to put his life together, to repent, as much as a year – a rather undetermined length of time. Maybe Luke remembers what he wrote in an earlier chapter when, quoting Isaiah, Christ spoke of "a year of the Lord's favor," a year of reconciliation and healing.

One of the delights of life is the phenomenon of starting over, beginning anew, turning a new leaf. This poor tree was given a year to flower again and produce fruit. God's compassion goes further than mere leniency; it extends to coming to the aid of the tree, to "dig around it," and "put manure on it." The first five verses clearly say that God is not responsible for the evil in the world, and that he is more responsible for sustenance and restoration than for the destruction of peoples' lives and possessions often attributed to him. One might say about that famous fig tree what Augustine said about original sin: a "happy fault" that should have aroused such forbearance.

THE APPARITION OF LA SALETTE of and by itself is an act of leniency. Even if the Lady had done and said nothing but appear in tears, people would have understood the meaning of her action, that Heaven was steeped in sadness at the sight of what humans do to one another. The gardener of Luke's gospel intercedes for the fig tree and pleads for more time for renewal and repentance, and so does the Lady with her tears. She makes no mention of a year but pointedly reminds her people that "Forever have I suffered for you! If my Son is not to cast you off, I am obliged to entreat him without ceasing."

Reflection Question:

• With the occasion of the Millennium or of a Holy Year in mind, "a year of favor from the Lord," have you given those around you more time to put their lives together, to change, rather than condemning them and dismissing them without further ado?

Sunday, October 23 (#150)
Thirtieth Sunday in Ordinary Time

(Sirach 35:12-14, 16-18; 2 Timothy 4:6-8, 16-18; Luke 18:9-14)

Meditation: *Whole-truth Prayer*

> ## HUMILITY IS NOT THINKING LESS OF YOURSELF, BUT THINKING OF YOURSELF LESS.
>
> ~ CS LEWIS

It is clear that the Pharisee in today's famous parable is not making anything up, but telling the truth about his good deeds, that he has gone above and beyond the call of duty.

Last week's readings helped us focus on the fact of prayer, the need to pray always and well. This week adds another notion with respect to the quality of our prayer: total honesty.

We might say that the way Our Lady of La Salette describes her unceasing prayer on our behalf is a paraphrase of the words of the tax collector, "O God, be merciful."

The tax collector doesn't list his sins. He was a "public sinner" by the nature of his job as an agent of the hated Roman occupiers. That was enough for the Pharisee to make the odious comparison between himself and the other man.

We hear today St. Paul's celebrated words: "I have fought the good fight, I have finished the race." Isn't he boasting, just like the Pharisee? No, because time and time again Paul makes it clear that it is only by God's grace that he has been able to accomplish anything.

The Pharisee was taking the credit to himself, and drawing the conclusion that he was better than others. His "truth" was not the "whole truth."

When Mary reminds us of our faults, she isn't saying that we are worse than anyone else. The only "other" that we should be concerned about is her Son. On her breast we see him crucified, for our sake and in our place. How could we stand at the cross of Jesus and boast of anything we have done for him? Mary never boasted, but recognized, "The Lord has done great things for me."

The reading from Sirach, where we hear, "The Lord is not deaf to the wail of the orphan," reminds me of a magnificent song by Amy Grant, "Better than a Hallelujah." It begins:

> God loves a lullaby
> In a mother's tears in the dead of night
> Better than a Hallelujah sometimes.

Surely God loves Mary's tears at La Salette, soul-brought, whole-truth tears shed for all her people.

Monday, October 24, (#479)
Thirtieth Week in Ordinary Time

Luke 13:10-17: "... *she was bent double and quite unable to stand upright.*"

Meditation:

Luke may have been describing the physical condition of this poor woman's ailment -- but Jesus saw the spiritual malady as well. This woman was carrying, not only her own burdens of life, but the burdens of family who saw her as "just another mouth to feed." She carried the burdens of her society and culture and saw her affliction as a punishment from God for her sins and the sins of her ancestors. The woman was an outcast – stooped and burdened from so many crosses that were not meant for her to carry. Jesus lifted these burdens from her shoulder, *"Woman, you are freed from your disability,"* and he laid on her the one cross that was meant just for her alone. Indeed her one cross was a burden that was easy and a yoke that was light! She is now quite capable of standing erect of walking uprightly with dignity before her God.

Mary also appeared badly stooped – a telling symbol of how we see ourselves before God! She appears burdened and imprisoned by chains – our chains of guilt, anxiety, anger and resentment. But she stands up! And in her standing, she appears as the "Beautiful Lady" in all her splendor and light – another wonderful symbol of how God wants us to appear before him. She wears the roses of our dignity. The cross of our salvation shines brightly. It is a symbol of our own cross that is meant just for us to carry. This cross is indeed a burden, but that yoke is easy, that burden is light. That cross is very light: the light of the world, the light of our salvation.

Reflection Questions:

• What are the burdens that make you "quite incapable of standing erect'?" How many years have you been "stooped over" carrying the burdens of anger, resentment, another's guilt? What would happen if you dared lay down those burdens right now'?
• What is your own special cross that God alone has given you to carry?

Tuesday, October 25, (#480) Thirtieth Week in Ordinary Time

Luke 13:18-21: *"What is the kingdom of God like? What shall I compare it with? It is like…"*

Meditation:

Jesus uses many images to explain what heaven and God are like. Heaven is like a mustard seed or yeast mixed with bread. God is like a shepherd who searches for lost sheep, or a woman searching for a lost coin. Above all, heaven is like a Father yearning for his lost children – a God who comes running to welcome and embrace the one who abandoned him long ago. No mention of a stern, harsh Judge! Not one mention of the demanding Master who "gives us what we really deserve"! Rather there is a lot of rejoicing, gladness and joy over one sinner who dares *"turn away from sin"* and *"believe in the Good News!"*

These stories are about giving up what little we have and receiving much, much more than we give.

AT LA SALETTE, Mary also gives us little images of what heaven is like. Heaven is like *"rocks and stones"* turning into *"heaps of wheat."* Heaven is like *"potatoes being self-sown in the fields."* Our God is like a father giving bread to his child. If only we can change our ways! If only we can be converted! Heaven is like a Mother yearning for her children not to run away, but to *"come closer"* and *"not be afraid."* Like Jesus, Mary assures us that, if we repent, there will be *"much joy and rejoicing in heaven."*

Reflection Question:

- Using images from your own life, complete this sentence: "Heaven is like…"
- When did you intensely feel the love of God – in what place did this happen; what people were with you?

Wednesday, October 26, (#481)
Thirtieth Week in Ordinary Time

Luke 13:22-30: *"Try your hardest to enter by the narrow door."*

For Your Reflection:

This gospel reminds me of a house that some good friends of mine own. It has a beautiful front door that opens into a brick wall! Years ago, when the house was being constructed, the builders made a mistake and built a wall where the main entrance was supposed to be. But the woman and her husband said to leave it that way. They could use the extra space that would have been taken up by the doorway. Besides, they said, nobody will ever use the front door anyway, beautiful as it is. All their children, friends and family will be using the back door – that's the door that is important! Only those who don't know them – sales people, business people, strangers – will try the front door. And will they be in for a surprise!

MAYBE THAT'S WHY MARY AT LA SALETTE WAS DRESSED LIKE "ONE OF THE FOLKS" OF THAT TIME. A simple peasant dress, a bonnet, an apron. Her demeanor and attitude tell us that God doesn't want us coming to heaven with pretenses of importance. Nor does God want us to be strangers. We are not worthy of the front door of the kingdom of God! That's only for people with "false fronts." But if we can become God's children, sisters and brothers of Jesus, then we have free access to the back door. Come as you are and enjoy. No need to "dress up." Just bring your own, unique, special gifts and enjoy the potluck, heavenly feast of the kingdom of God.

Reflection Questions:

- What door in your house is used most often?
- When was the last time you felt "at home" with a friend or relative? What does it feel like to be "a guest?"
- Do you have friends or relatives with whom you can simply come and "be yourself?" If you went to heaven today, would you describe yourself as "a stranger?" "a guest" or just "one of the folks"?

Thursday, October 27, (#482) Thirtieth Week in Ordinary Time

Luke 13:31-35: *"Jerusalem, Jerusalem..."*

Meditation:

In this most poignant lament of Jesus, one cannot help but take note of the longing, yearning, pining ache of a man deeply in love with his people – even though those same people are seeking to destroy him! Jesus pines for us. Jesus aches to be our Emmanuel, our "God with us." So often in our prayers, we express our hunger for God. In this particular prayer, Jesus expresses his longing for us! He longs to gather us in *"as a hen gathers her brood under her wing"* (Luke 13:34).

How often we turn away from God, not out of stubbornness of heart, but, surprisingly, because we feel we are not worthy enough to merit such a love. Yet, God deems us worthy enough! *"For God loved the world so much,"* says John, *"that he gave his only Son ... that the world might be saved through him"* (John 3:16). It is our freedom of will and our choice to decide to accept graciously this profound gift. And, even when we refuse, our God will continue to pine for our presence with Him.

Mary's apparition at La Salette mirrors so well this gospel reflection. The Mother of God continues to expound on the longing of the Divine for us. *"How long a time do I suffer for you? And, as for you, you pay no heed."* Pray that we live to see the day when the words so often prayed in our *Prayer of Dedication to Our Lady of La Salette* may come true: "From this day my glory shall be to know that I am your child. May I so live as to dry your tears and console your afflicted heart."

Reflection Question:

•Pray Psalms 42, 43 and 63 – all three psalms contain a deep hunger and longing for God. Think about God's longing for you in much the same way. What would be your response if you realized that God was praying these same psalms for you?

Friday, October 28, (#666)
Sts. Simon and Jude, Apostles

Luke 6:12-16: *"(Jesus) summoned his disciples and picked out twelve of them; he called them 'apostles…'"*

Meditation:

Although we may be Catholics from birth, often people get confused about some basic notions of faith. For example, the word "disciple" refers to a "learner" or "follower", of which there were many. The word "apostle" refers to one who is "sent out" of which an initial twelve were named, as in the gospel for today. Simon was called the Zealot because he was a member of a group of Zealots who refused to recognize any foreign power over Palestine. Jude was an actual cousin of Jesus. A tradition states that the two Apostles went to evangelize Armenia and Persia, and that they suffered martyrdom in the city of Suanir in the year 47AD.

Mary at La Salette also chose people to spread her message: at first, Maximin and Melanie, who shared Mary's message and thereby brought countless pilgrims to the apparition site. And as with Jesus, these initial two children, in turn, caused many others to become "evangelizers" and spread her message. It is simply remarkable that Mary's message is still being spread from person to person, across the face of the earth. At La Salette "her" message was, in fact, the message of her Son, Jesus. She called for daily prayer, making holy the Lord's

Day, an active Lenten season and other practices of faith, and reverence for the Name of the Lord. These are some of the basics of our Catholic faith.

Reflection Questions:

- How well do you pray and share your faith with others? Do you encourage others to be active followers of Jesus?
- When was the last time you supported others in their faith?

Saturday, October 29, (#484)
Thirtieth Week in Ordinary Time

Luke 14:1,7-11: *"My friend, move up higher."*

Meditation:

There is an airline company that prides itself on its "first class" service. When one plans a trip with that airline, one is pleasantly surprised to find that the whole airplane is first class – wide, comfortable, leather seats, champagne, a menu with several choices of nice hot meals served with real napkins and china. Everyone is equal on that plane. Everyone is seen as valuable and served with grace, dignity and respect. I suppose that the folks who expect better treatment than the rest would be a little disappointed at first, while those expecting the minimum would be amazed at the quality of service. That's what Jesus means when he talks about the heavenly banquet. There are no "head tables" in heaven. Everyone is treated equally as a son and daughter of God. Everything is "first class" in heaven. Those who expect better treatment than the rest will be sorely disappointed; those who think they are unworthy of heaven will be amazed at how their dignity is restored and enhanced in God's heavenly kingdom.

MARY CAME TO LA SALETTE to speak to the poorest of the poor – children from broken homes who did not expect better than their lot in life– to remind them that they, as well as all of God's children, are first class citizens in the kingdom of heaven. We are all pearls of great price in the eyes of God, pearls that are not to be tossed to the indignity of bias, prejudice, self-righteousness or belittlement. In God's sight there are no First World or Third World countries. As God secs the world, so should we see each other! Good News, indeed, Good

News worth tell-ing to all God's people!

Reflection Questions:

- What "class" does the world seem to put you in? What "class" do you put yourself in?
- What sort of treatment would you expect if you were in heaven today? Or, do you think that you're not worthy of heaven? Why or why not?

Sunday, October 30 (#153)
Thirty-First Sunday in Ordinary Time

(Wisdom 11:22—12:2; 2 Thessalonians 1:11—2:2; Luke 19:1-10)

Meditation: *Why They Came*

In today's Gospel we have one of many passages where Jesus states why he has come; in this case it is "to seek and to save what was lost."

The Beautiful Lady of La Salette also says why she has come—"to tell you great news."

No matter the words used, the purpose is the same. Mary's great news reminds us of why her Son came. She speaks, as Jesus does, to those who were lost or in danger of being lost, in order to "warn them and remind them of the sins they are committing, that they may abandon their wickedness," as we hear in the first reading.

But wait! There's more!

No one ever became a saint simply by giving up a sinful way of life. The Blessed Virgin didn't envision only that we would stop abusing her Son's name, but that we would return to the practice of the faith, in simplicity and sincerity. She speaks of submission and conversion. These are not negative notions. Zacchaeus was transformed when he submitted to God's grace and was converted.

It is precisely this transformation that is understood by the word "save." Salvation is not first and foremost about going to heaven when we die. It is about breaking with one way of life and entering upon a new one.

In Zacchaeus' case, he breaks with the greed that has marked his life until this moment, and his new life is marked by justice and generosity. And who knows where that may lead him?

In the case of those hearing and responding to the message of Our Lady of La Salette, the break is with indifference and the new life is characterized by respect for the Lord, by worship and prayer, and the consequences that flow from these.

Why Jesus came, why Mary came, was not just to take us away from something evil, but to offer us something good and beautiful and wonderful. Both came because we are loved by God. They want us to respond to that love with all our heart, so that, in the words of today's second reading, "God may make us worthy of his calling."

Monday, October 31 (#485)
Thirty-First Week in Ordinary Time

Luke 14:12-14: *"When you have a party, invite the poor, the crippled, the lame, the blind."*

Meditation:

The setting for Jesus' words today is in the context of his dining on the Sabbath with a leader of the Pharisees. They watch him closely as he heals a crippled man, unaware that their own misguided notions of Sabbath rest blind them to the miracle of God's recreative love in their midst. Their pride in keeping the Torah Law has brought a forgetfulness of the Exodus God who saved them, healed them and fed them in their hour of deepest need. No one, Jesus reminds them, should be excluded from their bounty since they first shared in God's.

At La Salette, Mary came to call the people of God out of their blind pride and a forgetfulness which was keeping them, and the Anawim (the poor) God loves so much, from experiencing the banquet of God's healing, nourishing love awaiting them without money or price. The invitation went out to all because their need was so great. It is still so today.

Reflection Questions:

- Are you excluding people from the bounty of God's love and mercy by your attitudes?
- Do you refuse to heal in those situations which seem to stand "outside" the law of the Church?

Tuesday, Nov 1, (#667)
Feast of All Saints

[not a Holy Day of Obligation this year]

(Revelation 7:2-14; 1 John 3:1-3; Matthew 5:1-12)

Meditation: *Blessed*

A great many of the people who lived in the region around La Salette in 1846 were poor, but they did not feel blessed. Quite to the contrary, as Mary pointed out: ***When you found the potatoes spoiled, you swore, and threw in my Son's name.***

Still, the message of the Beautiful Lady has a lot in common with the Beatitudes. It is addressed to "the meek" in the persons of Maximin and Melanie. In its invitation to reconciliation it calls for *peacemakers.* "*They who hunger and thirst for uprightness*," can see in Mary's allusions to prayer and Eucharist the need for a right relationship with God. Those who "*mourn*" the loss of children dying "***in the arms of the persons who hold them***" will be "*comforted*" by the image of the Weeping Mother.

Our Lord's Sermon on the Mount is foundational for Christian life. It is a source of both challenge and encouragement. The Beatitudes in particular are, as the rest of the Sermon makes clear, a sort of rule of life. The unnamed multitude of saints whom we celebrate today lived by that rule.

Our Lady's message on another mountain serves as echo and reminder of our Lord's Sermon. The crucifix she wears reminds us also of his sacrifice offered out of love for us all. The hope she offers is not focused only on our ultimate salvation in the company of the saints, but also on our capacity to respond to his love as they did, even now—a response that St. John describes in these terms: *"Whoever treasures this hope of him purifies himself, to be as pure as he is."*

The Blessed Virgin, like St. John, wants to open our eyes to *"see what great love the Father has lavished on us by letting us be called God's children."* If all who glory in the name of Christian could take those words to heart, how eagerly we would respond to the message of La Salette. How humbly we would accept Mary's criticisms and warnings. How sincerely we would submit to her Son. How greatly we would *"rejoice and be glad,"* even in times of hardship. How deeply we would renew our life of prayer. And as a result, how *"blessed"* we would be!

Wednesday, November 2, (#668) Feast of All Souls

John 6:37-40: *"It is my Father's will that whoever sees the Son and believes in him should have eternal life, and that I should raise that person up on the last day."*

Meditation:

One of the central truths of the Catholic faith is that if we believe in Jesus and follow his way during our lifetime, we need not worry about the afterlife. Jesus promises that we will be raised up (to heaven) on the last day. It's as simple and as profound that that! There are times in our life which can be very challenging and, as Anthony Padovano writes, "we may feel more the dust of the earth than the breath of God." But we must choose to move on in hope. When we lose a loved one in death, we can certainly grieve at the loss but, with the passing of time, some of this grief will pass and we will, in a sense, rise with our loved one in the hope of their and our resurrection.

AT LA SALETTE, our Blessed Mother wept for our sins. The question may occur: "If Mary is in heaven and beholds the face of God, how can she visit us in tears?" Fr. Normand Theroux explains: "Without doubt those in heaven neither suffer nor weep... However the Virgin wept at La Salette not because she was sad but because she wanted to emphasize by her tears the alarming scope of her message as the Mother of the Lord. *'If my people will not submit, I will be forced to let go of the arm of my Son.'* She cried because she was speaking to human beings who need some signs. On earth, tears are the ultimate sign of sorrow. In addition, Mary's tears express her deep sadness at not being able to protect her people from coming misfortunes, although her capacity to suffer has passed." As we grieve for our loved ones, we know that Jesus' Holy Mother is concerned for us and prays always for our salvation and that of our loved ones. Let us take comfort in this truth of our faith.

Reflection Questions:

• Do you know of someone who is still grieving at the loss of a loved one? Why not say a prayer for them or go out of your way to comfort them by word or deed?
• When have you wept at the loss of a loved one? What memories of that person do you still treasure and why?

Thursday, November 3, (#488)
Thirty-First Week in Ordinary Time

Luke 15:1-10: *"This man welcomes sinners and eats with them."*

Meditation:

Jesus reminds his listeners that the God he proclaims is one who is always on the side of the lost, the stray, and the prodigal. He will not rest until they are safely home and in the divine embrace. While this does not sit well with those who have another view of who is inside or outside of God's care, Jesus courageously tries to broaden their horizons – even at the cost of being rejected.

At La Salette, Mary also comes to a people who have lost their vision of God and yet refused to admit it. For her the lost and the stray were not only those who were despised and outcast, but also those who by their words and deeds had made them so. Even these were important to God, but in ways their hearts had not yet come to understand. For the power of their acceptance, their ability to reach out to others in love and care she knew could make the miracle of God's healing possible. This message could have been rejected, but her maternal care for even those who did not know they were lost, began a most unique and ongoing homecoming.

Reflection Questions:

- Do you believe that God's love is partial or impartial?
- Do you believe that there are some people who are outside of God's love and mercy? Do your attitudes and actions betray that belief?

Friday, November 4, (#489)
Thirty-First Week in Ordinary Time

Luke 16:1-8: *"For the children of this world are more astute in dealing with their own kind than are the children of light."*

Meditation:

Jesus' story of the dishonest steward becomes clearer in the light of the practice of stewards, who represent their masters, often engaging in the practice of usury. Their greed made them tack on extra fees to an original loan to be repaid that they would then skim off as the top of the debt. Having been caught, the steward "converts," goes back to the debtors and has them rewrite the debt to the original, minus the "hidden" commission. The master applauds the ingenuity in light of his personal situation. This is Jesus' way of calling people to a prudent use of material goods in the light of imminent crisis.

THE MESSAGE OF LA SALETTE is just such a wake-up call. Mary reminds the people of God of the imminent crisis that has resulted from their unwise stewardship of the gifts of life provided by their gracious God. The misuse of God's Name and Day, the irreverence towards people and the unwillingness to use more faithfully the time God gave them. She reminded them that the crisis could be averted through a turning back to God in their lives, to again use their lives as instruments of justice, healing and peace.

Reflection Questions:

- Are you using well the "goods" of the earth, the gifts of life and the talents with which God has entrusted you?

•How can you enter into that process of conversion that will make you more prudent "children of the light?"

Saturday, November 5, (#490)
Thirty-First Week in Ordinary Time

Luke 16:9-15: *"And if you are not trustworthy with what is not yours, who will give you what is your very own?"*

Meditation:

Jesus calls the people of his time to order their lives in such a way that the of God will always be the goal. If dishonest people can order their lives and dealings in a way that wins them friends and gets them what they want, should not honest people think of divine life and adapt their lives to obtaining it. Victory comes from the wise and honest use of the graces God gives to his faithful. Our lives are filled with opportunities to test our character as believers. The goals we set will guide us and determine the outcome. These goals cannot be compromised without leading to a divided heart.

At La Salette, Mary echoes Christ by calling us back to God's plans for us and the world, to seeing each other and our daily efforts through God's eyes. We must use the resources God has placed in our care to foster the healing, forgiveness and reconciliation which are the hallmarks of God's Kingdom. There are consequences both here and hereafter if we do not.

Reflection Questions:

•How are we, as persons, communities and nations, using our giftedness, our creativity, and the resources of our hearts and the fruits of our labors for the good of God's people?
•In the opportunities set before us that can test our character, is our allegiance to the God of Life or to "other gods?"

Sunday, November 6 (#156)
Thirty-Second Sunday in Ordinary Time

(2 Maccabees 7:1-2, 9-14; 2 Thessalonians 2:16 to 3:5; Luke 20:27-38)

Meditation: *What to Expect*

The Sadducees were up to no good. They wanted to get Jesus on their side in their ongoing quarrel with the Pharisees about resurrection. Using the question of the woman married to seven successive brothers (which they surely had already used on the Pharisees), they thought they had an unassailable position

There is, of course, nothing unusual about this. It has long been a standard in any form of debate. You back your adversary into a corner, with no apparent means of escape.

The two children who witnessed the Apparition of Our Lady of La Salette were often confronted with a similar reality. Some tried to bribe them to say they had lied, or at least to stop talking about what they had seen and heard. Others tried to trick them into contradicting themselves.

It is amazing that Maximin and Mélanie, totally unequipped for dealing with such onslaughts, never wavered. In their simplicity, they stunned people with their replies. Here are some examples:

Questioner: Maybe it was the devil that spoke to you?

Maximin: No, the devil wouldn't forbid us to blaspheme.

Questioner: The Lady was nothing but a bright cloud, was she?
Answer: Clouds don't talk!

Questioner: The Lady you saw is in jail in Grenoble.
Answer: It would take a clever one to catch her!

Questioner: It's easy to wrap yourself up in a cloud and disappear.
Mélanie: Let's see you do it!

None of this qualifies as persecution, but it reflects the hostility that people of faith some-

In their simplicity,
their replies can surprise you.

times encounter. We Catholics can feel inadequate when challenged by others who swear only by science, or who know the Bible better than we do, or point to scandals as reasons not to believe.

It is in some ways comforting to know that we should expect this, that we cannot make anyone else believe. Faith is not just opinion, so rational argument is one of the least effective ways of communicating it. But if we live it deeply, we just might have the right answer at the right moment.

Monday, November 7, (#491)
Thirty-Second Week in Ordinary Time

Luke 17:1-6: *"If your brother does something wrong, rebuke him and, if he is sorry, forgive him."*

Meditation:

In this passage, Jesus is addressing those he is calling to positions of leadership in his mission. A good leader is to be both courageous and compassionate in setting in motion the process of reconciliation. Sin and alienation are seen as facts of life, but so are both the need and the opportunities for offering the gift of forgiveness. The number "7" points out the importance of such unlimited love. The mission needs and seeks a constant growth in the faith which inspires and nourishes the life of a reconciler.

At La Salette, Mary calls the entire people of God to be leaders in the work of reconciliation. In their conversion of heart they can confidently turn to the God who forgives 70 times 7 times and always trust in divine mercy. They in turn can call others, caught in the inevitability of human sin, to seek that forgiveness. They – through prayer, the Eucharist and works of repairing shattered lives – can grow in faith and be instruments of unlimited, prodigal mercy.

Reflection Questions:

- In what ways do you need to grow in your faith as a reconciler?
- In the arithmetic of forgiveness, do you conserve or liberate the power of God's mercy for others?

Tuesday, November 8, (#492)
Thirty-Second Week in Ordinary Time

Luke 17:7-10: "*... when you have done all you have been told to do, say, 'We are useless servants: we have done no more than our duty.'*"

Meditation:

Jesus warns his disciples against an attitude of arrogance in their ministry of service to the Reign of God. All we do – our prayer, ministry, teaching, witness — should be guided by an outpouring of love for God's most needy and not a self-serving fear that worries about power, prestige or the gratitude of others. Our satisfaction should be the deep conviction of a job well done for the Lord.

AT LA SALETTE, Mary came not in the glory of power but in the humility of a loving servant. She sought no prestige for herself but the reconciliation of the lost. She looked for no merit of honor. She sought only to be an instrument for the healing of hearts, homes and world. She sought no flattery but only for God's work to be done.

Reflection Questions:

• What do you "expect" from God for the work you do as a minister?
• In your service, how closely do you resemble and imitate the "Mother of Reconciliation?"

Wednesday, November 9, (#671)
Dedication of the Basilica of St. John Lateran

John 2:13-22: "*Making a whip out of cord, (Jesus) drove all (the money changers) out of the Temple.*"

Meditation:

With rapidly changing cultural customs, it's at times difficult to keep current or remain politically correct. For example, when someone says that they are going to see their doctor, do we presume that it is a man they are speaking about? Yet there are certain actions that are never allowed, such as one spouse beating another or someone using excessive force with another. In today's gospel, according to Jewish custom, Jesus went up with the entire population of the kingdom of Judah to the Jerusalem temple for the Passover, the seven-day holiday of the Feast of Unleavened Bread. In this passage, as the Jerome Biblical Commentary mentions, this incident emphasizes Jesus' opposition to the "sacrificial system of Judaism (which) made "a marketplace" of the Temple," his Father's house (1968 edition, Prentice-Hall Publishers, Bruce Vawter, paragraph 65:16).

OUR BLESSED LADY'S TEARFUL WORDS to the two children about *"How long a time I have suffered for you... As for you, you pay no heed..."* and I gave you six days to work... and no one will give it to me..." express her tearful upset with our thoughtless response to God's pleadings. She is rightfully upset with her children. Her compassionate words directed to the two children about her concerns for their faith and their bodily welfare express her desire and hopes for her wayward people. They have neglected her Son's commandment to "keep holy the Sabbath" entering the temple of God, their parish church, for worship. She even mentions that *"in the winter, when (people) don't know what to do, they go to Mass just to make fun of religion."* This too defiles God's temple.

Reflection Questions:

•There are many ways to honor the "temple of God", your parish church. Do you worship in it regularly, support the needs of your parish community, participate in parish ministries, and reach out to the needy?
•Are you a good example to others in your family by the way you worship – your regular participation, your generosity to the parish community and its members?

Thursday, November 10, (#494)
Thirty-Second Week in Ordinary Time

Luke 17:20-25: *"For look, the kingdom of God is among you."*

Meditation:

Jesus is forever teaching his disciples and his listeners about the true meaning of the coming of the Messiah. Who will he be? How will we know him? What will his reign resemble? When will it arrive? Jesus taught, patiently but firmly, that the Messiah was not the revolutionary, political liberator his nation sought. The "revolution" was to be one of hearts mending, attitudes changing, lives turning around. This Kingdom's reign was to be already seen in his tolerance, love and forgiveness, in his welcoming of outcasts and sinners. And such a vision was a challenge to those with other, more fixed ideas.

MARY'S APPARITION AT LA SALETTE came in a time and place in history when thoughts of political "revolutions" still filled people's minds and hearts. Who would lead the nation to true peace? What type of government could allow such poverty and injustice to continue? Mary's message was a challenge to people to look first within themselves in order to recreate their hearts, turn their lives around, convert their relationships with God, self, others, the earth so that new ways of being and living would take shape from the inside out. This would truly be a revolution based on the power of the reconciling reign of God.

Reflection Questions:

•Do you look for answers to the great questions of peace and justice today by first examining your own heart, attitudes and actions?

•What role do you play as a reconciler in shaping the conscience of your institutions so that they may fashion instruments of peace rather than weapons of war?

Friday, November 11, (#495)
Thirty-Second Week in Ordinary Time

Luke 17:26-37: *"Anyone who tries to preserve his life will lose it; and anyone who loses it will keep it safe."*

Meditation:

This statement of Jesus comes as he seeks to call people to be prepared for the reign of God coming in all its power in their midst. Those who were unprepared in the past times of Noah and Lot squandered their energy in activity that had no orientation to heaven and even resulted in disaster for them and for the earth. Such times and pursuits are not only past memories for us. They stand as present reminders of our need to pursue the work of the Savior – the journey of self-surrender which leads to the cross, and glory and communion beyond.

MARY CAME TO LA SALETTE to call us to a new period of preparation that, if taken seriously, would usher in a "new springtime" for the earth and the people whom God has invited to care for it. The signs of the Kingdom coming would be seen in renewed relationships and reconciled lives and families. People would "lose" themselves in the healing service of a loving God and "save" their lives in passionate stewardship. Following the way Mary indicates for conversion, becomes a committed following of "The Way" that leads from death to life.

Reflection Questions:

- Does your seeking to "preserve" your way of living betray an unwillingness to enter the paschal mystery? Do your pursuits have a hint of heaven about them?
- In what ways do you "lose" yourself in service to the Kingdom of peace, reconciliation and justice?

Saturday, November 12, (#496)
Thirty-Second Week in Ordinary Time

Luke 18:1-8: *"Then (Jesus) told them a parable about the need to pray continually and never lose heart."*

Meditation:

Jesus taught his disciples to pray for the coming of the kingdom. He also taught them that this prayer must be an ongoing, vital and courageous part of their daily lives. Wherever and whenever justice is threatened or the poor, defenseless, vulnerable and powerless suffer, we must pray and work so that those who can make things right will open their ears and hearts to the cries that summon them "in the middle of the night." Our faithful prayer to the God who will not abandon those who cry out in their deepest need, to the God who cannot condone injustice will be heard if we do not despair. Hearts will change, conversion will happen and the work of our good and just God will prevail.

At La Salette, Mary recalled us to that sacred conversation with the God of life and hope that we call prayer. She urged us to explore again its most personal and public forms for their potential to heal and bring life. She reminded us to sanctify time and our daily routine by those moments of grace. She proclaimed again the promise that those who "pray well" can help "make well," by God's grace, what is ill, hurting and suffering.

Reflection Questions:

- Do you take the time to "pray well" as a vital part of your ministry of reconciliation? Or is your inability to pray a sign that you are "losing heart?"

Sunday, November 13 (#159)
Thirty-Third Sunday in Ordinary Time

(Malachi 3:19-20a; 2 Thessalonians 3:7-12; Luke 21:5-19)

Meditation: *An Obvious Choice*

There is a famous passage in the book of Deuteronomy where Moses says: "See, I have set before you life and death, the blessing and the curse. Choose life!" It would seem, as the saying goes, a no-brainer.

Today's Gospel, and the first reading, too, present a similar choice, this time between fear and hope. Jesus describes a coming time of trial in which "they will put some of you to death," and concludes: "By your perseverance you will save your lives." The seeming contradiction is resolved by understanding that there's life as we know it, and then there's the Life that is fuller, deeper.

At La Salette, Mary has her eye also on both realities. Life as "her people" knew it was hard. Their very survival was threatened by the failing crops and the rising rate of infant mortality. And yet, the Beautiful Lady dared to hold out a prophetic vision of a future of abundance.

The little word "if" at the beginning and the middle of her message indicated that there was a choice to be made. Again, the choice seems simple. Who wouldn't choose life? Who wouldn't choose abundance?

If the choice were only that simple! But every choice implies other choices, some of which we might rather not make. How many people, for example, enter upon a particular career only to find that the demands are more than they are willing or able to accept?

At La Salette, the demands seem quite easy. But it is a not a question only of returning to the practice of the faith. For many—then as now—the challenge is a return to faith itself.

Believers are, first of all, disciples, devoted to Christ, eager for a deep relationship with him. Resuming religious practices is a good start, but if faith is not there, the practices may soon be abandoned.

For many, however, I believe faith is still alive. Mary's word to them is a call to take advantage of what the Church offers to nourish that faith.

Faith involves renewing choices. The obvious choice, life/death, hope/fear is not always easy.

Monday, November 14, (#497)
Thirty-Third Week in Ordinary Time

Luke 18:35-43: "… *(the blind man) only shouted all the louder, 'Son of David, have pity on me.'*"

Meditation:

It may be that there is a slim line between hope and desperation. This gospel passage gives us a story of risk. The blind man takes a risk in asking what the commotion is all about: he may have been ignored. He takes a risk in calling Jesus' name: he could be quieted. (Indeed, he was!) He risked calling out a second time: he could have called forth a sterner rebuke. He risked answering Jesus' question: he could have been refused. He risked wanting to see, not knowing what his eyes would behold.

The main character in any gospel story, of course, is Jesus; but we can lose track of that when presented with such a compelling secondary character, especially if the character portrays something of issue in our own lives. If we keep our attention on Jesus, however, we find God's answer to our desperation and our risking. Jesus asks that the man be brought forward; he asks him what he can do for him; he grants the request. Could it be that Jesus is asking us to come closer? That he waits to hear what we want from him? That he continues to grant such requests? Have we called out to see?

LA SALETTE SUGGESTS that such may still be the case. The Beautiful Lady, in inviting the children closer, echoes all the Biblical passages that issue a similar invitation. God always seems to be inviting us closer. Our Lady's discourse and the choice she offers for conversion ask us to be in touch with what we really want from this life. The stories of the people who flock to the site of the Apparition, stories of conversion and healing and forgiveness, tell us that God had not been deaf to the prayers of his people. Can we dare believe that God hears us still?

Reflection Questions:

• What is the deepest desire of your heart? What do you want Jesus to do for you? Have you risked formulating that desire in your prayer?
• When you ask for some favor from God, do you first thank God for all that God has given you?

Tuesday, November 15, (#498)
Thirty-Third Week in Ordinary Time

Luke 19:1-10: *"The Son of man has come to seek out and save what was lost."*

Meditation:

The words of Jesus to Zacchaeus recall so many of Jesus' remarks and teachings in other places. The parables in Luke 15 readily come to mind: the shepherd who leaves the ninety-nine sheep to go in search of the stray; the woman who diligently sweeps her house until she finds her lost money; the father who is found to be anxiously awaiting the return of his prodigal son. And yet this response to Zacchaeus seems somehow out of place. The full story makes it seem as if it were Zacchaeus' initiative that brought him into Jesus' sight. After all, he heard that Jesus was passing by; he sought for a way to see him; he ran ahead and climbed a tree. And yet Jesus says that he has been in search of the lost, and has found such a one here. And this is great news. Maybe Jesus is suggesting that God is always taking the initiative no matter what it looks like. All our efforts to seek God end in our realizing that God has been seeking us all along.

WHEN WE TURN OUR ATTENTION TO LA SALETTE – or to Marian apparitions in general – there is an underlying question that often goes ignored. Beyond the questions of what happened and what was said, there is the question of why this would happen in the first place. What is God doing in these graced events? The answer to that question seems so obvious at La Salette. It is obvious in Mary calling us her children; it's obvious in the way Maximin's father was convinced when he heard the story of his own experience at Corps on the lips of the Beautiful Lady. God has shown us once again that the lost continue to be God's concern. The words that Jesus spoke to Zacchaeus could very easily have been Mary's at La Salette: *"I have come to search out and save what was lost."* "Because I love you; because my Son gave his life for you; because you are precious in God's sight." ***"Make this known to all my people."***

Reflection Questions:

• Does the suggestion that God always takes the initiative ring true in your experience?
• Are there parts of your life that even now feel "lost" or "strayed?" Might God be seeking these out for God's forgiveness? How might you be called to share in the reconciliation ministry of Jesus?

Wednesday, November 16, (#499)
Thirty-Third Week in Ordinary Time

Luke 19:11-28: *"Take the (gold coin) from him and give it to the man who has ten (gold) coins."*

Meditation:

Jesus will borrow from all avenues of human experience in order to make the points in his stories. That is probably just another way of showing that all of experience is revelatory of God. In this parable there are elements of economics and politics with which the people of the time no doubt readily identified. But what is the point of this story about a dangerous and ruthless king? It appears to be one of those parables of contrast Luke is fond of recounting. *"If a friend would get up at midnight, won't your heavenly Father be quicker to answer?"* *"If you know how to give good things to your children, won't your heavenly Father give the Holy Spirit?"* *"If an unjust judge will give justice to an aggrieved widow, won't your heavenly Father give justice to his children who cry to him?"* Here we might paraphrase: *"If a ruthless ruler rewards faithfulness in the investing of time and property, won't God's reward be even greater?"*

IN REFLECTING UPON THE DISCOURSE AT LA SALETTE, we also find an economic and political aspect. The poverty that besets the people is reflected in their choices of working overtime. Their lives are consumed with worry about future harvests: will there be enough? Mary's words echo those of the Gospel: "If you are faithful, the harvest will be plentiful. You who choose to ignore God's invitation to life will find that there is nothing left." The invitation is to life, whether in the Gospel, at La Salette, in our prayer, or in our coming together as Church.

Reflection Questions:

•Have you experienced God's bounty as a result of conversion or faithfulness?
•Do you recognize the call to conversion as the invitation of a loving God?

Thursday, November 17, (#500)
Thirty-Third Week in Ordinary Time

Luke 19:41-44: *"If you too had only recognized on this day the way to peace! But in fact it is hidden from your eyes!"*

Meditation:

Jesus speaks the above line as he weeps over Jerusalem. And even though the words can seem like a final judgment, phrased as it is in the conditional past, that never seems to be the way it is with God. That's what upset Jonah, for example, when he preached God's judgment upon Nineveh, only to find that when the population repented in sackcloth and ashes, God "repented" of the destruction planned. So, too, with the people Moses was leading out of Egypt. When God looked upon their desertion and their worship of the molten calf, his judgment to Moses was that he was going to destroy all of them. Moses' intervention swayed God once again to repent. One has the distinct impression that Jesus in tears would still relent of the judgment against the rulers of the age, if even now they would recognize the path to peace being offered in the person of Jesus.

Mary's words at La Salette are similar and are also spoken in tears. "*If only* my people recognized how much I suffer for them! *If only* they recognized the power in the name of my Son! *If only* they would come again to church, to the banquet spread before them! *If only* they would be converted! *If only...*" The possibility exists that we might even now recognize the offer being made with tears, and return to the God who loves us. That possibility is never taken from us.

Reflection Questions:

• What could possibly be an obstacle to your knowing the path to peace or recognizing God present in your daily life?
• Are there times when you think God's offer of love has been revoked? What would convince you to keep your hope alive?

Friday, November 18, (#501)
Thirty-Third Week in Ordinary Time

Luke 19:45-48: *"... the whole people hung on his words."*

Meditation:

Well, maybe not the entire populace; after all, this Gospel says that the chief priests and scribes and leaders of the people were looking for a way to destroy Jesus. But you get the picture: a charismatic speaker, one whose message was eagerly received, one whose message captured the people's imagination, fired their hope. This is someone to reckon with, someone not to be ignored. And yet that was somehow not enough. How do people move from captivating words to a change of heart? What could God do to move that process along? And the answer God presents is Jesus on the Cross. It's God asking, "Can you ignore this? Is this convincing enough for you? What more can I do?"

WHAT MORE INDEED! And yet the event at La Salette is God trying to get our attention. "Look, I send the Mother of my Son in tears!" At La Salette the children also hung on Mary's words. Her discourse demanded attention. But the children recounted that their attention was drawn to the crucifix the Beautiful Lady wore on her breast. The light seemed to radiate from that point and the corpus seemed so life-like. Whatever the message God sends, whatever the promise, whatever the invitation, it has to be heard against the backdrop of the Cross. This shows how serious God is about wanting us, about loving us, about saving us.

Reflection Questions:

• Do you find the Cross compelling in your own life of faith, your own devotional practices?
• How has your understanding of the place of the Cross, at the center of Christian faith, changed over the years?

Saturday, November 19, (#502)
Thirty-Third Week in Ordinary Time

Luke 20:27-40: *"Now he is God, not of the dead, but of the living; for to him everyone is alive."*

Meditation:

Jesus' detractors could not have argued with the first part of his conclusion. That God is the God of the living is clear in the Old Testament. Isaiah 38:18-19, for example, says that it is not the dead who praise God, but the living. There are a number of Psalms that sing of praising God *"in the land of the living."* God is the one who confers life, calls to life, and through the Prophet asks the people to "choose life." Life is what God is all about, so it is not strange to see that Jesus would identify himself with that orientation.

In John's Gospel, Jesus declares that he is *"the resurrection and the life,"* and that he has come that we *"may have life and have it to the full."* But the second part of Jesus' argument poses a problem. To assert that *"all are alive in him"* suggest an inclusiveness in God that does not characterize the leaders of the people – at least as they are portrayed in the Gospel. It was Jesus' inclusivity that got him in trouble with the authorities: he *"ate with sinners,"* was seen in the company of "outcasts," invited a tax collector to be his disciple, told the lowly they were blessed. What he was saying is that God's love is extended to everyone. All need to have the good news preached to them. In God's eyes, everyone matters – *"all are alive in him."*

Mary's message at La Salette is just as inclusive. Her tears are for the cart drivers who take the name of her Son in vain, for those who never go to church and those who go only to mock religion, for those who hold the dying children in their arms, and for those who will suffer because of famine. Mary's maternal concern reaches out to all her children. All are to be the recipients of the message of hope that she entrusts to Maximin and Melanie – themselves counted as little in the eyes of the world, but of infinite value in God's eyes. *"Make this known to all my people,"* says the Beautiful Lady. All need to know they matter; all are alive for God.

Reflection Questions:

- Do you believe that you matter in the eyes of God? Did you always believe this? What changed your mind?
- Are there people (or groups of people) you "naturally" consider cut off from God's love and God's offer of salvation or forgiveness? Where does this come from? Is it in accord with the view of the Gospel?

Sunday, November 20, (#162)
Feast of Christ the King
(Our Lord Jesus Christ, King of the Universe)

(2 Samuel 5:1-3; Colossians 1:12-20; Luke 23:35-43)

Meditation: *Making Peace*

When explaining the notion of personal spirituality I often use the example of religious orders as they might contemplate the crucifixion. It seems to me that a Jesuit would see Christ "obedient unto death," while a Franciscan would be touched most deeply by the absolute poverty of Jesus on the cross. Today's second reading expresses the La Salette focus: Jesus is "reconciling all things for God, making peace by the blood of his cross."

It is curious that Mary at La Salette did not use the word "reconciliation" and yet, when after Vatican II all religious orders were asked to return to their roots and rediscover their charism (their distinct spirituality) the spirit of reconciliation is what emerged for the La Salette Missionaries. For us it is like the air we breathe, and it characterizes almost everything we do.

Very soon after the Apparition, it was the faithful who gave Mary the title, "Reconciler of Sinners." Six years later, when the Bishop of Grenoble founded the Missionaries of Our Lady of La Salette, he re-

ferred to them as destined to "exercise the ministry of reconciliation." It's what we do. It's who we are.

When Mary said, "You will make this known to all my people," she was not telling us only to repeat her words, but to bring the spirit of the Apparition to all people, to do what she herself came to do, namely to help her people —our people — respond to the love of him who died for us. We should resonate with every passage in the Bible that concerns reconciliation, especially where we see Jesus associating with sinners and outcasts, restoring lepers to their human dignity, forgiving those who nailed him to a cross, etc.

Of the Seven Last Words of Jesus, the one in today's Gospel is among those that speak most eloquently to all those devoted in any way to La Salette. Christ, obedient and poor, innocent of any crime, extends his reconciling love to a real criminal: "Today you will be with me in paradise."

La Salette Missionaries, La Salette Sisters, and La Salette Associates long to accomplish in our world what Jesus accomplished in that moment.

Monday, November 21, (#503) Thirty-Fourth Week in Ordinary Time

Luke 21:1-4: *"I tell you truly, this poor widow has put in more than any of them."*

Meditation:

I recall as a child hearing this "poor widow" praised for her generosity and held up as a model for us. "Don't give from your excess; give from what you need to live on." This would be an expression of our trust in God. Indeed there are some who continue to preach this "ideal" of trust: give away what you need and God will provide. But none of this is contained in this Gospel story found only in Mark and Luke. Luke especially critiques the rich in his Gospel; the rich too easily exploit the poor, too easily ignore the word of God. We might do well, then, to suspect an issue of justice is being raised in this story. "Widows and orphans" were two groups to be treated with care, respect, and justice in Israel. The sustaining relationships in their lives – those of husband and father respectively – had been taken away. It was incumbent on the community to support those so bereft. This widow should not have been expected to support the temple treasury, and yet gives the little she has – maybe in appreciation that she is cared for by the community. And Jesus, who says she has given so much, is judging as God judges: the little given is recognized as the gift of a generous heart.

THERE IS A SOCIO-ECONOMIC CRITIQUE inherent in La Salette as well. It may not be most obvious, but it is there. Our Lady's tears are for those who have been cut off from the church, those who no longer recognize her Son living among them. But often those working on Sunday were not doing so because they enjoyed it; they had no choice if they were to eke out a living. Landlords and tax collectors expected to be paid and didn't care what that meant for the people subjected to them. But conversion has amazing ramifications – *"a humble, contrite heart, O God, you will not spurn."* (Psalm 51) Yes, God loves generous hearts; but conversion is also needed on the part of society. The workers should not be enslaved; all human life is worthwhile; the Sabbath recalls our dignity and our relatedness. We are converted as we relearn those lessons together.

Reflection Questions:

•Do you act out of the belief that the community dimension of salvation is important? Where do you most feel or experience that dimension?

•How do you stand up for and speak out for the dignity of the lowly, those whose voices often go unheard?

Tuesday, November 22, (#504)
Thirty-Fourth Week in Ordinary Time

Luke 21:5-11: *"And when you hear of wars and revolutions, do not be terrified."*

Meditation:

There are many "background" themes in the Bible, themes to which we may not pay immediate attention as we focus on the dominant themes of God's love, forgiveness, salvation. One of these important background themes is that of the presence of fear and anxiety and the calming reassurance that these lose power in the face of faith in the presence of a loving God. Jesus had earlier declared that his disciples should not be anxious about what to eat and what to wear. God would provide those things (Luke 12: 22-32). Tomorrow's Gospel passage suggests the disciples should not worry about what to say when dragged before the magistrates. What is necessary for their defense will be provided.

And so today the words *"do not be terrified"* about wars and insurrections are meant to comfort. Even more, they are meant to focus the hearers: "Don't be sidetracked," Jesus might be saying. "If your fears and anxieties get the better of you, you will not be focused on my words, on the truth of my teachings, on the presence of the Spirit among you." Jesus never said we would not feel fear or anxiety. It is simply that every time we do feel those things, we should hear him saying to his disciples (and to us), "Don't be afraid; don't be anxious."

IT IS ALSO COMFORTING that at La Salette our Weeping Mother bid the children not to be afraid. But more than comforting, it is also focusing. Putting aside their fears, the children are able to hear clearly the message they are meant to retell. It is likely that through all the times ahead when they were questioned, put through examinations and accusations, they took courage and strength from Our Lady's words, *"Do not be afraid."* Our own lives are filled with fears and anxieties, trivial or sublime, about ourselves or those we love. On a larger scale, we live in a world of war and violence. "Where is God in all this?" we may ask. God is present in the midst of it, saying, "Don't be anxious or perturbed, otherwise you may miss the words and ways of peace I am even now speaking."

Reflection Questions:

• Are you aware of the things, the situations that stir up fears and anxieties in you?
• How has focusing on God's words (in Scripture, in Eucharist) or God's presence (in the Spirit, in the love of your friends) helped you make it through those anxious times?

Wednesday, November 23, (#505)
Thirty-Fourth Week in Ordinary Time

Luke 21:12-19: *"You will be handed over to the synagogues and to imprisonment... for the sake of my name."*

Meditation:

Throughout the New Testament it is evident that Jesus' name is special and important. Reflected back into the infancy narratives, the very story of the Annunciation, the name is given: *"Look! You are to conceive in your womb and bear a son, and you must name him Jesus"* (Luke 1:31). It is this name that has power to heal: *"In the name of Jesus Christ the Nazarene, walk!"* (Acts 3:6). It has the power to save: *"Only in him is there salvation; for of all the names in the world given to men, this is the only one by which we can be saved."'* (Acts 4:11-12). But that name also brings Jesus' disciples into conflict. This is the other side of the story, one not to be forgotten or denied. The choice for Jesus means standing beside him even when that incurs the loss of relationships and reputation. *"Your perseverance will win you your lives."* (Luke 21:19).

AT LA SALETTE, Mary reminded us that we had forgotten the power of the name of her Son. Instead, that name became a convenient "throw-in" when swearing. It no longer remained the source of healing, the source of salvation, the name that demanded a decision for discipleship. In calling her people to salvation, Mary was calling them to remember their own identity as disciples. Yes, that road is a rocky one. But it is the remembering of our identity as loved and blessed and saved that is at stake here. Only this sacred memory gives us the power to see those rocks on the road changed into *"heaps of wheat."*

Reflection Questions:

• Have you ever experienced rejection because of your own decision for Jesus? Or has fear of rejection kept you from acknowledging your own joy and blessedness in being a Christian? What did either of those experiences feel like?

• At what times have you known beyond a doubt that Jesus' name was a source of power in your life?

Thursday, November 24, (#506)
Thirty-Fourth Week in Ordinary Time

Luke 21:20-28: *"Alas for those with child, or with babies at the breast, when those days come!"*

Meditation:

The image of a nursing mother is a revered one in Scripture. It describes the tender love that exists between God and Israel; and should a mother forget the child in her arms (which cannot be imagined!), even then would God remember Israel, says Isaiah. " ... *like a little child in its mother's arms, like a little child, so I keep myself*" (Psalm 131:2). *"Blessed the womb that bore you and the breasts that fed you,"* shouts a woman from the crowd when Jesus had finished preaching (Luke 11: 27).

This symbol of life, of tender love, of goodness, then, becomes a source of great mourning when not fulfilled. When the world is a place of darkness, to have brought children into it is a great sorrow. When Jesus meets the sorrowing women on the way to Golgotha, he says, " ... *do not weep for me; weep rather for yourselves and for your children. For look, the days are surely coming when people will say, 'Blessed are those who are barren, the wombs that have never borne children, the breasts that have never suckled!'"* (Luke 23:28-29).

AMONG THE LIST OF DIRE SITUATIONS named by Our Lady at La Salette, the most difficult to hear is that of infants dying in the arms of those who hold them. This is made all the more terrible when spoken by our Weeping Mother, one who knows the sorrow of the loss of a child. There is no greater anguish than that experienced by a mother who says, "I wish I had never given birth!" And so this becomes an appropriate metaphor for existence in a world that has lost all meaning. It is only through the eyes of the converted that the ugliness and sin of the world can be redeemed at all. It is only in the hearts of the converted that there is enough space, enough courage, to hold grief and death until it become transformed by the Spirit of God residing there. That is why Our Lady begs us in tears to remember her Son and to submit our lives to him.

Reflection Questions:

- Have you ever felt that the world had become "too crazy" to endure? That your life had lost all meaning? What assured you that such was not the case? Do images of childbearing and nursing speak of God's tender love today?
- Are there other, more compelling images for you or for us? What might they be?

Friday, November 25, (#507)
Thirty-Fourth Week in Ordinary Time

Luke 21:29-33: *"Sky and earth will pass away, but my words will never pass away."*

Meditation:

When writing to his friend, Timothy, Paul is in prison. He says he is wearing chains for preaching the Gospel, the very Gospel he is urging Timothy to preach fearlessly. *"I have to put up with suffering, even to being chained like a criminal. But God's message cannot be chained up."* (2 Timothy 2:9)! This is an image with roots in the Old Testament, where God declares through the prophet Isaiah, *"the word that goes from my mouth … will not return to me unfulfilled or before having carried out my good pleasure and having achieved what it was sent to do."* (Isaiah 55:11). Our faith always calls us to discern that which is lasting, to note what is of value in a world where so much is transient and unimportant. It is listening (with the ears of our hearts) to the Word of God that allows this discernment to take place, recognizing that Word as incapable of being chained, recognizing that Word as always fruitful.

THAT MESSAGE OF SOMETHING LASTING at the heart of the world could be proclaimed from the mountains of France over 1,800 years after Jesus' death; that the words of the Gospel are still proclaimed among a people of faith today gives testimony to its lasting character. Even more amazing is when we recognize this Word in places we didn't expect – on the streets, at work, from our children, on the lips of the outcast – when we thought it was "only in church" or in the passages of Scripture. If that message could be heard (and proclaimed!) by two children who counted little in the eyes of the world on the barren slopes of the French Alps, then maybe that Word can be at work in our world today – maybe even in our own hearts and kept alive on own lips.

Reflection Questions:

- Where are the "normal" places you go to be nourished by the Word of God? How do you count on the Word being fruitful?
- Have you ever been surprised by hearing God's Word in places or from people where you never expected to hear it or recognize it?

Saturday, November 26, (#508) Thirty-Fourth Week in Ordinary Time

Luke 21:34-36: *"Stay awake, praying at all times ..."*

Meditation:

These are the last words Jesus speaks in the Gospel of Luke prior to the account of the Last Supper and his Passion and Death. They are words that have been spoken before as Jesus recounted parables of vigilance. They are words taken up especially by Paul as he writes to various communities of Christians. Watch and pray. Perhaps these are the hallmarks of the Christian life, interwoven in the way we live out each day. We are alert for the signs of God's presence; we pray daily for God's coming. Our praying helps keep us vigilant; our vigilance shows us what to bring into our prayer. Once we have recognized our call to redemption in Jesus; once we have given our lives over to Christ in Baptism, this may be – surprisingly – the best description of what to do "until Jesus, comes again:" watch and pray.

OUR BLESSED MOTHER doesn't give us a very different message at La Salette. She calls us, through the message given to the children, to notice our own behavior as well as what goes on in the world. It's as if, being alert to God's presence in the world, we would never have forgotten the name of her Son, never have wanted to separate ourselves from the community that gathers to remember Jesus at Eucharist. Moreover, the poignant story Mary tells of Maximin and his father at the farm in Coin, suggests that God is ever alert to what happens in our lives. If we were as alert, we would notice God's loving gaze upon all that transpires. Maybe this is why Mary tells the children that prayer is so important: it's the activity that will help us notice that loving presence of God in our lives. Watch — and pray. Pray — and notice.

Reflection Questions:

- *"Do you pray well, my children?"* How well do I pray?
- Are there things I am becoming aware of that keep me from being watchful, alert to the presence or action of God's Spirit in my life?

Sunday, November 27 (#001)
First Sunday of Advent

(Isaiah 2:1-5; Romans 13:11-14; Matthew 24:37-44)

Meditation: *Awake in the Light*

Isaiah's image of the Mountain lends itself easily to a La Salette reading, especially in the words, "Come, let us climb the Lord's mountain... that he may instruct us in his ways and we may walk in his paths... Let us walk in the light of the Lord."

Mary appeared on a mountain, in light. Hers is a reflected light, the source of which is the crucifix she wears. When she invited Maximin and Mélanie to come to her, she was calling them to "walk in the light of the Lord."

St. Paul writes, "It is the hour now for you to awake from sleep... The day is at hand." That is the essence of Mary's message. It is a curious coincidence, but probably no more than that, that the two children had fallen asleep after their lunch and had just awakened when they saw the globe of light in which the Beautiful Lady gradually became visible.

Jesus tells us to "stay awake," to be ready for his return. He even compares himself to a thief, that comes by night.

If you have ever tried to stay awake when you are tired, you know it is not just an act of the will. You took means to stay awake: moving around, doing some work, engaging in a conversation.

Staying awake so as not to be caught off-guard when Jesus comes means not growing slack in our faith. St. Paul, in the same letter in which he insists over and over that faith is the source of salvation—not works—does not hesitate to insist also that we need to "conduct ourselves properly as in the day."

Mary came to La Salette precisely because her people were not awake and ready. They had grown indeed very slack in their faith. Neglecting the simplest requirements of Christian life, they had come to lose respect even for Jesus himself, who is the light of the world, in whose light we are called to walk.

Monday, November 28, (#175)
First Week of Advent

Matthew 8:5-11: *"...just give the word and my servant will be cured."*

Meditation:

Mother Teresa of Calcutta was asked in a television interview why she worked among the poorest of the poor. Her answer was simple and straightforward: "Because Jesus asked us to do it." There is no other reason to act, except for our faith in the person of Jesus.

"If you had faith the size of a mustard seed, you would be able to say to this mountain, 'Move from here to there,' and it would move" (Matt 17:20). This simple statement, "just say the word," is evidence of the father's faith. Strengthened by his desire to see his servant get better, he expresses not doubt but only true belief in the person of Jesus. "Jesus asked us to do it!" This is all we need do in order to act according to the Father's will. By retelling countless saving acts he performed in our midst, the Advent season helps strengthen our faith in preparation for the Savior's coming anew.

In Mary's message at La Salette we find this simple statement: "Rocks and stones will be changed into mounds of wheat and potatoes will be self-sown in the fields." Is this difficult to believe? "Just do it" and it shall come to pass. Mary seems not to favor a middle-of-the-road position either. With her it is all or nothing. The disciple must believe with undivided heart. "One cannot serve both God and money" (Matt 6:24b). Coming to believe with an undivided heart is possibly the greatest journey of all. It leads to the greatest gift of all, the freedom of the children of God.

Reflection Questions:

- Is your heart divided?
- What do you really care about?

Tuesday, November 29, 1, (#176)
First Week of Advent

Luke 10:21-24: *"I bless you, Father, Lord of heaven and of earth, for hiding these things from the learned and the clever and revealing them to little children."*

Meditation:

The Advent season is a time of preparation for a great happening, a revelation to "little children." Many people say that Christmas is for children. The true gift of Christmas does seem to be destined for the childlike, but this is far from saying that it is kid's stuff. *"I bless you, Father,"* Jesus prays, because it is the Father's choice that is manifested in those who believe.

Let us recall those words of the Lord in John's Gospel which clearly state that the believers were singled out by the Father himself and given to Jesus: *"I revealed your name to those whom you took out of the world to give to me"* (John 17:6). Candid trust opens *"little children"* to Jesus and prompts them to welcome his teachings. The same criterion holds true in our day. It is through Jesus that one enters the true life. Did he not say: *"I am the Way; I am Truth and Life"* (John 14:6a)?

THIS CHILDLIKE SPIRIT is very much at home at the site of the La Salette apparition. The witnesses to it were "little children" indeed.

They had no difficulty welcoming the revelation of the Beautiful Lady, dressed like a peasant woman. Maximin and Melanie typified the poorest in their small village, and for that reason they were chosen to be bearers of a message from heaven. Is this not the fundamental rule of the spiritual life? One must be entirely stripped of self in order to welcome God's revelation. In so many of its facets, the La Salette event reflects nothing but poverty and simplicity. Self-importance and self-reliance are nowhere to be seen. They obviously serve no lasting purpose!

Reflection Questions:

- What place does knowledge occupy in your life?
- Do you look down on the less fortunate and consider them inferior?

Wednesday, November 30, (#684)
St. Andrew, Apostle

Matthew 4:18-22: *"(Jesus) said to them, 'Come after me and I will make you fishers of people.' And at once they left their nets and followed him."*

Meditation:

Would that we were as instantly responsive to Jesus as the disciples in the gospel. In both Matthew and Luke, the point of this story is that the four disciples actually followed Jesus despite the fact that they did not know him. Perhaps a deeper point might be that, in the realm of faith, we can – and at time are urged to – "make a leap of faith", doing what would probably look quite reckless or thoughtless by those who insist on clear "reasoned decisions" from mature and responsible adults. When we look at the wider vision of what Jesus is doing – choosing specific men to become leaders in his church – perhaps we can sense a "joyful, inspired response" in this gospel event.

AT LA SALETTE, Mary chooses two unschooled children to be her messengers. They too respond quite spontaneously to her invitation to *"Come near"* and eventually to *"make (her) message know to all (her) people."* Certainly Mary is truly being led by the Holy Spirit in her mysterious choice of Maximin and Melanie. Yet surprisingly – and, it might be said, miraculously – they are true to their task until the end

338

of their days. At times we are a bit too cautious in matters of faith. When our pastor asks from the pulpit or elsewhere for assistance with this or that project, if we feel a mysterious urge to respond instantly, perhaps we should step out and take a chance, like in the instance with the disciples of old, that it might be God's spirit calling us to serve in some unexpected way.

Reflection Questions:

- Has there been an instance where you instantly felt an inner calling to step forth to help in a special situation and did so willingly?
- Whom do you know who often responds with generosity to help others in their need?

Thursday, December 1, (#178)
First Week of Advent

Matthew 7:21,24-27: *"Everyone who listens to these words of mine and acts on them will be like a sensible man who built his house on rock."*

Meditation:

The 14-year-old newspaper carrier blushed with embarrassment at the attention given him by the media. After noticing strange circumstances at a customer's residence, he had done no more than what he believed was the right thing to do. The elderly man had suffered a stroke and had been lying on his kitchen floor unable to move for some time. Because he had called for help, the teenager was credited with saving the man's life. Actions bring life into clear focus. Furthermore, putting Jesus' words into practice quickens the blessing of God's Spirit within us. Jesus showed us the way by living his life as the Father designed every human life to be lived, in deep trust and with loving submission to its Creator. And so his actions and deeds were grace-filled.

The Beautiful Lady of La Salette calls us to action. There is order in creation, she reminds us, and we must respect such order: *"And they will not give it to me ... "* Though we "will never be able to repay the pains she has taken for us," it is quite evident that the La Salette Event calls for a response. Her tears must not leave us unmoved. We are her people; her visit is designed to challenge us. Through it she begs us to find a better way of serving her Son. It is no less than a call to conversion: "Open your eyes to reality," the gracious Lady seems to be telling us. "Advent time is here. Prepare to welcome the Lord of your life!"

Reflection Questions:

- Can you list a few way that show you are living the gospel message?
- Do you know someone who is obviously living the gospel message?

Friday, December 2, (#179)
First Week of Advent

Matthew 9:27-31: *"Do you believe I can do this?"*

Meditation:

We learn from Scripture that while visiting his own town, Jesus could work no miracle there. The townspeople knew him too well as the son of Mary and Joseph, and as a result would put no faith in him (Matthew 13:58). His inquiry then, *"Do you believe I can do this?"* is not a mere rhetorical question, but one that is probing for trusting hearts, channels open to grace. Jesus seems to confirm this interpretation when he tells the blind men, "'According to your faith, let it be done to you.'" Life itself is gift. We should expect that each enhancement of life will be a gift as well. All things come to us as a blessing from God. Trust in God's goodness must mark each of our days. Jesus seems to be emphasizing this very fact by asking, *"Do you believe I can do this?"*

THE STORY OF THE APPARITION reveals a similar call. Mary prods Maximin's memory concerning spoiled wheat, recalling a walk back home to Corps with his father some time before. His dad had said to him, *"Here, my child, eat some bread while we still have it this year, because I don't know who will eat any next year if the wheat keeps up like this."* This very personal information startles the boy and jogs his memory. It further tells us that no human adventure eludes God's awareness. In visiting with us at La Salette, Mary attempts to reach that hidden core of goodness which is found in each and every one of us. Is this not a call to greater openness and deeper trust?

Reflection Questions:

- What is your part in God's creation?
- Do you trust that you can make a difference?

Saturday, December 3, (#180)
First Week of Advent

Matthew 9:35 to 10:1,5a,6-8: *"And as you go, proclaim that..."*

Meditation:

Quite popular is the following passage from the prophet Isaiah, *"How beautiful on the mountains are the feet of the messenger announcing peace, of the messenger of good news"* (Isaiah 52:7). Going about announcing that *"the kingdom of heaven is at hand"* (Matthew 10:7b) was Jesus' mission. It is also the mission of the disciples as they go through life. There is good news to be told. *"No one light a lamp and then put it under a tub; they put it on the lampstand where it shines for everyone in the house"* (Matthew 5:15). Making this announcement is part and parcel of the call to be a Christian. The gift is so great that it must be brought to the attention of all. The true blessing of the word is the life it bestows, a life it abundantly blesses with peace and joy, with hope and fulfillment. *"I have told you this so that my own joy may be in you and your joy be complete"* (John 15:11).

"**WELL, MY CHILDREN,** *you will make this known to all my people.*" Our Lady's closing words are similar. Since she said this twice, her commission also carries a note of urgency. Little Maximin was the first to share the exciting news of the visit from the Beautiful Lady with childlike excitement. Melanie was called away from her chores in the stable and asked whether she too had seen a lovely Lady. Without hesitation she confirmed the truth of her companion's report. The news spread like wildfire. After all, the episode included a number of startling aspects: the cowherds repeated the message the Lady had delivered in French, a language they were barely familiar with; questioned separately, the two witnesses related essentially the same rather detailed story; they would also subsequently remain steadfast in the testimony over a long period of time and under sometimes grueling questioning. The message is clearly good – and even great – news. The efforts we expend to spread this gift should be proportionate to our appreciation of its value.

Reflection Questions:

- Are you ready to share the tremendous blessing of your faith?
- What first step in this direction might you take today?

Sunday, December 4 (#004)
Second Sunday of Advent

(Isaiah 11:1-10; Romans 15:4-9; Matthew 3:1-12)

Meditation: *The Sin of Presumption*

John the Baptist didn't mince his words. He told the Pharisees and Sadducees not to presume that they were righteous simply because they were descendants of Abraham, but to "produce good fruits" to show that their repentance was genuine.

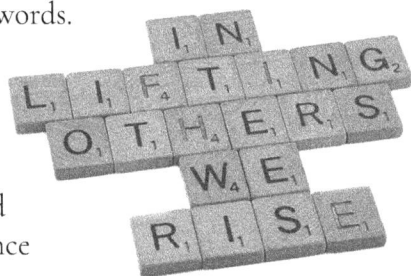

Today we can adapt this passage to read,
"Do not presume to say that you are righteous simply because you are baptized."

Most of the people of France in 1846 were baptized Catholics. In fact, the word "Christian" in French often was used as a synonym for "human being." At La Salette the Blessed Virgin showed in a variety of ways, however, that, of itself, just being baptized simply isn't good enough.

In fact, who offends more by blaspheming Jesus' name—the non-believer or the baptized Christian? How can a Christian swear, using the name of Jesus, and then claim that he doesn't "mean anything" by it?

At the very least, Mary shows us that the name of Christian isn't simply a label stuck on us when we were baptized. St. Paul puts it another way, reminding us that we should "with one voice glorify the

God and Father of our Lord Jesus Christ."

The fulfillment of Isaiah's vision of peace isn't automatic. Rather it anticipates a time when "the earth shall be filled with knowledge of the Lord." Our Lady of La Salette looked upon a "Christian" world and found it to be far from filled with that knowledge. And so she wept.

Advent by its nature invites us, like Isaiah, to look forward, as we say at every Mass after the Lord's Prayer, to "the blessed hope and the coming of our Savior, Jesus Christ."

Mary offers a vision of hope as well. But neither she nor the prophet implies that we should wait passively for these things to come about. Both of them challenge us to respond by showing our change of heart in our way of life, to "produce good fruits."

Mary's "people," in that time of famine, would have understood: planting the seed is not enough. The plant has to be cultivated. Anything else is mere presumption.

Monday, December 5, (#181)
Second Week of Advent

Luke 5:17-26: *"What are these thoughts you have in your hearts?"*

Meditation:

What lies in the heart distinguishes people one from another. One person will be capable of heroic sacrifice; another will be crassly self-serving. One will be happy and radiate enthusiasm; another will wrestle with doubt and court despair. Let us recall the fate his brothers visited upon Joseph because their hearts were jealous of the love their father lavished on this son (see Genesis 37). What is the difference between Cain and Abel? Is it not a decision reached in the recesses of the heart? The fully transparent heart is entirely of one mind, and the commandment of love requires us to be of undivided mind, the mind of God. It follows then that the heart of the Christian must be of Christ's mind, fully given over to the Father: *"My food is to do the will of the one who sent me ... "* (John 4:34). The thoughts of a heart divided will prove divisive and thereby contribute to the disintegration and destruction of life. *"Anyone who is not with me is against me,"* Jesus cautions, *"and anyone who does not gather in with me throws away"* (Matthew 12:30).

MARY'S WORDS AT LA SALETTE are a heartfelt plea for the people's return to their God, a single-minded and unyielding call for submission to his will in crucial areas of their religious practice: Sunday rest and worship, reverence for the Lord's holy name, fidelity to the church's precept of abstinence. The decision to make "a mockery of religion," she is at some pains to emphasize, can have rather adverse consequences: *"I warned you last year with the potatoes. You paid no heed."* Though we rarely carry the thought that far, our abuse, rather than proper use, of God's creation is a rebellious proposition – a perilous declaration of independence.

Reflection Questions:

- What lies in your heart? Dare you sound its depths in light of this day's gospel passage?
- How are you doing God's will for you today?

Tuesday, December 6, (#182) Second Week of Advent

Matthew 18:12-14: *"...it is never the will of your Father in heaven that one of these little ones should be lost."*

Meditation:

The Father's plan is fully revealed in Jesus. "[Jesus] went around all of Galilee, teaching in their synagogues, proclaiming the gospel of the kingdom, and curing every disease and illness among the people" (Matt 4:23). Because of Jesus' coming into our world, gifts of harmony and wholeness have been bestowed upon us. After being away from the church for a number of years, a woman approached the Sacrament of Reconciliation. Her life's journey had reached a graced and defining turning point. A marriage gone bad, acts of unfaithfulness, a divorce, years of alcohol abuse, and a successful 12-step rehabilitation program preceded it. She had carried within herself a deep feeling that, during her rebellious years, God had never withheld his fatherly care from her. Countless stories confirm this truth about the Father's exquisite care and concern. His plan is fully operative in the lives of all who turn to him in sincere repentance.

MARY AT LA SALETTE PAINTS A VIVID WORD PICTURE of creation's original wholeness as only conversion can restore it: "If they are converted, rocks and stones will be changed into heaps of wheat." This thorough renewal of creation fully reveals the Father's plan. To everything there is a place and a purpose in God's plan. Any distancing from this plan by the human stewards of creation results in disruption of right order. Away from the Lord, we display a spirit of independence rather than communion, a spirit of arrogance rather than reverence. It is this grave concern that the tearful mother of the Lord voices at the very outset of her address: "If my people will not submit..."

Reflection Questions:

• Where do you fit in the Father's plan?
• Do you lend your heart, mind and voice to creation that it might give your Creator fitting worship?

Wednesday, December 7, (#183)
Second Week of Advent

Matthew 11:28-30: *"Come to me ..."*

Meditation:

Most ailments now have a remedy. Various prescriptions for longevity abound. Many of them call for strange rituals or impose stringent regimens, submitting their clients to exotic potions or exerting postures. Jesus' prescription for a life of happiness and peace is unique. *"Come to me,"* says he, *"... and learn from me."* The important word here is the pronoun "me." Jesus prescribes his very self. Our personal relationship with him will open the way to a restored, restful and stress-free life. As he experienced God his Father, we are to experience Jesus. He would rise before dawn, steal away to an out-of-the-way place and commune there with the God of his life, mission and relationships. Our own personal relationship with Jesus grounds our day-to-day life and activity. It is the source of our refreshment and peace, of our insight and wisdom, of our inner composure and sense of purpose.

IN HER MESSAGE Our Lady exemplifies this very focus. She defines and describes her mission in constant reference to her Son: "the arm of my Son", *"If I want my Son not to abandon you"* and *"the name of my Son."* This emphasis is made clear from the very outset. There can be no mistaking the primary concern she brings to her people's attention.

Christ, her Son and Lord, is Healer, Savior, Shepherd, Teacher, and Friend to us all. In a sense, the words she spoke on the mountain of La Salette offer a commentary on the last of her words recorded in the New Testament: *"Do whatever he tells you"* (John 2:5).

Reflection Questions:

- What distracts you from a fuller communion with Jesus?
- How is Jesus a personal Savior to you? How often do you speak to him in prayer?

Thursday, December 8, (#689)
The Immaculate Conception
[Holy Day of Obligation]

Luke 1:26-38: *" … for nothing is impossible to God."*

Meditation:

It seems that God does not shy away from what we would consider impossible. As Jeremiah proclaims: *"Ah, Lord (God), you made the heavens and the earth by your great power and outstretched arm. To you nothing is impossible"* (Jeremiah 32:17). Even Job, struggling from the depths of utter loss professes: *"I know that you are all-powerful: what you conceive, you can perform"* (Job 42:2). In the New Testament the Matthean Jesus assures his weak-willed disciples: *"If your faith is the size of a mustard seed you will say to this mountain, 'Move from here to there,' and it will move; nothing will be impossible for you"* (Matthew 17:20). Again Jesus was explaining to his disciples how attachment to riches can prevent people from giving their lives to God. In response to his disciple's fearful question, *"Who can be saved, then?"*, Jesus simply states: *"By human resources, … this is impossible; for God everything is possible"* (Matthew 19:25-26). All in all, God will provide for God's creatures.

In the gospel for today, the words uttered by the angel to Mary were perhaps God's most marvelous impossibility: *"You are to conceive in your womb and bear a son, and you must name him Jesus"* (Luke 1:31). Motherhood and giving birth to a Son – the Son of God – this is an impossibly wonderful gift to give us, God's people!

At La Salette Mary concludes her visit by giving a seemingly impossible task to these two unschooled children: ***"You will make this message known to all my people."*** Yet by the grace of God they held true to her challenging task and did make her message known. The "impossible" was accomplished. Now it is our turn – all we who have heard her tearful and challenging message – to take up this seemingly impossible task and be evangelizers of her message, which is essentially the gospel message of her Son.

Reflection Questions:

• How did you first learn about the La Salette message?

• With whom have you shared it? If not, why not?

Friday, December 9, (#185)
Second Week Of Advent

Matthew 11:16-19: *"What comparison can I use to describe this breed?"*

Meditation:

No one likes to be told his or her "truth." Yet to know the error of one's ways is *essential* to spiritual growth. Such is the case also for the times in which we live. Every generation must evaluate its life and times, honestly assess its areas of potential growth and seriously devise means toward that growth. Jesus calls attention to the basic duplicity of the human heart. There is no integrity in the ways of people. Their views vary with the tides, their positions sway to suit the powers that be. It is our responsibility to come to grips with the ways of our own age and help it benefit from the liberating gift of God's word, that is a *"two-edged sword: it can seek out the place where soul is divided from spirit, or joints from marrow ... "* (Hebrews 4:12). This period of Christmas preparation offers a timely opportunity to evaluate the age in which we live and to speak to it by our very life the truth of God's word.

How specifically Mary at La Salette describes the spiritual climate of the times in which she appeared: *"I gave you six days to work; I have kept the seventh for myself and they will not give it to me. This is what makes the arm of my Son so heavy. And then, those who drive the carts cannot swear without bringing in my Son's name. These are the two things that make the arm of my Son so heavy."* We sense that the state of mid nineteenth-century European Christians had been carefully examined, that their spiritual health had been found wanting. Illness called for treatment. Appropriate and effective treatment required an accurate diagnosis. The Mother of Jesus pinpoints "the two things" most in need of her people's attention. If she were to return and underscore "two things" most in need of change in our own day and in our own land, what might they be?

Reflection Questions:
- How well do I know myself?
- How well do I know my "era" and surroundings?

Saturday, December 10, (#186)
Second Week of Advent

Matthew 17:9a,10-13: *"Then the disciples understood..."*

Meditation:

A number of realizations come to us thanks to the gift of God's word: the realization that we have been chosen by God; the realization that God first loved us into being; the realization that Jesus is the Son of God; the realization that he came into the world for the specific purpose of having us share his life. This realization opens up before the believer a whole new approach to life. "I had no idea. I didn't realize." Such words are among the saddest words in any language. As the late Anthony De Mello, in his book entitled, Awakening, wished people to acknowledge: most of us are asleep. We are sleepwalkers on a grand scale! We get up, we go to work, we get married, we raise a family, we read the newspaper, we go to church, we hear the word of God proclaimed. We are up and around. But how alert and awake are we? Advent issues a major wake-up call each year. It challenges us to arouse our awareness, to wake up to the true gift of life, the gift of the Kingdom in our midst, the ongoing gift of Christmas.

THE LA SALETTE APPARITION TOOK PLACE IN 1846, ON SEPTEMBER 19TH. "I am here," she matter-of-factly announces. A timeless presence. "I am here to tell you great news." A timeless call to heed a timely message. The Word incarnate is in our midst, the new Adam of a new human race. He has come to restore God's good creation to its original state. He has come to refurbish God's image in our hearts. "If the harvest is ruined it is only on account of yourselves," Mary tells us. She would have us realize that the fruits the earth bears are intimately linked with the fruits the human heart bears. She would make us aware that earth and fields, crops and harvests are submissive to hearts submissive to the Creator of all.

Reflection Questions:

- Are you fully aware of the ongoing grace of your baptism?
- How fruitful is your faith in good words and deeds?

Sunday, December 11 (#007)
Third Sunday of Advent

(Isaiah 35:1-6a,10; James 5:7-10; Matthew 11:2-11)

Meditation: *Are You the One?*

John's messengers had a question: "Are you the one?" Jesus answered with a list that can be summed up in one word: "Yes!"

The essence of the message of Our Lady of La Salette is that "yes," that affirmation that Jesus—her Son—is "the one." Unfortunately, we really have

John The Baptist prepares the way

to say she affirmed he "ought to be" the one. If her people had actually understood that he is "the one" and lived accordingly, she would not have needed to come.

Both the first reading and the Gospel speak of the blind seeing and the deaf hearing. In the former it is a prophetic vision, in the latter a statement of fact. La Salette invites us to see and hear, but in a particular way, as Mary sees and hears.

She saw the world through her tears. Her people were suffering, but their behavior showed they did not recognize her Son Jesus as "the one." Many Catholics today see the world in this same way. Not only is there tremendous suffering of all kinds, but fewer and fewer people seem willing to turn to the Lord for help. He is not "the one," it appears.

Mary heard her people ridiculing religion and faith, and at the same time blaming God for their troubles. We hear much the same today, and share the Beautiful Lady's sorrow.

But all is not lost. Today's reading from Isaiah ends with a magnificent image: "sorrow and mourning shall flee." Not "pass away," not "be no more," but "flee," as if to say sorrow and mourning will be utterly defeated by the everlasting joy with which "the ransomed" will be crowned.

Our Lady of La Salette wears a crown. It might be seen as representing this ultimate victory of joy over sadness. Theologians have wondered how the Blessed Virgin, in the blessedness and glory of heaven, can experience sorrow. But if we see her tears as a sharing in our own troubles and tears, they are the symbolic expression of her abiding love for us, reflecting the boundless love of her Son for us. He did everything possible to ensure our salvation. He reached out to the physically and spiritually poor, blind, deaf, lame, leprous. He was— and still is—"the one."

Monday, December 12, (#609A)
Our Lady of Guadalupe

Luke 1:26-38: *"Mary said, 'You see before you the Lord's servant, let it happen to me as you have said.'"*

Meditation:

Like La Salette, the story of the Apparition of Our Lady of Guadalupe is a simple but marvelous event "...on the morning of Dec. 9, 1531, Juan Diego saw an apparition of a young girl at the Hill of Tepeyac, near Mexico City. Speaking to him in Nahuatl, the girl asked that a church be built at that site in her honor; from her words, Juan Diego recognized the girl as the Virgin Mary. Diego shared his story with the Spanish Archbishop of Mexico City, who instructed him to return to Tepeyac Hill, and ask the "lady" for a miraculous sign to prove her identity. The first sign was the Virgin healing Juan's uncle. The Virgin told Juan Diego to gather flowers from the top of Tepeyac Hill. Although December was very late in the growing season for flowers to bloom, Juan Diego found Castilian roses, not native to Mexico, on the normally barren hilltop. The Virgin arranged these in his peasant cloak. When Juan Diego opened his cloak before the Archbishop on December 12, the flowers fell to the floor, and on the fabric was the image of the Virgin of Guadalupe" (summary quoted from *Wikipedia*).

WE SEE SOME SIMILARITIES between the Apparition at La Salette and the apparition of Our Lady of Guadalupe, In both apparitions the Virgin spoke in the native tongue and was dressed in native attire. Although no sign was asked from Mary at La Salette, the stream near her feet which flowed intermittently before the apparition, has not ceased flowing since her apparition. Also in both apparitions many miracles have happened in connection with the apparitions. Roses were also connected with the La Salette apparition; they surrounded her shoulders and her feet. And the devotion to Our Lady in both apparitions has strongly endured. It is appropriate that there be parallels in these two apparitions despite their three hundred year separation. In both apparitions Mary, in her usual role as a servant of God, touches the heart of pilgrims and brings them back to the way and message of her Son.

Reflection Questions:

• Can you say with Mary this phrase, but about you: "You see before you the Lord's servant . . ."?
• How do you "serve God" in your life?

Tuesday, December 13, (#188)
Third Week of Advent

Matthew 21:28-32: *"What do you think of this case?"*

Meditation:

In today's gospel Jesus continues with this parable to pursue the issue of sincerity and authority. Who does better, the one who agrees to do so but does not act, or the one who protests but after reflection comes around? When do most of us churchgoers fit into this scheme of things? Do we too quickly commit ourselves? Upon realizing the cost do we simply procrastinate, hoping it will all go away? Or do we hesitate, and wrestle with the pros and cons before committing ourselves? Jesus is likely to be more impressed with us if we don't rush in. Commitment was such an essential element in his life that he treasured - follow through.

AT LA SALETTE the two visionaries stayed committed to all they had seen and all they had heard. Conviction was the key element which allowed them to resist bribes and even threats. In no way were they to be coerced into negating the events that took place on the mountainside.

Reflection Questions:
- What does it take to convince me?
- At what cost am I willing to remain committed?

Wednesday, December 14, (#189)
Third Week of Advent

Luke 7:18b-23: *"John, summoning two of his disciples, sent them to the Lord to ask, 'Are you the one who is to come, or are we to expect someone else?'"*

Meditation:

Delivered by his disciples, John's question to Jesus reflects different possible expectations of Jesus' mission. Is John doubting who Jesus really is? Is John disappointed because Jesus is not turning out to be the kind of Messiah he had been expecting; that is, not enough of a freeing reformer? Or is John totally unaware of the healings, the liberation, the return to life, the restoration of sight to the blind, the cure of the lame, the cleansing of lepers? Jesus in Luke 4:17-23 had clearly stated what his mission was to be. In fact, he was rejected for it by his own townspeople.

Do our expectations at times do us in? We tend to narrow or to exaggerate what we think should be. People missioned around us have no choice but to measure up to it. Unfortunately, we can totally miss out on the witness the Lord is asking of them. Jesus reminds John, or is it a slight reprimand, that his zeal has blinded him to the Kingdom that is already blossoming before him! We need to change our premises: It's the Lord's call. It's his mission. Let's always allow ourselves the space to be surprised!

AT LA SALETTE THE VISIONARIES must have been taken aback at the various hostile reactions to Mary's apparition. Why wouldn't people rejoice? On the contrary many were disturbed because the event could raise havoc with their plan to secularize society. So they never wanted to hear about the healings, about the radios' changes in the hearts of people who came to the Holy Mountain. They wanted to control the situation by wishing it away, by ridiculing it or even by threatening those who believed.

Reflection Questions:

• How many situations have I refused to see and hear about simply because they did not measure up to my expectations?
• Do I allow myself the gift of being surprised?

Thursday, December 15, (#190)
Third Week of Advent

Luke 7:24-30: *"Prepare the way of the Lord."*

Meditation:

The call to dream dreams is the call of all Christians. Because we dream of being with Jesus in eternity, we embark daily on the project of living the day fully. Faith carries us into a future of dreams to be fulfilled. We all have in our personal stories of actions that helped us sacrifice for fhb sake of our tomorrows. We plant trees at times knowing full well we will never see them bearing fruit. We make decisions that can assure our children better lives even though we will not personally witness the wisdom of these choices. To be forerunner, to be prophet, to be messenger is a vocation we are called to embrace. It calls us to trust Jesus as Script-writer, it reinforces our mission to "prepare the way of the Lord" not only in our personal lives but also in the lives of others.

The children of La Salette possibly never imagined what their mission would one day produce. They only knew in their hearts that they were called to prepare the way of the Lord. From that conviction no one was to deter them. Mary's parting words: "Make this known to all my people" were deeply embedded in their young hearts!!

Reflection Questions:

- How do I do as a sower?
- Do I easily trust Jesus as Script-writer?

Friday, December 16 (#191)
Third Week of Advent

John 5:33-36: *"The lamp set aflame and burning bright."*

Meditation:

Today's gospel clarifies for us one of our callings as witnesses to the Light. We continue in the footsteps of many who preceded us and taught us how to reflect that gift to those in search of the Light. Though we are but examples of "indirect lighting," we, like John the Baptist, can motivate, inspire and convince others to pursue their need to be bathed in the Lord's love. Faith is a light needed to illuminate what is invisible and a necessary aid to its interpretation. Without it, we never dare trust those who are sent into our lives to give us direction and orientation.

We need to become addicted to the light. For it offers hope, especially if we have been victimized by darkness. Every time day breaks one becomes intensely aware of the first glimmer of dawn, aware of what yet needs to be awakened. Excite¬ment builds as it becomes clearer that our true calling is to be children of the light.

The children at La Salette saw Mary in a globe of light. It fascinated them be-cause of the hope it offered. In their circumstances - no education, no home life to speak of- Mary's light was a call now to More. From the darkness of their hope¬lessness, locked into very limited options, they now see their new potential, the greatest being the experience of calling and bringing others to the light.

Reflection Questions:

- Are we witnesses to the Light?
- Do we allow others through their indirect lighting to challenge us to more?

Saturday, December 17, (#193)
Third Week of Advent

Matthew 1:1-17: *The family record of Jesus Christ*

Meditation:

Because it is as important as it is off-putting, the late Scripture scholar, Father Raymond E. Brown, conducted a somewhat solitary campaign to make today's gospel passage a major Advent topic. If we were asked to tell the basic story of Christ to someone who knows nothing about Christianity, where would we begin? Surely not where St. Matthew does. His listing of Jesus' ancestors contains some of Israel's most prominent names, those of patriarchs and kings; it also includes a number of unknown and unexpected entries. It teaches that God did not hesitate to enlist schemers as well as noble folks, outsiders as well as insiders, the lowly as well as the mighty. The first fruit of the Incarnation is that we should be God's children, that Christ should be born in us. The all-inclusive lineage of Jesus assures us that God can bring Him to birth in our hearts, their waning good and evil impulses notwithstanding.

THOUGH SHE REPROVES OUR INDIFFERENCE and our straying, Mary at La Salette nonetheless addresses us in our essential dignity as a holy nation, a people of God's own choosing, though a people of saints and sinners. *"If my people are converted,"* she promises, *"rocks and stones will be changed into mounds of wheat."* Her words bring to mind the picture Jesus painted in the parable of God's field: wheat and stones ... side by side.

Reflection Questions:

- How literally do I take the statement that Christ is to be born in me?
- What might that mean in practical terms?

Sunday, December 18 (#010)
Fourth Sunday of Advent

(Isaiah 7:10-14; Romans 1:1-7; Matthew 1:18-24)

🔊 **Immanuel** also romanized: Emmanuel
/NOUN/
(meaning: "God is with us")

The virgin will conceive and give birth to a son, and will call him Immanuel.

Meditation: *The Sign*

We can paraphrase Isaiah's challenge to King Ahaz in these words: "Ask for a sign, any sign!" Ahaz was less than honest when he refused. Yes, the Scripture says, "You shall not tempt the Lord," but this case was different. God wanted to convince the king that he would deliver Jerusalem from enemy forces. The only conclusion to be drawn from Ahaz's refusal is that he did not trust the Lord to keep his promise.

So God decided what the sign would be—and what a sign it was! Actually, it's two signs: first, that a virgin will bear a son; second, that his name, in other words, his identity, will be "God with us."

The Apparition of La Salette is a sign made up of many signs. There are, of course, the words Mary spoke, which "signify" a prophetic message. There are the tears, the light, the roses, the heavy chain around her shoulders, the cross with the hammer and pincers, her peasant garb, her movement, the spring that has flowed ever since that event, the place itself, even the children chosen as witnesses. Something for everyone, so to speak.

And, above all, there are the two other persons, namely Mary herself, the Virgin who conceived, and Jesus, the Son she bore, whom she now bears, crucified, over her heart, truly God with us.

All of the above, like all signs, point beyond themselves, give us a direction. In today's readings that direction is indicated by a phrase in St. Paul's letter to the Romans. He writes that his role as an apostle is "to bring about the obedience of faith."

That was also the Beautiful Lady's purpose in coming to La Salette. Often, because of the message, I apply to Our Lady of La Salette the title "Queen of Prophets" from the Litany of Loreto; but today we are reminded that she is also "Queen of Apostles."

Ordinary signs are useful things. Some are even necessary. But a few signs, like those in today's readings and at La Salette, besides being useful and necessary, are wondrous, magnificent!

Monday, December 19, (#195)
Third Week of Advent

Luke 1:5-25: "… 'The Lord has done this for me, now that it has pleased him to take away the humiliation I suffered in public.'"

Meditation:

Not unlike ourselves most probably, Elizabeth thought of God's mighty deeds as something done for others a very long time ago – until something wondrous happened to her. She recognized in her totally unexpected pregnancy the Lord's power to overcome obstacles as daunting as age and sterility. God's might, she learned, is not something restricted to bygone days but something that touched her own life: "*So has the Lord done for me at a time when he has seen fit to take away my disgrace before others*" (Luke 1:25).

WE MIGHT THINK OF MARY'S APPARITION at La Salette as belonging entirely to nineteenth-century Europe and the spiritual challenges and concerns of that time period. We might manage to situate her coming to earth in a longstanding series of divine interventions in human history. Our challenge in this second Christian millennium, however, is to claim its timeless call to reconciliation and reflect that ever-timely grace "in these days." The Lord is "acting on our behalf," surely this makes us ambassadors of God's good will.

Reflection Questions:

- Where have I recently detected the Lord at work in my own life?
- In what way can I make the Lord's action on my behalf a gift to others?

Tuesday, December 20, (#196)
Fourth Week of Advent

Luke 1:26-38: *"Mary said to the angel, 'But how can this come about…?"*

Meditation:

In announcing his marvels to us and in eliciting our misting response, God seems to place major emphasis on the "what" and always skim over the "how". Though she might have kept a prudent silence, Mary responded to the news that the angel had brought with the words, "How can this be?" She does not doubt the event, but wonders how it shall come about. She is not asking whether it will happen, whether God can make it happen, but how. Her faith and her question are not at odds. Informed by the angel's evocative yet very mysterious reply, she acquiesces freely and fully.

Not surprisingly, at La Salette Mary puts questions to Melanie and Maximin: "Do you say your prayers well, my children?… Have you never seen wheat gone bad?" In each instance a faith dialogue is opened. Questions and answers give shape to a conversation that plumbs unseen depths, the depths of God and those of the believer. Questions and answers underscore the need to communicate with God in regular moments of prayer, the value of viewing the happenings of our everyday life and the events of history in the light of faith.

Some Reflection Questions:

- What feelings come over you when you struggle with the "hows" of God's action in your life?
- What in the message of Our Lady at La Salette is best suited to your own day?

Wednesday, December 21, (#197)
Fourth Week of Advent

Luke 1:39-45: *"Mary set out at that time and went as quickly as she could into the hill country to a town in Judah. She went into Zechariah's house and greeted Elizabeth."*

Meditation:

Mary had just heard the incredible news of her own pregnancy yet her first thoughts are for her elderly kinswoman Elizabeth, now with child as well, It is this remarkable ability to focus first on the needs of others rather than her own that Mary will pass on to her child. Learning from the self-forgetfulness of his mother, Jesus, who first surrendered his divinity in order to share in our humanity, will learn to pour out his very life in opening the gift of life and sharing it with all.

Mary's caring for others is evident at La Salette, as she shares with us there a twofold concern: God's grief at the sight of human sinfulness and humanity's sinful squandering of opportunity. Prayer gives roots to faith. Faith blossoms into love. Love in turn bears fruit in selfless service. Mary's journey to the Judean hill country and her coming to the mountains of southeastern France offer striking examples of timely assistance. Errands of mercy in time of need.

Reflection Questions:

• How deeply convinced am I that as a Christian I am to love, not in word, but in deed?
• How will I put my love for God in action today?

Thursday, December 22, (#198)
Fourth Week of Advent

Luke 1:46-56: *"(God's) faithful love extends age after age."*

Meditation:

The Dominican theologian, Edward Schillebeeckx, has aptly called Our Lady's canticle "A Toast to God." The core of her *Magnificat* contrasts the drastically different fates of the humble, the lowly, the hungry and the haughty, the proud, the rich. It is, essentially, a hymn of praise for the liberation a God ever mindful of his mercy is bringing about. On the doorstep of her kinswoman's house, his Mother proclaims her unborn Child to be the absolute and definitive manifestation of God's ageless mercy. Because human history can be rather resistant to God's loving purpose, believers in Christ never cease to proclaim that "God's mercy is from age to age."

MARY'S VISIT TO LA SALETTE should be seen as part of that ongoing outpouring of mercy. We need not be content with the ripples radiating from events in the remote past. The Advent of God's mercy takes place in our own time. New life and moral rebirth are gifts being offered to us today as surely as they were being offered to their world through Elizabeth and Mary.

Reflection Questions:

- What are some of the signs of God's mercy in my life?
- What new insight into the La Salette apparition and its relevance for these times have I gained?

Friday, December 23, (#199)
Fourth Week of Advent

Luke 1:57-66: *"All their neighbors were filled with awe and the whole affair was talked about throughout the hill country of Judaea."*

Meditation:

Events of special significance we tend to tell and retell. In each retelling, different details are highlighted and take on new significance. Such repeated telling breathes fresh life into these happenings and can bring to light insights and meanings that may have previously gone unnoticed. The birth and naming of John the Baptizer, prelude to those of Jesus himself, were such events in that hill country neighborhood. Generations of Christians have tirelessly told and retold the circumstances surrounding these mysteries, pondered them in their hearts and claimed their spiritual fruitfulness.

NEWS OF WHAT MAXIMIN AND MELANIE saw and heard that memorable day in September of 1846 spread rapidly through mountain villages and was greeted with utter amazement. People who had felt abandoned learned that they were anything but forsaken by the God whose "mercy is from age to age" Their difficulties were part of the larger problems the world was grappling with at the dawn of the industrial age. These difficulties, however, were not going unnoticed by heaven. Early reflection on Mary's message made it clear that it restates the gospel challenge to discern the signs of the times, signs of this particular time and particular day.

Reflection Questions:

- How do you make sense of what takes place in the world around you?
- Where do you seek God's concrete will for the times we are now living?

Saturday, December 24, (#200)
Fourth Week of Advent

Luke 1:67-79: *"... because of the faithful love of our God ... the rising Sun has come from on high to visit us."*

Meditation:

On the threshold of the Nativity, we hear a closing Advent hymn of praise that the promises God made to Abraham and to David will soon come true. We meditate today on a poetic prelude to the dawning of our Dayspring. The One whose coming we await once more will enflesh "the bowels of God's compassion." Jesus comes to make known the inmost depths of God, to translate the mystery of God into terms we can grasp, into a reality that will grasp us. God's love for us in Christ is not a cool, detached Platonic benevolence but manifests itself as a visceral love, a love felt in the pit of the stomach, a lump in the throat, a welling up of tears.

THE MOTHER OF JESUS REMINDS US at La Salette that, if she knew the unspeakable joy of giving this world its Hope and Light, she also experienced an unspeakable depth of pain and sorrow. On the day of her apparition, two innocent cowherds witnessed an astonishing anguish, an anguish only an overflow of maternal tears could convey, an anguish they surely could not fathom.

Reflection Questions:

- "The hopes and fears of all the years" will meet in Bethlehem this night. Do I have a dream for our entire world?
- This Christmas Eve, do I dare bid the "heart-felt kindness of God" make its home in my heart?

Sunday, December 25, (#016)
The Nativity of the Lord

John 1:1-5,9-14: *"The Word became flesh, he lived among us, and we saw his glory..."*

Meditation:

St. Irenaeus once said: "The glory of God is (humanity) fully alive." In today's parlance, we understand this to mean that when we are the best we can be – that is, the most Christ-like that we can be – then God is truly glorified in us. God's wish, as we hear in John's introduction to his gospel, is that, in the Word's "dwelling ("pitching his tent") among us, helps us see God's glory and, in turn, we show it ourselves by how we love and serve in Jesus' name. We are to bring Christ and his light into the darkness of our daily living and show others that God is alive in us and all that we do. This is one aspect of the meaning of the mystery of the Incarnation which we celebrate today.

MARY AT LA SALETTE literally appears in a globe of light and when she stands, the children confessed that it was difficult to see the face of the Beautiful Lady due to the brilliance of the figure of Christ on the cross. Jesus is our light. Mary came to remind us, her children, that because of our actions – disrespect for her Son's name, not celebrating the Eucharist regularly, not praying well, not using the Lenten habits of faith to support and deepen our spiritual life – we need to be reconciled once again with her Son, allow him to change our lives for the better. In a sense, our life was a plant that was withering due to a lack of the Light that is Christ himself.

Reflection Questions:

- Whom do you know who "shines with the light of God" in their life?
- How do you "show God's glory" to others by the way you live and love, serve and sacrifice, or for whom you are a reconciler?

Monday, December 26, (#696) St. Stephen, First Martyr,

Matthew 10:17-22: *"You will be universally hated on account of my name; but anyone who stands firm to the end will be saved."*

Meditation:

It would be easy to become fearful and discouraged the moment one realizes the truth of what Jesus says, "If the world hates you, remember that it hated me first." For Jesus the word "world" indicates a center of resistance, the place of sin and death. But by his coming as a man, he tells us, he has "overcome the world." In this one phrase, we can understand the meaning of new life through the incarnation of the Son. What seemed impossible, and what is "impossible for man," is not "impossible for God." St. Stephen stands out as the first witness to this new possibility when he says, "I can see heaven thrown open and the Son of Man standing at the right hand of God."

Joined to Jesus, being one with him by believing in him, each of us has hope for that salvation which is beyond any human power. It springs forth from God through the power of the Holy Spirit as one of his principal gifts, a supernatural virtue. Anyone who endures in hope, relying upon God's grace to the end, will be saved.

To Maximin and Melanie Our Lady brings the hope of what seemed impossible, great news indeed. In her presence the children immediately become aware of heaven. Their hearts are transformed by the possibility, and the desire to be there makes them willing to leave everything else to follow her back there.

Reflection Questions:

- How does Our Lady, the mother of Jesus and my mother, show me the meaning of hope in her divine Son?
- How do I share the hope that Jesus gives me by sharing it concretely with others through my words or deeds?

Tuesday, December 27, (#697) St. John, Apostle and Evangelist

John 20:1a,2-8: *"He saw and he believed."*

Meditation:

This was not a simple case of "seeing is believing." Rather, St. John saw only an empty tomb that day. The absence of the Lord's body could have meant that "they have taken the Lord and we don't know where they have laid him." Presented with the facts, however, John made a choice. He chose the option that Jesus had arisen as he said. This brings the gift of faith into perspective.

What we do with faith and the knowledge it brings to us is a matter of choosing one option over another. The virtue of faith makes it possible for us to trust in the Lord's word and to choose the options which correspond to the truth of that word. Some schools of thought which influence us tend to equate observation with proof. Sadly, however, the meaning of the proof is often predetermined. Thus, some would always tend to deny the things we cannot see. Faith makes it possible for us to see the things we Christians must not deny.

THE MOCKING OF RELIGION WHICH OUR LADY SPOKE ABOUT does not necessarily mean a blatant lack of religion, though it often is. Failure to honor and worship God as we should is characterized by callousness toward the saints and the things which are especially consecrated to God. It can also be marked by insensitivity toward another's piety and devotion. The presence of Our Lady inclined the children toward deeper faith.

Some Reflection Questions:

- Have you attempted to help others grow in faith in legitimate ways?
- Or have you taunted them by mocking their faith at times?

Wednesday, December 28, (#698) Holy Innocents,

Matthew 2:13-18: *"Then were fulfilled the words spoken through the prophet Jeremiah: A voice is heard in Ramah, lamenting and weeping bitterly: it is Rachel weeping for her children, refusing to be comforted because they are no more."*

Meditation:

Innocent children were put to death by Herod so that he might not have to face a rival to his kingship. All the male children two years and under were killed with the intent of eliminating Jesus. These children became victims to the totalitarian exercise of power which places the State before the inherent dignity of the person. They had no defense. Today, the failure to respect innocent life, the crimes of abortion and euthanasia, are the results of policies and attitudes which over time place the "cult of having" above the basic rights of persons.

OUR LADY'S PREDICTION that children would be seized with trembling and die in the arms of those who hold them, stands as a warning of the consequences of sin. The weakest always suffer most. Our Lady calls even the most hard-hearted to repentance with her tears. The voice of the Beautiful Lady of La Salette is heard, she is weeping for all her children.

Reflection Questions:

- Who has the power of Herod today in our society?
- Have I acted responsibly in fulfilling my civic duties in order to create a more just society where all Mary's children, human embryos, the unborn, the disabled, the elderly, and the dying will he protected from the violence which would deprive them of the

fundamental right to life?

Thursday, December 29, (#202)
Fifth Day Within the Octave of Christmas

Luke 2:22-35: *"My eyes have seen your salvation, which you have made ready in the sight of the peoples."*

Meditation:

When Simeon took Jesus in his arms and blessed God, he proclaimed the universal scope of Jesus' saving work. He came that all may have life and have it to the fullest. Yet, the message must still be proclaimed in every corner of the world, and effectively in every aspect of culture from the arts to the realm of technology. Each Christian has a role to play in the evangelization of culture, in his or her circle of friends, work, and entertainment. No place or culture, no aspect of human existence is to be ignored in the proclamation of the Good News of salvation in Christ.

Our Lady's marching orders could not be clearer: *"Make this known to all my people."* We have seen the salvation that the Lord has prepared. We have heard the message of La Salette which speaks to us of God's great mercy. What was first proclaimed to the children as a way to avoid human tragedy still stands as a model for action. *"If they are converted,"* she indicates, justice will be restored. But justice, in order to reach its perfection, begins and ends as the work of God, who first justifies us and then perfects us by his love. A call to the heart for conversion opens up the way for the saving grace of God. "I come to bring you great news."

Reflection Questions:

• Do I believe that the merciful apparition at La Salette has the power of the gospel to transform the world and so help bring light to all peoples?
• Have I helped the sinful to repent by announcing to them the great mercy of God with the enthusiasm and love of Mary?

Friday, December 30 (#017A)
The Holy Family

(Sirach 3:2-6,12-14; Colossians 3:12-21 or 3:12-17; Matthew 2:13-15,19-23)

Meditation: *Mother and Child*

In religious art, the "Madonna and Child" holds pride of place. Within the basic similarity of Mary holding the child Jesus, there are infinite variations depending not only on the medium, but also on how the artist chooses to depict the relationship between Jesus and Mary, and between them and us.

Twice in today's Gospel Joseph is told to "take the child and his mother" and travel, first escaping to Egypt, later returning to Israel. Paintings or sculptures of Madonna and Child in these two circumstances would no doubt differ greatly.

La Salette does not present Madonna and Child in the classic sense. There is another name for the image of Mary and her Son that applies here. We know it as the "Pietà," Mary grieving over the lifeless body of Jesus after he is taken down from the cross. The crucifix the Beautiful Lady wears reminds us vividly of that scene.

Farther removed from the usual Madonna and Child, but important in its own way, is the fact that Mary calls Maximin and Mélanie "my children"—seven times, in fact! Her own words paint the image of her caring, motherly attitude toward them and us.

In today's first reading we find mention of "a mother's authority." La Salette gives an excellent illustration of that authority, exercised firmly in much of Mary's message but never harshly, especially not towards the children. "Don't be afraid," spoken right after she calls them "my children" the first time, penetrates the entire event. She demonstrates the "heartfelt compassion, kindness, humility, gentleness, and patience" that St. Paul invites us to in the second reading.

In the light of all this, we might allow ourselves a flight of fancy and wonder what the Madonna and Child might look like if we put ourselves in Mary's arms in Jesus' place. How does she look at us? How do we look at her? How does she invite us to look out on the world? What does she ask?

Saturday, December 31, (#204)
Seventh Day Within the Octave of Christmas

John 1:1-18: *"… from his fullness we have, all of us, received – one gift replacing another."*

Meditation:

There are two principles that God provides us with as means to goodness. One is the law and the other is grace. John tells us that grace and truth came through Jesus Christ. The New Law of the Gospel has as its primary element the grace of the Holy Spirit. In baptism, we receive this grace which recreates us to new life, joining each of us individually to the Risen Jesus. This is the gift that keeps on giving. For throughout our lives the Holy Spirit perfects our spiritual capacities with his gifts, purifying and elevating all of our dispositions, leading us on to greater goodness.

Our Lady helps us to understand, however, that these gifts may be rejected. As she indicates, we can refuse these graces and reject – even the grace of salvation itself. The submission of which she speaks has as its most fundamental characteristic the humility required to receive the grace and gifts of the Holy Spirit by acknowledging our need of them. Conversion follows. Prayer, the Sacraments, the Scriptures, and the Magisterium of the Church all assist us in our spiritual and moral growth. A sincere appreciation of these elements of the Evangelical Law of Christ enhances the life of grace. Saying, *"If they are converted,"* Our Lady promises a consequent abundance of food. This material abundance becomes the sign of the spiritual bounty, grace in place of grace, available to each believer.

Reflection Questions:

- In what ways does my daily living reflect thankfulness and praise for the gift of new life which I received through the Holy Spirit?
- Are there signs of the spiritual bounty which I have been promised? For what special blessings in your life should you give thanks to God?

APPENDIX:

What is a Novena?

A novena is a traditional devotion consisting of specific prayers recited on nine successive days. Besides being a form of praise, a novena is frequently offered for a particular intention. This practice began in 12th century Christianity and continues to be beneficial today as a way of praying for healing, protection or other blessings for ourselves or others.

This particular novena is prayed to God through the intercession of Our Lady of La Salette. In praying this Novena, as in the case of all prayer, it is good to begin by opening ourselves wholeheartedly to God's will, offering a simple act of trust in God's wisdom and love for us all.

Since Our Lady's apparition was on September 19th, 1846, the novena offered in her name is usually prayed on the eleventh to the nineteenth of each month. May Our Lady of La Salette guide you and God bless you.

How to Pray This Novena

This novena is based on the message of Our Lady of La Salette. Each day of the novena is divided into the following parts:

1. Scripture quote for reflection:
2. Words from the apparition dialogue of Mary at La Salette;
3. Meditation followed by quiet reflection;
4. Our Prayer;
5. After mentioning your intention, pray the Lord's Prayer and the Hail Mary;
6. Closing prayer (La Salette invocation).

This novena can be prayed alone or with others. To set the stage for praying this novena, you are invited to read the story and full dialogue of the apparition of Our Lady of La Salette."

First Day of Novena – Welcome

Scripture Says: "Come to me, all you who labor and are burdened, and I will give you rest. For my yoke is easy, and my burden light" (Matt 11:28, 30).

Mary Said: *"Come near, my children."*

Meditation: What a wonderful invitation! In all simplicity Mary at La Salette calls the two children to come near. Her words echo her Son's invitation to come to him that we may find rest from our burdens and refreshment for our spirits. This too is Mary's desire: that her children — meaning us as well — should feel welcomed and loved.

Mary wishes us to come nearer to God who desires only good for us. We must approach and listen to her words, spoken with the love and concern of Jesus. She and her Son wish that during this La Salette Novena of prayer, we may "have life and have it more abundantly" (John 10:10b). This special time of prayer can help us experience the welcoming presence of Mary and her loving Son. [Quiet Reflection]

Our Prayer: Virgin Mother of La Salette, we approach your loving Son with confidence. During these days of prayer and reflection, we place before our Savior our labors and burdens, our thoughts and feelings, our words and actions. May Christ ease our burdens, and fill us with his presence. With faith, we ask for his blessings on us and on those whom we hold close to our hearts. [Mention Intention]

Pray: the Lord's Prayer and Hail Mary

Invocation: Our Lady of La Salette, Reconciler of Sinners, pray without ceasing for us who have recourse to you.

Second Day of Novena – Freedom from Fear

Scripture Says: "Do not be afraid, Mary, for you have found favor with God" (Luke 1:30b).

Mary Said: *"Do not be afraid."*

Meditation: At her Annunciation, Mary's initial response to the presence and words of the angel was anxious fear. She could easily sympathize with the reaction of fear which overcame the two children at her sudden appearance on the Holy Mountain of La Salette. Her words, like those of the angel, were most welcome and reassuring.

Mary, who was relieved of her fears, now relieves us of our own. She who "found favor with God," in turn finds favor for us. Mary who knew the God of her ancestors as a God of power and might now encounters God in a personal and intimate way. At La Salette she speaks from that privileged relationship with God to teach us that we too are "beloved of the Father."

Saint John declares, "perfect love drives out fear" (1 John 4:18a). Mary came to know that "perfect love" as her own Son. May he cast out our fear as well, and perfect his love in us. [Quiet Reflection]

Our Prayer: Remember, Mother of Sorrows, how often fear keeps us from God. Lovingly guide us to Jesus, the source of grace. As we take comfort in your invitation to draw ever closer to your Son, may your words melt our hearts, dispel our fears, and increase his peace within us. [Mention Intention]

Pray: the Lord's Prayer and Hail Mary

Invocation: Our Lady of La Salette, Reconciler of Sinners, pray without ceasing for us who have recourse to you.

Third Day of Novena – Joy

Scripture Says: "The angel of the Lord appeared to [the shepherds] and said, 'For behold, I proclaim to you good news of great joy that will be for all the people'" (Luke 2:9a, 10b).

Mary Said: *"I am here to tell you great news."*

Meditation: The good news spoken to Mary at her Annunciation brought forth a prayer of praise. This prayer, the Magnificat, not only expresses her deep joy and the conviction of her strong faith; it also recounts how God cares for and helps the needy, the downtrodden, the lost.

Like the Gospel, the message of Mary at La Salette is one of good news. Her words announce great joy — the joy of our salvation: sin is forgiven, death is destroyed, a broken world has been renewed.

The angels announced the Good News of Jesus' birth —God breaking forth into our world. Mary at La Salette reminds us that God continues to break into our world, restoring and renewing the face of the earth. This is the Good News! This is the source of our joy! [Quiet Reflection]

Our Prayer: Gentle Virgin of La Salette, you urge us to find joy in God our Savior. Gladly we hear your words and pledge to spread this good news. May our lives give glory to your Son and be filled with joy in serving Christ, now and forever. [Mention Intention]

Pray: the Lord's Prayer and Hail Mary

Invocation: Our Lady of La Salette, Reconciler of Sinners, pray without ceasing for us who have recourse to you.

Fourth Day of Novena – Rest

Scripture Says: "Six days you may labor and do all your work; but the seventh day is the sabbath of the Lord, your God... For remember that you too were once slaves in Egypt, and the Lord, your God, brought you from there with his strong hand and outstretched arm. That is why the Lord, your God, has commanded you to observe the sabbath day" (Deut 5:13-14a, 15).

Mary Said: *"I gave you six days to work; I kept the seventh for myself..."*

Meditation: Yes, the seventh day belongs to God and God shares this gift with us. This consecrated time is meant to free us from the vicious cycle of production and consumerism. It points us to the greater reality of God's presence and our life of grace. We are restored to the divine image.

The One who made the heavens and the earth has reserved this day for himself to remind us that we are "children of God" (Rom 8:16). This day, then, is also meant to restore our community. In sharing the Body of Christ we are called to be the Body of Christ. "given into one another's care as were Jesus' mother and disciple at the foot of his cross. [Quiet Reflection]

Our Prayer: Faithful Virgin of La Salette, you uphold our dignity as free people and as children of God. May the Day of the Lord shine on us and give meaning to our work and our relationships so that in Jesus Christ we may give thanks to God. [Mention Intention]

Pray: the Lord's Prayer and Hail Mary

Invocation: Our Lady of La Salette, Reconciler of Sinners, pray without ceasing for us who have recourse to you.

Fifth Day of Novena – True Fasting

Scripture Says: "This, rather, is the fasting that I wish: releasing those bound unjustly, untying the thongs of the yoke; Setting free the oppressed, breaking every yoke; Sharing your bread with the hungry, sheltering the oppressed and the homeless; Clothing the naked when you see them, and not turning your back on your own" (Isa 58:6-7).

Mary Said: *"If the harvest is ruined, it is only on account of yourselves. I warned you last year. You paid no heed! Instead, you swore. The rest will do penance through the famine!"*

Meditation: Mary's message startles us to an awareness of the evils of our world and to our own indifference. Today two-thirds of the world suffers or dies from hunger. Human rights are ignored across the face of the earth and injustice lies on our very doorstep. These signs cry out for our response.

If we listen to and act upon her words and those of her Son, she promises that one day Jesus will say to us: "Come, you who are blessed by my Father... "For I was hungry and you gave me food, I was thirsty and you gave me drink, a stranger and you welcomed me, naked and you clothed me, ill and you cared for me, in prison and you visited me... whatever you did for one of these least [ones] of mine, you did for me" (Matt 25:34a, 35-36, 40b). [Quiet Reflection]

Our Prayer: Mother of Compassion, open our eyes to the sufferings of our sisters and brothers. Open our hearts and hands to share with the most needy of your children the plenteous blessings of this earth. Inspired by your words, Mary, may your people continue to nourish and heal, to love and forgive, to build the world our God desires. [Mention Intention]

Pray: the Lord's Prayer and Hail Mary

Invocation: Our Lady of La Salette, Reconciler of Sinners, pray without ceasing for us who have recourse to you.

Sixth Day of Novena – Promised Blessings

Scripture Says: "The desert and the parched land will exult; the steppe will rejoice and bloom. They will bloom with abundant flowers, and rejoice with joyful song...They will see the glory of the Lord, the splendor of our God" (Isa 35:1, 2b).

Mary Said: *"If [my people] are converted, rocks and stones will turn into heaps of wheat..."*

Meditation: Jesus who opens the eyes of the blind and makes the lame dance, comes to restore us to life. The constant temptation is to harden our hearts and narrow our vision, so that we miss his very presence.

Let us come to Jesus, who is the Way to follow, the Truth to be discovered, the Life to be enjoyed and shared. He is the One who can make the desert of our heart — and of our world — bloom and bear abundant fruit.

Mary's apparition on the mountain near the village of La Salette has unleashed a stream of life-giving water, bearing the promise of refreshment and renewal. Heeding Mary's call to conversion makes our own lives rich and fruitful. [Quiet Reflection]

Our Prayer: Virgin Reconciler, "may your unceasing prayer and loving concern for us bear fruit in the constant conversion of our minds and hearts. May our lives burst forth anew with love for your Son. May we obtain the blessings you and your Son have promised and faithfully give him thanks as our Savior and Lord. [Mention Intention]

Pray: the Lord's Prayer and Hail Mary

Invocation: Our Lady of La Salette, Reconciler of Sinners, pray without ceasing for us who have recourse to you.

Seventh Day of Novena – Prayer

Scripture Says: "Rejoice always. Pray without ceasing. In all circumstances give thanks, for this is the will of God for you in Christ Jesus" (1 Thess 5:16-18).

Mary Said: *"Do you say your prayers well, my children? You should say them well, at night and in the morning...[people] go to Mass just to make fun of religion. In Lent they go to the butcher shops like dogs."*

Meditation: The Virgin at La Salette questions us on the quality of those gestures of faith which link us to God, and serve as the source of our ongoing conversion.

Each day, we are invited to express in prayer our free and constant dialogue with God. We remember the words of Jesus' own prayer: "Father... not my will but yours be done" (Luke 22:42).

Each week, we are called to celebrate the Eucharist, the central memorial of the death and resurrection of Christ. The presence of the Risen Lord in our gathering revives our faith, and helps us wait in hope until he comes again.

Each year, our Lenten penance, prayer and sharing strengthens our faith. With renewed vigor, we give our lives to God daily in service "to our sisters and brothers. [Quiet Reflection]

Our Prayer: Mary, first disciple of Jesus, make our lives a living prayer. May we always be ready to pray, to celebrate God's presence and to follow Jesus faithfully every day. Hold us close beside you in the heart of the Church, ready to share the struggles and sufferings of all your people. [Mention Intention]

Pray: the Lord's Prayer and Hail Mary

Invocation: Our Lady of La Salette, Reconciler of Sinners, pray without ceasing for us who have recourse to you."

Eighth Day of Novena – Bread of Life

Scripture Says: "Jesus said to them, "I am the bread of life; whoever comes to me will never hunger, and whoever believes in me will never thirst" (John 6:35).

Mary Said: *"But you, [Maximin], surely you must have seen some (spoiled wheat) once, at [the field of] Coin... your father gave you a piece of bread and said to you: 'Here, my child, eat some bread while we still have it this year...'"*

Meditation: The fear of a future evil, the carefree attitude of a child, the concern of parents for their family, the sharing of bread — all details of life held in the memory and heart of the Virgin Mary at La Salette. Her solicitude invites us to trust in her concern for our welfare.

Her loving Son, Jesus, also reminded people how much our Heavenly Father watches out for our welfare. "If you, then, who are wicked, know how to give good gifts to your children, how much more will your heavenly Father give good things to those who ask him" (Matt 7:11).

The promise of shared bread and good gifts is a consoling message. This pledge reminds us that the Bread of Life willingly broke and "gave himself to satisfy our deepest hunger for God. He continues to do so, and invites us to do the same. [Quiet Reflection]

Our Prayer: Mother, ever attentive to our needs, awaken in us compassion for the hungry and the needy. Help us to share our Creator's concern for all human hungers — of body, heart, or spirit. Give us always a yearning for the Bread of Life, Jesus, your Son and our Lord. [Mention Intention]

Pray: the Lord's Prayer and Hail Mary

Invocation: Our Lady of La Salette, Reconciler of Sinners, pray without ceasing for us who have recourse to you.

Ninth Day of Novena—Our Mission

Scripture Says: "Then Jesus... said to them... 'Go, therefore, and make disciples of all nations, baptizing them in the name of the Father, and of the Son, and of the holy Spirit, teaching them to observe all that I have commanded you. And behold, I am with you always, until the end of [time]" (Matt 28:18-20).

Mary Said: *"Well, my children, you will make this known to all my peo-*

ple."

Meditation: As Mary challenges and encourages us to follow her Son, she reminds us of our mission. We are to bring to the whole world the Good News of Jesus Christ. Marked by his Spirit and consecrated in truth and love, the followers of Jesus work together to advance the Kingdom of God.

The "great news" of Mary is the Gospel of Jesus Christ. Like Mary, as we hear and bear the Word of God, we carry on the mission of Jesus, the mission entrusted to his apostles and to all the baptized. Such is our mission – so plain and simple that it was entrusted to two young children on the mountain of La Salette.

With maternal concern, the Virgin encourages us one final time: "Well, my children, you will make this known to all my people." [Quiet Reflection]

Our Prayer: Mother of the Church, watch over us, your people. Help us who have heard the Word of God to proclaim it in word and deed. As you were filled with the Spirit and gave birth to the Savior, may we, filled with that same Spirit, advance the kingdom of unity and peace for which Jesus gave his life on the cross. [Mention Intention]

Pray: the Lord's Prayer and Hail Mary

Invocation: Our Lady of La Salette, Reconciler of Sinners, pray without ceasing for us who have recourse to you.

Nihil Obstat: *Very Rev. Timothy J. Shea, V.F.; Imprimatur: Bernard Cardinal Law, Sept. 19, 1989; Copyright © 1989, Missionaries of La Salette Corp., 915 Maple Ave., Hartford, CT 06114; All rights reserved. Written by La Salette Frs. Joseph Bachand, James Kuczynski, Ron Gagné, and Thomas Leclerc.*

La Salette Prayers

Memorare to Our Lady of La Salette

Remember, Our Lady of La Salette, true Mother of Sorrows, the tears you shed for us on Calvary. Remember also the care you have taken to keep us faithful to Christ, your Son. Having done so much for your children, you will not now abandon us. Comforted by this consoling thought, we come to you pleading, despite our infidelities and ingratitude.

Virgin of Reconciliation, do not reject our prayers, but intercede for us, obtain for us the grace to love Jesus above all else. May we console you by a holy life and so come to share the eternal life Christ gained by his cross. Amen.

Dedication to Our Lady of La Salette

Most holy Mother, Our Lady of La Salette, who for love of me shed such bitter tears in your merciful apparition, look down with kindness upon me, as I consecrate myself to you without reserve. From this day, my glory shall be to know that I am your child. May I so live as to dry your tears and console your afflicted heart.

Beloved Mother, to you and to your blessed charge and sacred keeping and into the bosom of your mercy, for this day and for every day, and for the hour of my death I commend myself, body and soul, every hope and every joy, every trouble and every sorrow, my life and my life's end.

O dearest Mother, enlighten my understanding, direct my steps, console me by your maternal protection, so that exempt from all error, sheltered from every danger of sin, I may, with ardor and invincible courage, walk in the paths traced out for me by you and your Son. Amen.

La Salette Invocation

Our Lady of La Salette, reconciler of sinners,
pray without ceasing for us who have recourse to you.